To Roger W. Fjeld

from *[illegible]* Father

for *[illegible]* ...alog

August, 1986

SET APART TO SERVE

SET APART TO SERVE

The Meaning and Role of Episcopacy
in the
Wesleyan Tradition

JAMES K. MATHEWS

ABINGDON PRESS *NASHVILLE*

SET APART TO SERVE
*The Meaning and Role of Episcopacy
in the Wesleyan Tradition*

This book is printed on acid-free paper.

ISBN 0-687-38100-2

Library of Congress Cataloging in Publication Data

Mathews, James K. (James Kenneth), 1913-
    Set apart to serve.

    Bibliography: p.
    1. Methodist Church—Bishops. 2. Methodist Church
—Government. 3. Methodist Church—Doctrines.
I. Title.
BX8345.M27 1985   262'.12   85-4009
ISBN 0-687-38100-2 (pbk. : alk. paper)

MANUFACTURED BY THE PARTHENON PRESS AT
NASHVILLE, TENNESSEE, UNITED STATES OF AMERICA

To All Bishops of the Wesleyan Tradition

CONTENTS

INTRODUCTION

This volume is a study undertaken in part as a special assignment by the Council of Bishops of The United Methodist Church. It has taken a major amount of my time since retirement on August 31, 1980. It has proved a far more formidable task than I had supposed; therefore, I have extended it to book length. It has been a rewarding experience throughout and satisfying to complete it during the Bicentennial Year of American Methodism. In fact, we as a denomination have grown up with the republic, and in some respects the shape of our federal government structure was borrowed from Methodism.

The title, *Set Apart to Serve,* comes from the service of consecration. These words seem to sum up what essentially episcopacy is supposed to be among us. Bishops in the Wesleyan experience are presbyters or elders set apart to serve the church in well-defined ways. One contemporary writer has suggested in jest that presbyters are deacons with fuller powers, though they prefer to think of themselves as bishops with lesser powers. The point is that bishops *are* presbyter-bishops and also presbyter-deacons; that is, quite literally, they are intended to be servants of the church.

The thread running through this study has been the

meaning and role of episcopacy in the Wesleyan tradition. It seemed, first of all, important to root this in Scripture. Then the theme of the episcopate is traced through church history as well as through its more specific Methodist development during the past two centuries and more since John Wesley, our father in the faith and the wellspring of our episcopacy.

Because of this approach to the subject those who may be especially interested in bishops in Methodism may do well to begin their reading with Chapter 3. The first two chapters may then be read to make the account more complete.

Recently I heard a strange reference to the "Asbury family"—strange because Asbury was a bachelor. It may seem odd that I do not write more about the Evangelical United Brethren stream, for that too is, broadly speaking, a part of the "Asbury family." However, a colleague, Bishop Paul. A. Washburn, has just completed an account of the 1968 union of The Methodist Church and the Evangelical United Brethren Church titled *An Unfinished Church* and has covered some of that ground. I therefore found it unwise to try to weave too much of the latter into this treatment. I am grateful for the help Bishop Paul W. Milhouse and Bishop Washburn have given in regard to bishops in the Evangelical United Brethren heritage.

Of course, a great deal has already been written in the general field of Methodist bishops. Much of the earlier work was polemic or apologetic in nature. In each generation bishops have engaged in various studies: John Emory, Robert Paine, Matthew Simpson, Holland N. McTyeire, Stephen M. Merrill, Thomas B. Neely, John J. Tigert III, Richard J. Cooke, Frederick D. Leete, Roy H. Short, and Nolan B. Harmon. Mention must be made also of the discerning study of our episcopacy by Dr. Gerald F. Moede, published in 1964. Nevertheless, a comprehensive survey of the meaning and role of episcopacy has not been undertaken lately; hence, this effort.

This study has corrected or confirmed many widespread impressions of the episcopal office. Its classic roles of defending the faith against false doctrine, of teaching the faith, of stationing the clergy, and of disciplining the church are all strongly present with us.

Regrettably, I have not said much about individual bishops. They have ofttimes hovered over my shoulder, as it were. I am made proud by so many who have honored the episcopacy in our tradition and am humbled to be a part of that company. From the reading of their biographies and autobiographies I have profited greatly.

Naturally I am indebted to a multitude of people who have helped me. These include library staff members at Boston University School of Theology, Drew, Garrett-Evangelical, Wesley, the Archives of The United Methodist Church in Madison, New Jersey, and others. Then I am grateful for three colleagues who have read these pages and made helpful suggestions, namely, Bishops Nolan B. Harmon, Roy H. Short, and John B. Warman. I am thankful also to Professor Albert C. Outler for a critical reading of the manuscript and for repeated instances of friendly counsel along the way. With respect to British Methodism, Professors Rupert E. Davies and A. Raymond George have given many suggestions. Regarding Old Testament usage, Professor Dewey M. Beegle of Wesley Seminary came to my aid.

For assistance concerning episcopacy in the Orthodox tradition, gratitude is expressed to Archbishop Iakovos of the Archdiocese of North and South America, and to Professor John S. Romanides of the Church of Greece. With regard to Russian Orthodox practice, help was given by Professor John Meyendorff, Orthodox Church of America. Special mention must be made also for guidance concerning Roman Catholic episcopal practice given by Professor Gerard S. Sloyan of Temple University.

Most of all I am indebted to my wife, Eunice, who read critically and typed these pages. She has proved of the same help to me as she long was to her father. If I may be allowed to approve what she has done in the way the people used to approve their bishops, I would say, "She is worthy!"

This book is being completed during my twenty-fifth year as a bishop. One cannot stand in too grateful appreciation to God and to the people called Methodists for this privilege of service. Naturally I have drawn deeply on experiences along the road. It is astonishing to be able to state in 1984 that I have been personally acquainted in some degree with well over half of those who have ever been bishops in our church! Moreover, in this ecumenical day I have enjoyed friendship with bishops of every Christian tradition and of many nations. To all of them I am a debtor.

—James K. Mathews
Washington, D.C.
Good Friday, 1984

I

"A SCRIPTURAL EPISKOPOS"

A study of episcopacy in the Wesleyan tradition by its very nature leads us to John Wesley. He wrote his brother Charles on August 19, 1785: "I firmly believe I am a scriptural ἐπίσκοπος as much as any man in England or in Europe."[1] Even earlier, under the date of March 25, 1785, he had written, "I know myself to be as real a Christian bishop as the Archbishop of Canterbury."[2] Wesley surely meant no disrespect to bishops by expressing himself in this way. Charles Wesley could at times refer to some of them as "mitred infidels," but John had written long ago, "We can never enough reverence those of the Episcopal Orders. They are the angels of the Church, the stars in the right hand of God."[3] But in this same context John made clear that he reverenced the Bible far more than he did bishops. He had been weaned on the Scriptures at his mother's knee. He read the Bible daily; he had translated it; he commented upon it; he preached biblical truth with careful attention to text and context. He aimed at "spreading scriptural holiness throughout the land." "I wish to be in every point, great and small, a *scriptural,* rational Christian."[4]

As a "man of one book" he would not lightly claim to be

"a scriptural ἐπίσκοπος." But what did he mean by this? This question must be examined against the background of Christian ministry generally. To consider any dimension of Christian ministry requires that we acknowledge the whole ministry exemplified by our Lord Jesus Christ himself. John Wesley's view leads us also to examine how the early church governed itself.

The Church is variously known as the people of God; the congregation of God (I Cor. 1:2); the congregation of Christ (Rom. 16:16); and the community of the Holy Spirit (Phil. 2:1). The perspective is of God's calling a whole people into covenant relationship with himself and the sending of a whole people to fulfill his will in the world. Jesus Christ *is* the head of the Church (Col. 1:18), not *was* the head. He has no successor and still lives in his Church. It is his body. Just as Jesus' earthly body was the instrument for performing the Father's will in the world, so the Church as the body of Christ continues to be an instrument by which God's will is done in the world.

Jesus left the church with no prescribed governing order other than the Twelve.* At first the church gave little thought to instituting organized offices of ministry. This was because of eschatological ideas—the conviction that they were living in the "end time." The first Christians were therefore not passionately interested in organization as such. Moreover, the earliest disciples existed within the context of Judaism and had no intention or expectation of this being otherwise. Thus some notions of leadership for the community came to them from Judaism, and this was augmented by the emergence of charismatic leadership supplied by the Holy Spirit as necessity required.

---

*Cf. John L. McKenzie, *Authority in the Church* (New York: Sheed & Ward, 1966), 32: Jesus "left instructions on how the Church is not to be governed, and that is according to the model of secular power."

Old Testament Format of Leadership

Turning first to the Jewish context of the early church, we find that the roots of Christian ministry are clearly found in the Old Testament—the Scriptures. One root is, of course, the priestly role. Originally exercised merely by family heads and by patriarchs, an *office* of priesthood finally emerged. The priests' functions were teaching, ascertaining the will of God and making it known, mediating between God and man, and especially the offering of sacrifices. They were reminders to all Israel of who it was: a holy, elect people, a kingdom of priests.

The Old Testament gives a fairly straightforward and detailed account of the development of the priesthood. This is set forth in the Pentateuch with large sections of the last four books given to priestly origins and ritual. Moses, of the tribe of Levi, is portrayed as consecrating his brother Aaron and Aaron's sons as priests. This is the origin of the Levitical priesthood. All priests were Levites. The Levites were a separated people, substitutes for the firstborn, and so were representative of all Israel, the covenant people of God.

This rather simple account of priestly origins has been subjected to intense critical study and proves not to be so simple after all. The priesthood is seen as emerging after the exile with a hierarchy of high priest, priests, and Levites. The high priest was an office of great prestige and even splendor, a role much sought after. It was usually an hereditary position; the rites, ceremonies, and vestments associated with it were elaborate in the extreme. The high priest's representative character is seen especially on the Day of Atonement, when he alone enters the Holy of Holies and offers atonement for himself and all the people. For Christians the high priesthood is understood as culminating in Christ, as the book of Hebrews makes clear.

The ordinary priests shared with the high priest cultic responsibilities. The Levites had lesser responsibilities related to the sanctuary.

All three of these roles continued into New Testament times, and they are mentioned in the four Gospels and in the Acts of the Apostles. As has been said, they were doubtless taken for granted by the first Christians at Jerusalem in their Jewish setting. The New Testament, however, makes no reference to an office of priest as related to Christian leadership.

Several reasons are advanced for this. First of all, Jesus himself is seen as the high priest. John 17 shows him uttering his high priestly prayer. More significantly, the writer of Hebrews likens Jesus' death and ascension to the high priest's entering into the Holy of Holies on the Day of Atonement in behalf of not just Israel but all humankind. Recurrent priestly sacrifice was therefore no longer needed, for Jesus once and for all offered himself as a single sacrifice for everyone and for all time (Heb. 9–10).

In time, too, some Christians may have reacted against a priestly system in Judaism which would have been seen as inimical to their Lord and to themselves. More importantly, the Christians came to see that they had no need for a sacerdotal system because every Christian was a priest. This idea is already present in the Jewish Scriptures. For example, in Exodus 19:6 the children of Israel are called "a kingdom of priests and a holy nation." Numbers 8:10 graphically portrays all Israelites delegating their priesthood to the Levites by laying hands on their heads (cf. Isa. 61:6). In the New Testament this view is grasped by the early church. In I Peter 2:9 the writer reminds the Christians: "You are a chosen race, a royal priesthood, a holy nation, God's own people." This position was emphasized by the Reformers in the "priesthood of all believers" and affirmed also by the Roman Catholics in

Vatican II. Present-day scholars would tend to interpret the intention here as referring to priestly holiness and not to priestly function.[5]

This view of universal priesthood is set forth elaborately in a famous essay, "The Christian Ministry," which the great Bishop J. B. Lightfoot incorporates in his commentary on Philippians.[6] He speaks of the Christian ideal of the kingdom without sacred times and seasons, without sacred places, and without sacrificial or sacerdotal class. This extreme view he tempers by admitting to the reality that no society or religious institution can in fact be exempt from the universal need for appropriate leadership of various levels and kinds. The ideal of Israel's universal priesthood assumed by the church was of necessity qualified; thus an organized ministry emerged even in the earliest apostolic period recorded in the New Testament.

A Christian priesthood did eventually develop in spite of the fact that no individual member or leader of the church is in the New Testament called "priest." This development was influenced by the priestly tradition of Judaism. As time elasped and the return of the Lord was deferred, the church became less and less an eschatological community. The need for organized and not just charismatic leadership became apparent.

At the same time, the church outgrew its Jewish context by geographical extension and greater inclusiveness among its adherents of those of non-Jewish origin who finally became dominant. This trend was accelerated with the destruction of the Temple which was at the same time a loss of a common symbol and a sign to the Christians of God's rejection of the Jews who had rejected the Messiah. The Jews, on their part, excommunicated the Christians who were viewed as more and more suspect and disloyal to the tradition. A separate Christian religion developed with its own ministry or priesthood, its own forms and rites, and its increasing understanding of the Lord's Supper as a bloodless sacrifice (see Heb. 13:15; Rom. 12:1; 15:16; Phil. 4:18). Episcopacy developed with a part of its function the presiding at the Eucharist. This role was then shared with all the priests.

John Wesley was of course a part of this priestly tradition. As a presbyter in the Church of England he was a participant in this long heritage. A "scriptural *episkopos*," among other functions, fufills priestly roles.

In its concept and ideal of ministry, the church was profoundly influenced by another powerful Jewish tradition, namely, the prophets. The classic prophetic stream of Israel had ceased a long time before Jesus appeared. Nevertheless the early church saw itself as a part of this tradition. Luke's Gospel bursts forth in an atmosphere of prophecy. Zechariah, Simeon, and Anna are illustrations. John the Baptist appears as a prophet after the model of Elijah. Jesus himself is acclaimed as a prophet in all four Gospels.

In Israel, just as priests were those who spoke to God on behalf of humanity, so prophets spoke to humanity on behalf of God. Prophetic monotheism is often said to express the whole mood and tone of Judaism. It stands for spiritual and ethical religion as opposed to idolatrous nature worship. Moses is understood as the forerunner of this tradition and is regarded in Judaism as the greatest of prophets. Prophets were not just seers who forecasted the future. They were forthseers who spoke for Yahweh and declared that God was active in history, working out his will and purpose, judging and redeeming humankind, endowing life and history with meaning. Much of the Old Testament writings are made up of exactly this understanding.

Emerging from rather misty origins, prophetism cleared

itself from mere augury, priestly divination, and ecstasy and entered its classic period in the eighth and seventh centuries B.C. Here the great names arise—Hosea, Amos, Micah, the Isaiahs, Jeremiah. They were called of God, sometimes from humble origin, to speak the timely word for a particular historical situation, making clear the true situation and uttering the clear demand of God's will. A kind of "prophetic cycle" was manifested: disobedience, rebellion, and sin; followed by disaster and judgment; followed by invitation to return to Yahweh's righteousness and mercy; followed by repentance, redemption, and restoration. The prophets were concerned about Israel as a covenant community bound to Yahweh and to one another. Yahweh's righteous will and his prophets proclaimed: "Thus saith the Lord." God was exalted as a living, ethical, personal Being; not remote from human beings but an active participant in their lives inviting their response, trust, and obedience. Prophetism at its best reached beyond Israel to the universal, with Israel thus becoming a light to all the nations.

This whole tradition is taken seriously by the first Christians; both men and women were termed "prophets" (Acts 11:27-28; 15:32; 21:9-10). Prophesying became a mark of the primitive church. Peter's sermon at Pentecost (Acts 2) sees the prophetic role as a fulfillment of the promises uttered by Joel. The Book of Acts mentions a number of prophets and prophetesses. Prophecy in the New Testament is understood as faithful and intelligent interpretation of the word of God, in other words, as inspired preaching. The prophet was ranked next to apostle in importance and respect. Great and effective preaching is in this stream and was so understood and practiced by John Wesley; therefore, it may properly be regarded as a part of the meaning of "scriptural *episkopos.*"

Emerging Leadership in the New Testament

We have observed that Jesus made no other provisions
for leadership among the disciples than calling the Twelve.
They may be viewed as prior to the church; they were there
at the beginning of primitive Christianity. Thus in a sense
we may say that the ministry produced the church and not
the church the ministry.

The Twelve were chosen by Jesus from among the larger
circle of his disciples. They are termed *"the* Twelve" in all
four of the Gospels, in Acts, in Paul, and in Revelation.
They are designated either as apostles or disciples. They
were called by Jesus "to be with him," trained, sent out,
and commanded by him to preach the gospel of the
kingdom and to heal, just as he himself did all these things.
Just as Jesus was chief shepherd, so they were under-
shepherds (John 10). Theirs also was a symbolic role in the
eschatological congregation of sitting on twelve thrones
and judging the twelve tribes of Israel (Matt. 19:28; Luke
22:28-30; Rev. 21:14).

Their names are listed four times, once in each of the
Synoptic Gospels and once in Acts. A rudimentary organization must have been understood as attaching to them, for
Peter is always mentioned first on the lists and the first
four, in one or another order, always include Peter, James,
John, and Andrew. Moreover, in all four lists Philip's
name always heads the second set of four names and James
the son of Alpheus heads the third set of four names. The
Twelve (or the eleven) are all credited with having seen the
risen Lord, and this is kept in mind as the first disciples
voted to replace Judas with Matthias (Acts 1:16-26).

The direction of the church was, at the beginning, in
their hands. The Twelve represented and served the whole
community of believers. They were preachers of the Word
in the congregation and outside as well, for some of them

left on missionary journeys. They were guardians of the tradition and assured continuity in the community. Peter clearly played a leading role of spokesman, as Acts records and the Gospels reflect. Associated with him were John, the son of Zebedee, and James, the Lord's brother (who was not an apostle). Paul terms these three as "pillars" (Gal. 2:9). The Twelve served as a part of a council of advisors as recorded in Acts 6 and 15. They dealt with issues that concerned the welfare of the whole church. They were not bishops, and nowhere in the New Testament are they called "bishops." They did not preside over local churches. They did exercise some supervisory functions *(episkopé)* either individually or collectively. Therefore, the Twelve give us insight into some aspects of the episcopal role.

The New Testament affords more than one view of the apostle, as we shall see more elaborately later on. The Twelve clearly were apostles and are repeatedly termed such in the Gospels and Acts. An *apostle* is literally "one who is sent out." A word of equivalent meaning was used in Jewish tradition. Jesus himself had a deep sense of himself being sent of God. He, in turn, sent out his disciples (cf. John 20:21). Luke speaks not only of the Twelve but also of the seventy (or seventy-two) who are sent out on a task similar to those assigned the Twelve (Luke 10:1, 17). The Twelve were a part of a company with Jesus throughout his ministry and a witness of his resurrection (save Judas). As companions of Jesus they were in particular guardians and guarantors of the purity of the tradition. According to all four Gospels they were also commanded to go forth on mission for their Lord. The mark of apostleship was witness and service for their Lord and to people according to their needs. The apostles were essentially missionaries who founded new Christian communities.

At the same time the New Testament gives very little

detail about the precise missionary activity of the Twelve, so this has long been the focus of lively and imaginative speculation. For example, apostles other than Paul surely planted the church in Antioch, Rome, and Alexandria. Luke largely restricts the use of *apostle* to the Twelve, but he also applies the term to Barnabas and Paul (Acts 14:14).

Paul makes a somewhat different use of the word *apostle*. First of all, he applies it to himself. He had seen the risen Lord (I Cor. 9:1-2; 15:8; Gal. 1:12). He was called by Jesus Christ and commissioned by him (Rom. 1:1; Gal. 1:1). Although we lack details of the missionary activities of the Twelve, we have the most elaborate details of Paul's mission to the Gentiles. He regards himself in no way inferior to those whom he calls "superlative apostles" (II Cor. 11:5; 12:11). Again and again he defends his own apostleship and repeatedly speaks of his suffering for the gospel (cf. II Cor. 11–12; I Cor. 4:8-13; II Cor. 6:3ff; Phil. 3:10). Yet he acknowledges the apostleship of the Twelve and calls some others apostles, too (Rom. 16:7; I Cor. 15:7). He speaks also of "false apostles" (II Cor. 11:13).

Paul could not himself lay claim to having been a companion of Jesus, but if he lacked this dimension of apostleship, he added other dimensions not inconsistent with it and in fact displayed an intensification of it in his imitation of the Lord. Thus he is appropriately restrained in his references to the earthly Jesus and only infrequently quotes his words. On the other hand, he interprets the *meaning* of the gospel in the most penetrating fashion, a fact from which the whole church has subsequently profited. He did fervently preach the gospel (I Cor. 9:16). Paul does not hesitate to assert authority, but in the main he seeks to serve and not to rule.

Paul was not a local church leader nor was he called a "bishop," but he was a missionary extraordinary and exercised the most careful overseership of the churches.

He is therefore an appropriate episcopal model, and John Wesley rightly saw him as the very ideal of the "scriptural *episkopos.*"

By definition throughout the later history of the church a bishop could not be apostolic in the Lucan sense for he had not *seen* the Lord, but a bishop could be apostolic in some Pauline sense; that is, in the missionary sense. In many respects throughout history some bishops have been such apostolic figures. So too was John Wesley apostolic as were some bishops in the Wesleyan tradition. Examples would be Francis Asbury himself, or Bishops James M. Thoburn, William Taylor, and Walter R. Lambuth.

We have noted that Jesus did not provide for formal ministry other than the Twelve and that this was augmented by charismatic forms of ministry as necessity demanded, followed later by a more formal and ordered ministry. The forms of ministry were the products of experience and history responding to needs in mission, worship, order, and service.

Fortunately, the New Testament is quite specific with regard to gifts for the ministry granted by the work of the Holy Spirit. In I Corinthians 12:28 we find a list of seven types of leaders: "And God has appointed in the church first apostles, second prophets, third teachers, then workers of miracles, then healers, helpers, administrators, speakers in various kinds of tongues." (RSV).

In Ephesians 4:11-13 the list is shorter, but their functions are elaborately stated:

> And his gifts were that some should be apostles, some prophets, some evangelists, some pastors and teachers, to equip the saints for the work of ministry, for building up the body of Christ, until we all attain to the unity of the faith and of the knowledge of the Son of God, to mature manhood, to the measure of the stature of the fulness of Christ.

Similarly Romans 12:6-8 refers to gifts in terms of qualities, seven in number, rather than offices:

> Having gifts that differ according to the grace given to us, let us use them: if prophecy, in proportion to our faith; if service, in our serving; he who teaches, in his teaching; he who exhorts, in his exhortation; he who contributes, in liberality; he who gives aid, with zeal; he who does acts of mercy with cheerfulness.

In all three instances the various aspects of ministry are gifts of the Spirit on God's initiative. All are to be used for the benefit and building up of the whole community. In all cases they are given to be used. None of the lists is exhaustive. All the gifts have their appropriate place with no apparent value attached to rank or status. No one person has all the gifts. The apostle is named first in both of the first two lists, but this term gradually went out of use, except metaphorically. Prophets and teachers appear on all three. Prophets, as we have seen, are essentially preachers. They usually are regarded as itinerant; the teachers as local residents.

In the first list the function of governance, administration, or oversight appears specifically and would be associated with the episcopal or overseeing type of responsibility (see also I Tim. 3:4-5); though other functions such as preaching, evangelism, and pastoral care would no less relate to this role. Leadership is not singled out as a mark of superiority but as an obligation of service owed to the fellowship and to all. This note of servanthood is constantly sounded by Jesus who himself came not to be served but to serve. It is the undeniable and indispensable mark of the leader among Christians. A "scriptural *episkopos*" is a servant!

It should be emphasized that these charismatic leaders

were not just ideal figures but real people who arose spontaneously within the Christian communities according to God's will. Paul constantly refers to these persons, and at the beginning or ending of his letters he mentions many of them by name. Such persons have continued in the church, and no period has been entirely without them. We have them still.

It should be noted also that the New Testament is replete with informal designations for Christian workers which do not demand distinction between clergy and laity. Among these are "laborers," "fellow workers," "fellow soldiers," "helpers," "leaders," "counselors," "partners," "servants," "messengers," and so on. The Christian community has never been able to do without them. First Thessalonians 5:12-13 makes an interesting reference: "But we beseech you, brethren, to respect those who labor among you and are over you in the Lord and admonish you, and to esteem them very highly in love because of their work." Such laborers sound very much like bishops.

Nevertheless, with the passage of time, reliance solely on a charismatic and somewhat informal ministry became less and less the rule, and clearer evidence of a more ordered and institutional ministry was gradually manifested. By at least the middle of the second century the local Christian churches had a threefold ministry of *deacons, elders or presbyters,* and *bishops.** These terms are also used in the New Testament during both apostolic and postapostolic periods. Their distinction and relationship are not always clear. We will later return in greater detail to this factor.

---

*Sometimes an effort has been made to show counterpart relationships in the Old and New Testaments between deacons and Levites, presbyters and priests, bishops and high priests.

A More Ordered Ministry

We must mention *deacon* which is often termed the oldest of the major orders of ministry. It may also be regarded a brand-new order without any clearly defined precedent. Traditionally the origin of the diaconate is understood to be recorded in Acts 6 when the early primitive fellowship was faced with the problem of fair distribution of daily food and alms to the widows of its Hellenist members. It is the fashion with present-day New Testament scholars to deny this origin. After all, the noun for "deacon" is not used in the passage but only the verb for "serving." In fact the word *deacon* does not itself occur in Acts. Rather, this event is seen as showing the increasing influence of the Hellenistic party in the earliest church *vis à vis* the Hebrew Christians loyal to the Temple (Acts 6). All the names listed there are Greek rather than Hebrew.

The incident is of interest in and of itself. It does tell of a group of men, constituted by the Twelve and the whole assembly of disciples, to free the apostles for preaching and to relieve them from "serving tables." They were selected and appointed by the apostles to this duty with prayer and laying on of hands. The crisis was met successfully, and the church continued to prosper. Moreover at least two of these seven men superseded in function the mere serving of tables. Stephen was an effective preacher and first martyr, and Philip became an outstanding missionary evangelist.

Regardless of origin, deacon (Phil. 1:1) and deaconess (Rom. 16:1; I Tim. 3:11) do have a clear and important place in the New Testament. Their role involved caring for the ill, the poor, and the needy, an office of serving that reflected the example of their serving Lord. Their work and personal qualities are clearly set forth in I Timothy 3:8-13:

Deacons likewise must be serious, not double-tongued, not addicted to much wine, not greedy for gain; they must hold the mystery of the faith with a clear conscience. And let them also be tested first; then if they prove themselves blameless let them serve as deacons. The women likewise must be serious, no slanderers, but temperate, faithful in all things. Let deacons be the husband of one wife, and let them manage their children and their households well; for those who serve well as deacons gain a good standing for themselves and also great confidence in the faith which is in Christ Jesus.

Deacons are especially linked with bishops not only in the New Testament (Phil. 1:1; I Tim. 3) but also throughout church history. They were and are (including in United Methodist practice) ordained by the bishop alone. They have been related to the bishops as assistants in liturgy, particularly in the Eucharist (especially prominent in the Orthodox tradition). There also seems to be a correlation between younger/deacon and elder/bishop (I Pet. 5:5); in other words, the term *younger* (Greek, *neoteros*) appears to be a synonym for *deacon,* just as *elder* (Greek, *presbuteros*) is a synonym for *bishop.* The New Testament makes clear that the office of deacon became widespread in the early church (see I Cor. 12:28; Rom. 12:7-8).

When we turn from deacon to elder or presbyter, it is extraordinarily difficult to decide where to begin. Whatever its precise origin the office of deacon, as we have seen, was brand-new in the early church. In the case of elder we have a usage already venerable not only in a long Jewish history but also in many societies and cultures throughout the world and throughout history. It is not as if we can move easily from the development of a lower order of deacon directly to a next higher one of presbyter and then finally to a third order of bishop. It is almost as if we come suddenly upon eldership and discover it in operation in the Christian community. And when we do, we find elder also equated with bishop—as we shall see more closely a little later.

Elder means, first of all, simply "older in years." It usually appears in the plural and refers to an aggregation of older men charged with a community's social and political responsibilities, which are based largely upon respect for their wisdom accruing from long experience. They are likely to be a part of any clan or patriarchal system. In the Pentateuch they are seen as representatives of all of Israel, and they played a leading role with Moses in the Exodus. Several accounts are given of their Hebrew origin (Exod. 18:13-20; Num. 11:16-17). By the third century B.C. there was established a Jewish Sanhedrin (possibly two: a political one and a religious one) made up of seventy or seventy-two elders. The Sanhedrin is familiar also from New Testament references. In addition there were similar town councils of elders as well as in synagogues. The term appears also in the Qumran community.

Luke is the first one to introduce the term *elder* in the context of *Christian* leadership (Acts 11:30). Here they are found as a council of elders in Jerusalem (Acts 21:18), with James,* the Lord's brother, as chairman, to whom Barnabas and Paul took famine relief collected from the Gentile church at Antioch.

It is interesting that this group of Hebrew Christians were engaged in an activity similar to the one that the seven "deacons" were charged with among the Hellenists (Acts

---

*Although James is not in the New Testament called "bishop," he is often referred to by scholars as filling this function in the primitive apostolic community and is therefore an episcopal model—a "scriptural *episkopos*."

6). These elders were a kind of Christian Sanhedrin and were closely related to the twelve apostles. These two groups—the Twelve and the elders—were closely interrelated in governance of the fellowship in Jerusalem. The phrase "apostles and elders" is used several times about the group which sat together in the council (ca. A.D. 40) assembled to consider the question of Judaizing (Acts 15:2, 4, 6). They came to a decision together and with the whole church (Acts 15:22ff.). This decision was then communicated to all the churches including those of Gentile origin (Acts 15:30; 16:4). Paul also met with James "and all the elders" when he returned from his third missionary journey (Acts 21:18-25).

In Acts 14:23 Paul and Barnabas are reported as having "appointed elders for them in every church, with prayer and fasting." Elders are mentioned as existing in Ephesus (Acts 20:17) where Paul had evangelized. In none of his undisputed letters, however, does Paul himself refer to elders. Yet Titus is directed to "appoint elders in every town" (1:5). This may imply that Paul did not actually appoint elders everywhere he went and this was yet to be done.

References are made to elders in James (5:14), where this role is taken for granted, and also in II and III John and in some of the Pastoral Epistles. In the Book of Revelation a heavenly group of twenty-four are mentioned a number of times, possibly a symbolic allusion to twelve patriarchs and twelve apostles. By the end of the first century there were presbyters in many places participating in the governance of the church.

While the designation of elder (presbyter) or its equivalent was common in many cultures and had a long history in the Jewish tradition, a less familiar term began to appear in the leadership category among the Christian churches, namely, *bishop*. The earliest New Testament reference is in Paul's letter to the Philippians (1:1) where in greeting the saints he includes also "the *bishops* and *deacons*" (note plural; italics mine). The term also appears in Greek in Acts 20:28 (the only mention of bishop in Acts) where it is used interchangeably with *elders* to refer to the leaders of the church at Ephesus when Paul gave his farewell address to them. The word *bishop* occurs, together with related verb forms, only a very few times in the New Testament but it was, of course, destined for a great future in the developing church, alongside the functions of deacon and elder.

The fact is that in the New Testament the designations *presbuteros* ("elder") and *episkopos* ("bishop") are equivalent terms; there is no perceptible difference between them.[7] As used in the apostolic and postapostolic periods of the New Testament they are essentially interchangeable, so much so that it is appropriate to use the term *presbyter-bishop,* or *bishop-presbyter.* Both titles are used to describe leadership functions in the congregation, and the emphasis upon one word or the other may have been due simply to divergent practice from region to region. Some authorities have suggested that *presbuteros* emphasizes the dignity ("venerable") and *episkopos* the function (literally, "overseeing") of one role. Others have implied that *elder* was the term more appropriate and familiar among Jewish Christians while *bishop* was commonly used among Gentile Christians, but it is hard to sustain this point of view.

In any event there is abundant New Testament evidence for the equating of the two terms, and there is very general agreement on this point. The following arguments support this view:

1. Acts 20:17 refers to the assembly of the "elders" at Ephesus to hear Paul's farewell address, and in Acts 20:28

these same persons are addressed by the apostle as "bishops" ("overseers," RSV).

2. In a somewhat similar fashion a usage is found in I Peter. In 5:1-2 the elders are addressed by a fellow elder and advised "to tend or oversee" (verb form for "exercising the role of bishop") the flock of God.

3. In I Timothy the writer speaks of the qualifications for bishop (3:1-7), but later in the same letter the same persons are addressed as "elders" (5:17).

4. Once again in Titus the young representative of the apostle is advised to appoint "elders" in every place in Crete who are to be "blameless" (1:5-6). Then these same persons in the next verse are called "bishops" (v. 7), who "must be *blameless*" (italics mine).

This equation of terms continued for some time after the New Testament period, and it was only after the elapse of many decades that a distinction between them became clear and universal.

Further attention needs now to be given to the term *bishop*. The noun form, *episkopos*, is used infrequently in the New Testament and carries the overtones of supervisor, watchman, guardian, inspector. We have already referred to the elders or bishops of Ephesus (Acts 20:28); to the leaders addressed at Philippi (Phil. 1:1); and to bishops in I Timothy 3:2 and Titus 1:7, where the *qualities* of these officers are given. There is one other use of *episkopos*, namely, in I Peter 2:25, where reference is made to Christ as "the Shepherd and *Bishop* [from the Greek; "Guardian," RSV] of your souls." There are no other New Testament uses of this word.

A related word, *episkopé*, having to do with the *function* of superintending, overseeing, or visitation, appears four times in the New Testament. One instance is in Acts 1:20, actually a quotation from Psalm 109:8, and pertains to a replacement for Judas among the Twelve. Matthias was chosen. Another instance is in I Timothy 3:1 and refers to aspiration to the "office of bishop" as being worthy. Two other instances (I Pet. 2:12; Luke 19:44) relate to the meaning of visitation, as in "visitation of an affliction," and are not pertinent to ministry as such.

The word used as a verb, *episkopein* ("to oversee" or "to supervise"), is found in I Peter 5:2 and has already been referred to in the discussion of equating elder and bishop. One final use as a verb appears in Hebrews 12:15, but here too it has no relevance for our discussion and merely refers to "looking out for" or "seeing to" something.

In striking contrast *episkopos* and related words are used scores of times in the Septuagint edition (LXX) of the Old Testament. The noun refers to "inspector," "superintendent," sometimes "captain," or less happily "taskmaster" or "visitor in order to examine and punish." The noun *episkopé* occurs very often in the LXX with the root meaning of "inspection with responsibility to a higher authority" and "introduction of a new order of things." Sometimes the reference is to military officers. *Episkopoi* (plural) are charged with seeing to it that things are done rightly. The Old Testament usage is sometimes in the context of definite religious office. Both *episkopos* and *episkopé* are used in Numbers 4:16 where Eleazar "has charge of the oil" and "oversight of all the tabernacle." Other usages have to do with appointing "a man over the congregation." Two verses in II Kings (11:18; 12:11) mention oversight of "the house of the LORD."

These words occur also in classical Greek where the emphasis is on examination, scrutiny, reviewing, and inspection. *Episkopos* was an office of commissioner, especially in relation to new colonies, an inspector or manager or magistrate. It referred also to officials who reported to a king, curators, stewards, overseers of religious or political groups, even "heads of a road gang."

In the mystery religions the highest grades of initiates who had "seen" the deity were referred to by this word. No wonder that scholars of an earlier day felt that this word was of pagan origin and therefore was not likely to be used by Jewish Christians.

Nevertheless, examination of the Dead Sea Scrolls reveals in the Qumran community a figure remarkably like a bishop. Indeed the word *pāqêd* is a direct Hebrew equivalent of *bishop*. He was an overseer, lay or priestly, who knew the law and made doctrinal and administrative decisions and was related to a council of twelve:

> The highest office of the Essene community, aside from that of the presiding priest, was that of inspector, *mᵉbaqqēr* (related to *pāqêd*). He was the president of the "Many," fiscal agent of the community, director of labor, religious and secular, in charge of training and examining those who applied for membership in the community. He was to act as shepherd.[8]

The use of *bishop* then has had a fairly long history, and its adoption for use for leadership in the Christian community is understandable. Even the etymology of the related words gives insights into the episcopal role throughout the centuries.

We turn again to the Pastoral Epistles and to I Peter for what they have to say about the office of bishop. First and Second Timothy and Titus are generally regarded as not having been written by Paul himself. They were not addressed to churches as Paul's letters generally were but to individuals. Clearly they were written by one who knew the mind of Paul and wrote as in his name or in his behalf to individuals, but more than that, to pastors in general. They are reflections of and reflections on what Paul suggests elsewhere. Timothy and Titus are addressed in roles which are not strictly apostolic but rather what may be termed "apostolic delegates" (cf. I Cor. 4:16-17).

These letters specifically have something to say about the functions and qualities of bishops:

> Now a bishop must be above reproach, the husband of one wife, temperate, sensible, dignified, hospitable, an apt teacher, no drunkard, not violent but gentle, not quarrelsome, and no lover of money. He must manage his own household well, keeping his children submissive and respectful in every way; for if a man does not know how to manage his own household, how can he care for God's church? He must not be a recent convert, or he may be puffed up with conceit and fall into the condemnation of the devil; moreover he must be well thought of by outsiders, or he may fall into reproach and the snare of the devil (I Tim. 3:2-7).

Here we have not so much a description of the functions of a bishop as of the qualities that should attach to one called to that responsibility. They are indeed very demanding ones.

The counsel proceeds with reference to deacons:

> Deacons likewise must be serious, not double-tongued, not addicted to much wine, not greedy for gain; they must hold the mystery of the faith with a clear conscience. And let them also be tested first; then if they prove themselves blameless let them serve as deacons. The women likewise must be serious, no slanderers, but temperate, faithful in all things. Let deacons be the husband of one wife, and let them manage their children and their households well; for those who serve well as deacons gain a good standing for themselves and also great confidence in the faith which is in Christ Jesus (I Tim. 3:8-13).

It is of interest to compare and contrast these qualities with those required of a bishop.

Later on the writer turns attention to the importance of sound teaching and of avoiding quarrels and to the evils of love of money. Then he proceeds: "But as for you, man of God, shun all this; aim at righteousness, godliness, faith, love, steadfastness, gentleness" (I Tim. 6:11). Or looking to the letter to Titus we find a similar strain:

> This is why I left you in Crete, that you might amend what was defective, and appoint elders in every town as I directed you, if any man is blameless, the husband of one wife, and his children are believers and not open to the charge of being profligate or insubordinate. For a bishop, as God's steward, must be blameless; he must not be arrogant or quick-tempered or a drunkard or violent or greedy for gain, but hospitable, a lover of goodness, master of himself, upright, holy, and self-controlled; he must hold firm to the sure word as taught, so that he may be able to give instruction in sound doctrine and also to confute those who contradict it (Titus 1:5-9).

No less demanding!

Once again, in I Peter we find the writer expressing himself in these terms:

> So I exhort the elders among you, as a fellow elder and a witness of the sufferings of Christ as well as a partaker in the glory that is to be revealed. Tend the flock of God that is your charge, not by constraint but willingly, not for shameful gain but eagerly, not as domineering over those in your charge but being examples to the flock (5:1-4).

These searching requirements are enough to give anyone pause who may perchance aspire to the honorable office of bishop. One wonders how well Peter or Paul themselves might have done with respect to these requirements, in the light of their renowned weaknesses candidly recorded in Scripture. And what of John Wesley? And what of bishops today? Surely a "scriptural *episkopos*" ought in large measure to reflect such ideals as are set forth here.

Even more is demanded of the "scriptural *episkopos.*" Some of these demands are embodied in the Order for Consecration of Bishops: in the readings from Acts 20:17-24, 28-32 and John 21:15-17; in the questions with which bishops-elect are examined; in the prayers that are uttered; in the vows exacted and the authority given; and in the blessings evoked upon them. The demands are implicit in the ideals set forth and the exemplary conduct required: to be good ministers of Jesus Christ; to be persons of prayer and the Word; to be willing to spend and be spent; to be all things to all people; to be true shepherds and guardians or watchmen—as both Old Testament and New Testament require and empower; to be faithful teachers and exemplary liturgical leaders; and above all to be loyal followers of Jesus Christ and like him humble, obedient servants. Was not John Wesley then such a "scriptural *episkopos*"?

We have tried to explore the meaning of episcopacy as it appears in the Scriptures and early secular usage. It is clear that in the New Testament it does not denote an office but a function. It does not mean there what we mean nowadays by *bishop*. It refers to a person who exercises charge or overseership in the church. Bishops were presbyters who also exercised oversight (*episkopé*) (cf. I Tim. 5:17), for not all presbyters filled this latter role. Though John Wesley did not in the Church of England enjoy the title and office of bishop, he did over the Methodist societies exercise the function of bishop. According to the Scriptures, bishops partook something of the role of the Old Testament priest (or high priest) and prophet; something of the role of the New Testament apostle of the

Pauline variety; and something of the roles of Jesus whom they imitated—shepherd, high priest, guardian, teacher, servant. The Scriptures suggest many models which have proved instructive to the church. It is therefore legitimate and helpful to speak of "scriptural *episkopos.*"

Notes

1. *The Letters of the Rev. John Wesley, A.M.,* ed. John Telford, standard ed., 8 vols. (London: Epworth Press, 1931), 7:284. (Note: this reference and the following one are both dated *after* the British ordinations.)

2. Ibid., 262.

3. Ibid. 1:158; see also 274.

4. Ibid. 8:112 (italics mine).

5. See J. H. Elliott, *The Elect and the Holy,* supplements to *Novum Testamentum* (Leiden: Brill, 1966), passim.

6. J. B. Lightfoot, *Saint Paul's Epistle to the Philippians* (London: Macmillan, 1890).

7. So John Wesley believed. "When I said 'I believe I am a scriptural Bishop,' I spoke on Lord King's supposition that bishops and presbyters are essentially one order." Wesley, *Letters* 8:143.

8. Frank M. Cross, Jr., *The Ancient Library of Qumran and Modern Biblical Studies* (Garden City, N.Y.: Doubleday, 1958), 175-76.

II

A BRIEF ACCOUNT OF THE
DEVELOPMENT OF EPISCOPACY

John Wesley was a "scriptural *episkopos*" and so also, in some sense is a bishop in the Wesleyan tradition. The role is also recognizably akin to the office of bishop as it has emerged through the centuries, though of course mingled with elements peculiar to our own denominational ethos and combined with features appropriate to the contemporary scene. We must sketch the historical development.

Some form of *episkopé* ("oversight"; "supervision") is essential to the effective functioning of the Christian church. This is evident, as we have seen, in the New Testament itself. Yet no one form of church government is specifically prescribed in the Scriptures. Warrant can be found there for congregational (or independent), presbyterial, and episcopal governance, but none of these can claim exclusive sanction.[1] These all afford ways of fulfilling *episkopé*.

In their time the leading apostle among the Twelve, Peter, as well as James and Paul, exercised such a function as the New Testament makes clear. Yet even their roles were varied: Peter was the spokesman for the Twelve;

James was the leader in Jerusalem, possibly so because he was the eldest surviving male of Joseph's family; Paul was the pioneer missionary among the Gentiles. Some of the variety of "charismatic ministers" also fufilled such a role. Sometimes supervision was cared for personally and individually; sometimes this was done corporately or collegially. Sometimes it was done only locally (James in Jerusalem) and sometimes regionally (e.g., Paul and the church at Corinth). How did the various local groups relate to one another? How did the primitive church order its life, worship, and mission for the fulfilling of this function of oversight?

Though elements of the three basic shapes of church government—congregational, presbyterial, and episcopal—can be found in the New Testament (Canon B. H. Streeter once observed that all three have won and received prizes), it is significant that in the historical development of the church the episcopal form of supervision has emerged as prevalent for most centuries in most of Christendom. This does not mean that the other two forms of superintendence are completely lost sight of; and even episcopacy relates in some sense with the collegial and congregational modes.

Episcopacy, of course, has throughout history been constantly under scrutiny, criticism, and not infrequently resistance and protest. Some groups have rejected it out of hand. Others have insisted that it is of the very *esse* of the church, or at the very least of the *bene esse* or *plenum esse* (essential to the nature of the church, or to its well-being, or to its fullness of being).

Regardless of these matters the necessity of some mode of oversight has always been understood. It is of interest that more recently many of the very communions traditionally and stoutly opposed to episcopacy have, as they restructure their lives for contemporary mission, been making provision for regional supervisory ministries which closely resemble episcopacy in role and function. Moreover, in current ecumenical discussion a positive attitude of acceptance toward the episcopal office is nowadays evident, and greater readiness is being shown toward making provision for it in polities for which it has long been alien.

We have seen that in the New Testament bishops and presbyters were for all intents and purposes the same. The words are used interchangeably in the Pastoral Epistles, Acts, and I Peter. The earlier modes of supervision varied as we have already seen, but after Paul's death there emerged a pattern of two orders of ministry, presbyter-bishop and deacons, which prevailed nearly everywhere. This became more or less uniform by the end of the first century. Then, by the time of Ignatius of Antioch early in the second century, one bishop emerged as leader over a college of presbyters. By the end of the second century this model was virtually universal.

The Rise of Episcopacy

The first development took in precisely a "tunnel period," between about A.D. 65 or 70 and as late as A.D. 150, concerning which we have the least historical information. Therefore, an interpretation of development in this interval is likely to be more theological than historical in nature. Yet Rupert E. Davies has stated, "All that the historian can do is to show as far as possible what bishops have been in the sight of man, not of God."[2] The problem is complicated by the fact that the scraps of historical information we do have are at times inconsistent and ambiguous.

We have already cited a famous and well-documented essay by Bishop J. B. Lightfoot in which he asserts that the office of bishop did not develop from the apostolate by localization but from the synonomous presbyteral order "by elevation; and the title, which originally was common to all, came at length to be appropriated to the chief among them."[3] This appears to have occurred during a gap of about fifty years following the end of Luke's narrative of Acts.

This period was marked by a series of crises in the life of the primitive church. First of all, there occurred about A.D. 65 within a short span the death of the three most influential early leaders whom we have just named: Peter, Paul, and James. Other apostles were also dying, and only a few could have survived into the latter decades of the century, though those who did survive were doubtless quite influential. Later the subapostolic figures who might be called "apostolic delegates," such as Timothy and Titus, also finally disappeared from the scene.* Another crisis occurred in A.D. 70 with the fall of Jerusalem and the consequent scattering of the Christians to the Judeo-Christian communities in other parts of Palestine, Egypt, and Syria. Partly prompted by this event, tensions increased between Jewish and Gentile converts calling for adjudication by some supervisory authority.

Yet another factor was the missionary effort of the church which resulted in the rapid and widespread growth in the number of Christians of Gentile origin and the consequent reduction of both the proportion and influence of Jewish Christians. There came a time, too, when a more settled and local rule had to replace missionary rule. Added to this was the concurrent threatening issue of Gnosticism, not to mention other jealousies and rivalries

---

*Paul in Philippians 2:14-24 seems to be preoccupied with the problem of leadership after his death.

which were bound to arise in the Christian community itself and of which we may see a foretaste in I Corinthians 1–3. To combat heresy and schism, to meet the other growing crises confronting the church, and to enforce discipline and unity in doctrine, a strong authority was required and indeed was forthcoming. In fact, the kind of authority and leadership that emerged was directed exactly toward meeting the demands just enumerated.

In the early church in Jerusalem there was clearly a council of elders. A similar circle of elders (also called "bishops") existed in Antioch, Ephesus, and elsewhere. The Acts of the Apostles records that James, the brother of our Lord, both because of family connection and because of personal qualities and character became the acknowledged leader of the council of presbyters in Jerusalem. The existence of such a body implies the necessity of some sort of presiding officer, and James was the one chosen. Even if not specifically so designated, James for all practical purposes filled the role of bishop and was certainly afterward regarded as such.[4]

Here then was a ready model of the kind of leader called for by the various crises. The survivors among the Twelve would doubtless have given their sanction and encouragement for this now familiar pattern of leadership. Some scholars have supposed that a second "Council of Jerusalem," similar to the one described in Acts 15, was summoned to meet these crises, but the support for this is pure speculation. Government by bishops and presbyters simply emerged gradually and pragmatically during the lacuna of some fifty years, to which reference has been made. By the time reliable historical documents are again available to us, the episcopal office had already rather fully matured and had been consolidated over a wide area.

Thus when the veil is again lifted in the early part of the second century, episcopacy had become the almost universal custom and practice of the primitive church. Bishop Lightfoot[5] calls the roll, as it were, of the ancient Christian world and finds evidence of it nearly everywhere during the second century: in Jerusalem and elsewhere in Palestine; in Antioch and other parts of Syria; throughout Asia Minor; in Macedonia and Greece. Philippi was a possible exception, and in Corinth too the episcopal office emerged later than in some other regions.

In Rome also, evidence for a very early unitary episcopate is confused and contradictory. Second-century evidence is also found for bishops in Crete, Gaul, and Africa. Alexandria is hazy and its early approach to the episcopal office exceptional. The evidence shows episcopacy gradually developing everywhere, not always at the same rate. It developed rapidly in the East where oriental and apostolic influences prevailed, with a unitary, monarchical figure emerging. This pattern took shape more slowly in the West where Greek influences were dominant, and a more plural type of *episkopé* prevailed longer. Added to this is the indirect testimony of many quite early writers—Irenaeus, Tertullian, Origen, and others—all suggesting that episcopacy was universal. They betray no knowledge of any time when the monarchical type was not the main pattern, and they take it for granted.

This development may be reinforced by reference to Ignatius, Bishop of Antioch, who died about A.D. 110. Ignatius was his Latin name; his Greek name was Theophoros ("God-bearer"). He was neither Greek nor Roman in temperament but oriental. It is astonishing that such an early witness should prove to be so staunch an advocate and example of episcopacy as reflected in his many letters. With Ignatius we find reference to three orders of clergy—bishop, presbyters, and deacons—long before this arrangement manifested itself concretely elsewhere. Already for him presbyter-bishop had ceased to be entirely synonymous. But Ignatius did not understand the bishop apart from the council of elders, the presbytery.[6] They related to him as strings to a harp.[7]

After the fall of Jerusalem, Antioch became very influential and prominent. Its leading figure toward the end of the first century was Ignatius who also terms himself "Bishop of Syria." He was finally a martyr in Rome, and his writings are preoccupied with the fact of his approaching death. Nevertheless he incidentally gives us much information about his own churches and others in Asia Minor. His letters are addressed to churches we know from the New Testament, such as Rome, Ephesus, Philadelphia, and Smyrna, and to others that are not mentioned in the New Testament, such as Tralles and Magnesia.

His theology is thoroughly ecclesiological, eschatological, mystical, and sacramental. Ignatius is not legalistic in his approach and offers no theories. He simply portrays what a bishop is and does as he himself experiences it, and he assumes this pattern prevails in other places as well. What he describes is so pronounced and detailed that it can hardly be regarded as his own innovation but rather common practice in the primitive church. He is, however, passionate and even poetic in his speech. For example, for him Holy Communion is the "medicine of immortality." He likens a bishop to a helmsman in a storm-tossed sea;* or to a physician applying cold compresses to a swelling; or to an athlete in disciplined training for the Olympic Games (see *Letter to Polycarp*). He is the earnest pastor deeply concerned about the welfare of every member of his flock and readily accessible to them.

---

*An architectural note: The elevated *cathedra* has been likened to the seat of a steersman looking out over the nave (From Latin, *navis,* "ship"), steering by his navigational knowledge (theology) through a troubled world. Yet *cathedra* means also a "teacher's chair."

Ignatius is likewise troubled about discipline in the church. His anxiety is that the bishop may be strong enough to be able to exercise discipline effectively. This is a part of the reason why he concentrates on the nature of the office: "The bishops represent the will of Jesus Christ"[8]; "Render obedience to the bishop and presbyters"[9]; "He who deceives his bishop plays false with God."[10] But he is far more concerned about their possibly succumbing to the Docetic heresy and to Gnosticism. Thus we find him insisting: "Shun these false teachers and cling to Christ and to your bishop."[11] He is no less concerned that Christians show their solidarity with fellow Christians by showing hospitality to them—a mark of sincerity of faith and an episcopal obligation. He is interested in preserving unity and sees unity of the faithful with the bishop (and presbyters) as the way of maintaining it: "No schismatic shall inherit the Kingdom."[12]

Above all, Ignatius is concerned about agreement in matters of doctrine, and he would secure this through the most careful administration of the sacraments, with the bishop as the visible center of unity in the rites. If his claims for episcopacy seem extravagant, as surely they must by present-day understanding, then we must recall the extreme and crucial pressures upon the infant church of that earlier day. But even in his day Ignatius' claims did not go entirely unchallenged; indeed, they were challenged by the Montanists. They would rely upon the Holy Spirit to protect against heresy and maintain unity, and not just rely upon bishops. Ignatius is not really clerical but ecclesiastical in his thinking, and he manages to accommodate the pneumatic dimension to his ecclesiology.

According to Ignatius, the bishop is set aside primarily to offer the Eucharist and to maintain its purity by his being also the ordaining officer. This role for the bishop is clearly evident in the oldest extant description of the Liturgy from

Justin Martyr (ca. A.D. 150). The local church is the body of Christ and sustains its ecclesial unity as it participates in the sacramental body of Christ. The gathered Christian community is an eucharistic assembly making a "pure offering" in every place. In each place Christ himself is present in and with his followers. This is symbolized by the presence of the bishop with his helpers, the presbyters, deacons, and the people.[13] The bishop on earth represents the true Bishop—Christ. This wholeness manifested locally and implied universally *is* the Church Catholic. (Indeed, Ignatius was the first Father to use the term *Catholic Church.*[14]) "The bishops established in the farthest parts of the world are in the counsels of Jesus Christ."[15] "As many as are of God and Jesus Christ are with the bishop."[16]

The bishop is the president of the eucharistic assembly. He alone says the eucharistic prayer to which the people say "Amen." What we call "concelebration" would not have been possible in the primitive church because no fixed prayer was yet used. Ignatius, declares, "The united prayer of the bishop and the congregation is all powerful."[17]

The presiding officer (the bishop) sits in the place of God (or of Christ) surrounded by the presbyters who symbolize the apostles. For Ignatius, the bishop is after the image of Christ, and the presbyters are after the image of the apostles. He admonishes the people, "As the Lord was united to the Father and never acted independently of Him . . . so you yourselves must never act independently of your bishop and presbyters."[18] He advises them to "make sure that no step affecting the Church (especially the Eucharist) is ever taken without the bishop."[19] "Obey your bishop. The bishop is the center of the individual congregation as Christ is the center of the universal Church."[20] It is the distinctive characteristic of the bishop's office that the sacraments be under his supervision: "Let that be deemed a firm Eucharist which is under the bishop, or under one to whom he has entrusted it"[21]; "It is not lawful without the bishop either to baptize or to celebrate an *agape.*"[22] It should be observed that nothing in the New Testament would sanction this. With the growth of the church, this provision had to be altered in practice in the church both East and West. For centuries, however, some episcopal tokens were present in the worship, and to this day the bishops are mentioned in the Catholic liturgy. Ordination, in principal part, is a conveying of sacramental, particularly eucharistic, authority to the presbyter.

Such an idea of monarchical bishop is more than slightly offensive to us nowadays. This did not mean, however, that Ignatius was autocratic or dictatorial; that developed in later history in many times and places. Eastern Orthodox writers are insistent that the Ignatian bishop was not really monarchical at all in that he never acted without his circle of presbyters. So the monarchical concept can be badly distorted if it is understood too rigidly.

Then, too, the picture must be corrected geographically. The Ignatian bishop, and even Cyprian or Chrysostom, must be seen in connection with small local churches, much like a pastor and his assistants in a relatively small community. All the faithful would know the bishop well, and his human qualities would show through to them. Each town had its bishops and presbyters to begin with. Rural bishops were often known as *chorepiskopoi.* This term persists in some traditions to the present time, and in fact Orthodox presbyters today are according to their function what the *chorepiskopoi* once were, except they do not have the right to ordain. But for the most part these rural bishoprics were absorbed to become parts of larger urban dioceses.

The various bishops kept in touch with one another through correspondence and through meetings of synods, thus sustaining a linkage and solidarity both regionally and universally. The factor of growth of the church made it necessary for the bishop to delegate his eucharistic responsibility to presbyters.

Without elaborating upon it, it needs to be emphasized once again that although the notion of a unitary episcopate was well developed early in the East, west of the Aegean Sea the development was slower. In the West a collegiate or plural style of episcopacy persisted until well into the second century. Different political realities existed there, and nothing like the manifold pressures and crises of the East were experienced. In any event the term *bishop* does not appear to have attached solely to the presiding officer of the presbytery as quickly in the West. He presided and ordained but had not yet emerged in a singular or monarchical sense.

In contrast to his usual practice, in writing to Rome Ignatius does not address a bishop by name, for Rome apparently had none in the sense that he intended, and uncharacteristically, he does not mention the episcopal office at all. It is surmised that his presence at the time of his martyrdom and his testimony there may have influenced the church in Rome to turn to a unitary episcopate. In lists of bishops of Rome compiled later, reference is made to those who had played the role but had not yet enjoyed the designation as bishop. The first century in Rome ended with Clement, a mild and unpretentious presbyter-bishop, and the second century ended with an autocratic Pope Victor. Between these two poles the change took place.

If for Ignatius the bishop is the "center of Unity," then for Irenaeus he is the "repository of truth." Irenaeus grew up in Asia Minor and was a pupil of Polycarp. In all probability the church in Gaul came from Asia Minor, and Irenaeus became bishop in Lyons in the latter part of the second century, dying about A.D. 202 or 203. He emphasizes the bishop's teaching authority and affirms that the bishop possesses a "charisma of truth."[23] Even in his day the term *presbuteros* is still used interchangeably with *episkopos,* and in accordance with Western practice he is slow to replace the first with the second. Nevertheless, he may at times term *bishops* as *presbyters,* but he never terms *presbyters* as *bishops.* With respect to teaching authority he early acknowledges the primacy of Rome and uses its apostolic tradition in his appeal against heretics. It should be of particular interest to those of the Wesleyan tradition that Irenaeus appears to regard episcopacy as a distinct office but not as a separate order.[24] He overcomes Gnosticism by arguing from the unbroken apostolic teaching tradition, which did not uphold Gnostic ideas. He therefore is staunchly christological, and he strongly affirms the Incarnation. He is, in fact, regarded as the founder of Christian theology. One of his famous aphorisms is that "Christ became what we are so that we might become what he is."

The next leading figure in the development of episcopacy is Cyprian, Bishop of Carthage in the third century. He is the most outstanding churchman of his century. As such, he outstrips all his predecessors in the vigor with which he asserts the status and prerogatives of episcopal office. He holds his own episcopal role as being the "absolute vicegerent of Christ." The bishop is the indispensable conduit of God's grace. He is the high priest. The bishop is appointed by God and is responsible directly to him. He is under God's inspiration and illumination. In a word, just as Cyprian argues that without the Church there is no salvation, so without the bishop there is no Church. Therefore, without the bishop there is no salvation. Cyprian's ecclesiology is very "high" indeed. The Church is Mother, Bride of Christ, and a person cannot have God for his Father without the Church as his Mother. Ignatius' ecclesiology is also strong, but he is not "clerical" or "ecclesiastical" in the sense of Cyprian, for whom laity are essentially set aside entirely. Needless to say not all of his notions were universally accepted. He separates also from Ignatius in a christological sense. The bishop stands not so much in the place of Christ as in the place of the apostles, whose ministry he sees himself and other bishops as continuing. Thus the roles of episcopacy and presbytery are essentially reversed for him. Cyprian is known also for his insistence on Christian priesthood and sacrifice. In this he follows Tertullian.

Of course Cyprian operated in the midst of much controversy where he had to be stoutly assertive. The first issue he confronted was the status of Christians who had lapsed under persecution. His viewpoint was that only the bishop had the power of absolving and restoring them. He successfully called upon and received the support of the Bishop of Rome for this view. The second issue was the famous one on whether or not baptism by heretics and schismatics was valid. He stood for rebaptism in such cases. Here again he called upon Rome but was refused support. Various synods in Africa and Asia Minor, however, supported him, and he stood his ground. He was a man of very strong principle and helped to affirm the supremacy of the episcopal office. Nevertheless, he never entirely lost the sense of the importance of the local church as the eucharistic community, the view characteristic of Ignatius. His intention was to consult his colleagues and followers, but in practice he did not always do this. Cyprian believed also that the episcopal office is a whole, indivisible, and that all bishops share in it, a notion first manifested in Ignatius. As the sacramental and ecclesiastical body of Christ is one and bishops preside over the Eucharist, so the bishops in each locality are a vehicle of ecumenical unity. Cyprian died a martyr in A.D. 258.

Apostolic Succession

It has been emphasized here that the early development of episcopacy is clouded with uncertainty and is therefore more a matter of theological interpretation than of history. The very period in which it emerged is one for which documentary support is entirely lacking. Therefore, theories abound.

The viewpoint which seems to have weightiest support later in Reformed circles is that the bishop arose as leader or chairman from a body or council of coequal presbyter-bishops. Even in the middle of the third century the bishop was appointed or elected by the presbyterial college and consecrated by them. The practice continued in the church of Alexandria, a fact that John Wesley often emphasized. It would be both natural and necessary for this to occur, particularly in an atmosphere of crisis and multiple emergencies. This is not out of accord with known facts of the New Testament period as well as with existing conditions in the postapostolic era at the end of the first century and the beginning of the second century. This interpretation is congenial to a Protestant perspective. It emphasizes history rather than theology and does not insist on special divine or apostolic sanction of the episcopal office.

Attention needs to be given also to what may be termed a "Catholic perspective," namely, apostolic succession. It began to make itself felt at a time when Gnosticism was being combated and when a self-conscious priesthood was emerging. There is a hint of this notion in II Timothy 2:2 where it is recorded: "What you have heard from me before many witnesses entrust to faithful men who will be able to teach others also." Certainly the time came when this position was strongly affirmed, and this having been done, it is possible to derive considerable historical support for it. For example, Clement of Rome, writing to the church at Corinth toward the end of the first century, states somewhat ambiguously that the apostles appointed their "first fruits" to be bishops.[25] They knew there would be strife over the office of bishop. The apostles were said to have anticipated these disputes and therefore directed "that if they should fall asleep, other approved men should succeed to their office."[26] This reference has often been cited as containing the "germ" of apostolic succession and of papal primacy. What kind of apostles did Clement have in mind: the Twelve (i.e., Lucan) or Pauline apostles? Paul is reported to have appointed presbyter-bishops, but the New Testament gives no evidence that the Twelve did. Besides, apostolic succession is not Clement's focal issue: he desires rather to rectify injustices against leaders of the church in Corinth.

Then Ignatius is often cited in support of this theory of apostolic succession. He does indeed write with apostolic authority. Yet he specifically states in his Roman epistle: "I do not as Peter and Paul issue commandments unto you. They were apostles; I am but a condemned man; they were free, while I am even until now a servant."[27] He apparently makes no claim to apostleship. Moreover, we have seen that Ignatius likens the bishop to one who sits in the place of God or Christ. It is the *presbyters* who are likened to the circle of apostles.

The name of Hegesippus is also often mentioned in support of this theory. He visited Rome about the middle of the second century. He is cited by Eusebius as having drawn up lists of bishops in various churches. His aim was to affirm the orthodoxy of these churches by demonstrating that they upheld orthodoxy because they preserved the apostolic teachings. He seems to trace successions of bishops back to the apostles themselves. He is supported by Irenaeus, a somewhat later contemporary, who may quote Hegesippus in his own writings. Irenaeus, as we have seen, particularly appeals to the Roman succession as guaranteeing pure doctrine thereby opposing Gnostic heresy.

Another contemporary, Tertullian, takes a similar approach. He is followed a little later by Hippolytus who also emphasizes that the bishop is filled with the Holy Spirit. Thus he adds to linkage with the historical Jesus the contemporary power of the Holy Spirit in ordinations. It is no surprise that Cyprian supports apostolic succession in the strongest possible terms. For him bishops are not merely in succession *from* the apostles but are successors *of* the apostles. In other words, for him bishops *are* apostles. Repeatedly this notion is resorted to in order to establish priestly teaching authority against heretics. Here again we see the mingling of theology and history. Its supporters would insist that it was a fact before it was a doctrine. The Orthodox tradition, however, lays stress on continuity of apostolic faith, not of function. A fairly classic statement asserts:

> The Church founded by Jesus Christ is apostolic; it was to the Apostles that our Lord confided the deposit of the faith, the mission to teach all nations, the power to administer the sacraments, the task to lead the faithful into the way of salvation. The Apostles were mortal; their ministry is to be exercised until the consummation of the ages. They must therefore have successors: these are the bishops. The bishops are doctors; that is to say, guardians, interpreters, and judges of doctrine. They have the fulness of the priesthood; not only do they administer the sacraments, but they confer the power to administer them. They are pastors; to them belongs the care of leading and feeding the flock of

Jesus Christ. What the bishops have received from the Apostles they transmit to their successors; and thus is formed in the Church a chain, of which not a link is broken—an uninterrupted tradition by which, from generation to generation, pass the teaching, the episcopal character, and authority.[28]

Apostolic succession would attribute the origin of episcopacy to divine initiative and therefore make it indispensable to the church. Stated boldly, it would have bishops as successors to the apostles by virtue of divine right, though they may be so seen as successors collectively or as a college, and not just as individuals. They are seen as in an "unbroken line" of tactile succession from the apostles who transmitted to bishops what they had received from Christ, especially orthodoxy of doctrine and power of ordination. Some would soften this view and refer to "the historic episcopate," but others would reject such terminology, insisting on a hard doctrine of episcopacy, thus making only episcopally ordained ministry valid and all nonepiscopally ordained ministry invalid.[29] It should be stated that Eastern Orthodoxy accepts this view in the sense of continuity of faith and not of function.

Of course, Wesley himself rejected such a staunch view,[30] and it is rejected also by the Wesleyan tradition. It is not our purpose here to try to prove or disprove apostolic succession but simply to state it as very powerful and influential in the Catholic tradition.* Nevertheless, even the Presbyterians have a similar idea of succession

---

*Bishop R. J. Cooke in *The Historic Episcopate* does decisively reject the claims. Likewise, Bishop John A. Subhan attacks it in a pamphlet, *The Episcopacy in the Church of England.* So does the *Discipline* of the African Methodist Episcopal Church, 1976 edition, p. 29. See also Thomas Coke's ordination sermon (1784) and annotated *Discipline* (1798).

attaching to the presbyterate's acting as a whole which would assure continuity and purity in ministry which dates from the apostles. After all, the Church is one, holy, catholic, and *apostolic*.

With whatever vigor it is argued, it can scarcely be established that there is identity of the office of bishop with that of apostle. After all, the apostles (the Twelve) are gone; they alone were companions of Jesus and witnesses to the resurrection. Assuredly tactile succession cannot be proved. At the same time a succession from apostolic times of faith, of apostolic teaching and doctrine, of ministry, of mission, liturgy, and Spirit is recognized nowadays as very important by most traditions. A sense of continuity with the past in the church as a whole and in the experience of every Christian is a significant truth. Episcopacy clearly is designed in part to uphold and embody this under the free sway of the Holy Spirit, and in history it has often performed an invaluble and continuous function in safeguarding truth and unity, in offering pastoral care, and in transmitting authority through ordination for word, sacrament, and order.

Regardless of means and upon whatever theory or theology, a strong, monarchical, diocesan episcopacy had been established throughout the church by the end of the third century. Nor was this the only controlling factor. "To order the life and teaching of the church and to preserve the apostolic witness against Gnostic perversions and Montanist extravagances the episcopate, the canon and the creed were developed."[31] Though it arose in the midst of crisis the office of bishop became fixed and permanent in fact if not in function. The bishop was long chosen by the people, and from an early date and with some exceptions, he was ordained by three other bishops[32]—this, to affirm universality of the office.

The bishop's roles were many but included preaching,

choosing and ordaining other ministers, confirming, consecrating churches, presiding over various councils, having responsibility over administration, including custody of church funds and care for the needy. He was also teacher and upholder of sound doctrine and unity, chief pastor, supervisor and principal actor in the Liturgy, dispenser of discipline and judicial authority; he cared for the household of God, visited the parishes, served and built up the church. In some early traditions the bishop was seen as wedded to his diocese and could not be translated or transferred.

Most of these functions are recognizable with regard to the episcopal office today. Though representative bishops in various centuries of Christian history would be very different from one another, there would be a continuum of role which in some sense would unite them. In the Apostolic Constitutions (8.28) we find these words: "The bishop blesses; but does not receive the blessing; he lays on hands, ordains, offers the Eucharist; . . . the bishop exercises discipline, except over a bishop for alone he cannot do this."[33]

So it was that during the first three centuries a threefold ministry of bishop, elder or presbyter, and deacon developed. We have already observed that Jesus left no blueprint for ministry or episcopacy, but the New Testament and apostolic tradition contributed to the shaping of the office, infuenced by historical and sociological factors, by the guidance of the Holy Spirit, and by experience. The same factors have continued to influence the shaping of the office throughout history.

A Fourth Century Change, and Later

In the fourth century very great changes took place with respect to the ministry of episcopacy prompted by developments within the church and from the outside as well. The principal internal element has already been referred to briefly: apostolic succession. With Ignatius the responsibility of *episkopé* is a shared one by the bishop and presbyters together. We have seen how their very designations were interchangeable: *episkopoi* and *presbuteroi*. Then the president of the council became known as *the* bishop; consequently the responsibility divided. The bishop was seen in a christological and eschatological role—an eucharistic role—for he alone at first uttered the eucharistic prayer, he alone ordained. The circle of presbyters were after the model of apostles and were charged with being teachers and administrators.

As the church grew and parishes multiplied, having one bishop for each church became unwieldy and finally virtually impossible. This meant that the eucharistic role could no longer be reserved solely for the bishop and was undertaken by delegation to the presbyters. The earlier liturgical documents show that authority was conveyed by the bishop to presbyters to celebrate the Eucharist. This meant there was a reversal of role. The bishop became the coordinator and administrator among the several parishes. Likewise, since authoritative and unitary decisions had to be made in doctrinal disputes and in the combating of heretics, the *magisterium,* the teaching authority, also was concentrated in the hands of the bishop. Both of these functions—administration and teaching—had formerly belonged to the presbyters. Meanwhile, with the scattering of presbyters, in the exercise of their new eucharistic role, the practice of there being a council of presbyters was effectively lost. Both offices became more individual than collegial. At the same time the ministry became a priesthood. The stage was set for a true *monarchical* bishop who was at the same time less collegial and more autocratic. The notion of apostolic succession tended to fix this new distribution of authority; hence, a new idea of episcopate was brought into being. Symbolically, the bishop ceased to represent Christ while the presbyters represented the apostles; the situation was now reversed.

During the same period, but especially from Cyprian onward, all bishops were seen as coequal for a time. Each had a responsibility also for the whole church. Each bishop was a successor of Peter. By letters and encyclicals, by synods and councils, this community sense was made real, and the ground was prepared for a more universal structure and finally for the papacy.

The external developments in the fourth century that effected a drastic change in the course of episcopacy were the conversion of Constantine (A.D. 313) and the Roman Empire's subsequently becoming officially Christian with the Edict of Milan the same year. The bishops gradually became officials of state and a part of a system of secular dignitaries. With the barbarian invasions the power of bishops increased even more. They were among the best educated and most experienced administrative persons in society. They were well known and inspired confidence and respect among the populace. At the time of the invasions the church was probably better organized than the empire. Thus bishops became civil authorities. In the Middle Ages in many parts of Europe they became temporal lords, leaders of armies, and a privileged part of the feudal system. A subject could scarcely distinguish his prince from his bishop. So it was that they were even more truly monarchical bishops.

At one time the bishop had been a local church leader, and the local chuch was thereby exalted. Now the local church's significance was lost in the midst of an exalted superstructure. The bishops were priests of a religion officially sanctioned by the imperial power. It was such an episcopacy that the Reformation resisted. There were undoubtedly many conscientious and saintly bishops, but this was not the prevailing pattern. Augustine, for example, called the episcopal office "a duty" and not an honor. He also said, "*For* you I am a bishop but *with* you I am a Christian"[34] (italics mine). The shape of ministry and episcopacy which was formed in the fourth and fifth centuries differed sharply from the model that emerged during the first three centuries. In its new form it persisted until the Reformation. In fact these changes in episcopacy and church organization accommodating itself to a nominal Christian society, Christendom, have predominated until our own century. In the East episcopacy has had an even more static and fixed character than in the West.

This is not the place for detailed discussion of the papacy, but the pope is, after all, a bishop too. By Roman Catholics he is regarded as vicar of Christ and successor to Peter. He is Patriarch of the West and Bishop of Rome, acknowledged primate of all Roman Catholics.

Peter clearly stood out among the Twelve in a special way. The Gospels reflect this throughout. Tradition, but not concrete history, places him in Rome. If so, he was *apostle* there together with Paul and never specifically called "bishop" there or anywhere else. He was the principal spokesman of the leaders of the early church and presumably continued to be until he finished his course.

Rome as a Christian center was prominent very early since it was the focus of the Roman Empire. At an early date other churches began to look to Rome for appeal, for guidance, and for support. This is clear in the writings of Clement, Ignatius, Irenaeus, Cyprian, and many other church fathers. From the second century and afterward the Bishop of Rome was looked to for deciding questions of doctrinal controversy. The pope played an ever-increasing role in matters of determining doctrine, of opposing heretics, of establishing the canon of Scripture. Naturally the status of Rome's bishop increased, and in time these prerogatives were aggressively asserted by the pope as his right. In any event the primacy of the pope was recognized by the church both East and West for many centuries.

At times, however, there was a contest between those who supported the theocratic imperialism of Rome, on the one hand, and the Caesaropapism of Constantinople, on the other. Many powerful figures appeared in the papal chair, some of whom were outstanding in their efforts to reform the excesses and corruption that plagued the church. The papacy began its ascent in the sixth century, reached its climax in the twelfth and thirteenth centuries, and began to decline in the two centuries that followed. Very often there was tension between popes and the episcopacy in general. Gradually the appointment of bishops was put into the hands of the papacy.

It is interesting that in the latter part of the twentieth century the papacy enjoys a new prestige in much of the world. Vatican I created a furor with its proclamation of infallibility, but Vatican II has succeeded in tempering that position with a reemphasis upon the collegiality of Roman Catholic bishops under papal primacy more in keeping with the Cyprian view.

Nevertheless, it was the abuses related to episcopacy—simony, pluralism, clerical marriage, nepotism—that led to the virtual abolishing of the office of bishop by the reformers on the European continent or the changing of the shape of the office drastically from what it had become in the medieval period.* This criticism did not go unnoticed by Rome, and the Council of Trent laid great stress on correcting abuses and corruption among the

---

*There was a saying about some bishops of the Middle Ages that though they had the title of shepherd, they played the part of wolves.

hierarchy. Since that time the aim at least has been to see to it that able administrators and authentic spiritual guides rule Roman Catholic dioceses, and once again Vatican II has greatly extended this process.

Some mention must be made of women and episcopacy. There were many women who were overseers in the history of the church, that is, abbesses and *episcopae*. "A great number of communities headed by abbesses with independent jurisdiction exempt from bishops were spread throughout Italy, Spain, France, Germany, Poland, England and Ireland."[35] Gradually this practice was phased out or suppressed, however. There is evidence of a number of stone carvings and mosaics of *episcopae* in episcopal regalia, with stoles and miters. They had all the duties of bishops and enjoyed at least quasi-episcopal status. They were not ordained to the priesthood, although abbesses seem to have had a kind of ordination. They could not themselves ordain others. Therefore, though "functional" bishops, they were not sacramentally bishops. The Council of Trent imposed restrictions on such practice, although some bishops opposed this. In France such roles for abbesses continued until well into the nineteenth century.[36]

In England episcopacy was never abandoned, despite the insistence of reformers on the Continent. In fact episcopacy has continued much the same since the missionary Augustine arrived in Kent in 597 to become the first Archbishop of Canterbury (601). This has meant a greater continuity in the Church of England and, at times at any rate, an insistence upon apostolic succession that would outpace Roman Catholic apologists. Despite this, Pope Leo XIII in 1896 declared Anglican orders invalid through defect of form and intention, just as Pope Pius V had excommunicated Queen Elizabeth I in 1570. The road was at times rocky, however, and British monarchs kept their hands in the appointment of bishops whose fate then tended to rise and fall with that of their sovereigns. There are genuine reasons to question the uninterrupted tactile succession of Anglican bishops at the beginning of this period. On the other hand, the intention of continuity is fairly clear, and there were fortunately many outstanding bishops during the crises of the English Reformation and the Civil War. Later on some English bishops so persecuted and hounded the Puritans that the scars have not been entirely erased to this day.

By the time John Wesley appeared on the scene the persecution had ceased, but many bishops were time-servers, seekers after status and little interested in vital religion. There were exceptions, of course, but they only served to prove the prevailing pattern. The wonder is that Wesley was as patient and supportive of his mostly indifferent episcopal superiors as he was. Fortunately the nineteenth and twentieth centuries brought change, and many Anglican bishops of this later period have been in every way exemplary.

For our purposes it is of great interest that the Moravian church (Unitas Fratrum) had and still has bishops for whom the claim of historic succession is made by some. The validity of this was admitted also by Dr. Potter, Archbishop of Canterbury, who while Bishop of Oxford had ordained John Wesley. It was through the Eastern rather than the Western church that the succession was conveyed. John Amos Comenius was a Moravian bishop and conveyed the episcopal order to his son-in-law, Daniel Ernst Jablonski, who consecrated Count Nicolaus Ludwig Zinzendorf bishop, and he in turn ordained Peter Boehler. While in Georgia, John Wesley was deeply moved as he witnessed the ordination of a Moravian bishop.[37] Wesley equivocated on his attitude toward Moravian bishops and other orders of their ministry.[38] Episcopacy among them was and continues to be very limited in its function and authority. Their bishops are nevertheless the ordaining officers, as a German couplet states:

Der Bischof ist ein Mann
Der ordiniren kann.
(A bishop is a man
Who can ordain.)

Some branches of the Lutheran family of churches also have maintained an episcopacy, through without claim of historic succession. This was particularly true in Scandinavia.[39] Martin Luther preferred the congregational structure but was open also to the episcopal or presbyteral, as not being contrary to Holy Scripture. Indeed, Luther engaged with others in the ordination of bishops. One example is Nicholas Amsdorf who was consecrated on January 20, 1542. In 1970 the American Lutheran Church authorized the use of the title for appropriate officers, and in 1980 the Lutheran Church in America approved the use of the designation *bishop,* which is now widely employed in these denominations. The change was one of title only, not of power or authority.

This essay concludes as it began by affirming that bishops of the Wesleyan tradition have some kinship with bishops throughout history. We are recognizably a part of a common stream. Diversity is a hallmark of the development of episcopal tradition so there is plenty of room under the ample spread of the trees. We can trace our roots with some clarity. Yet Wesley was more interested in a scriptural episcopacy than an historical episcopacy. This is where we episcopal Methodists come in.

Notes

1. This topic was discussed at Wesley's second conference in 1745. Cf. *Minutes of the Methodist Conference* (London: Mason, 1862), 1:26–27.

John Wesley believed the episcopal form of government to be scriptural, though not exclusively so (see his sermon on "Catholic Spirit," *Standard Sermons* 2:2). But to quote from the 1744 Minutes:

"Q. Is Episcopal, Presbyterian, or, Independent church-government most agreeable to reason?

A. The plain origin of church-government seems to be this. Christ sends forth a preacher of the Gospel. Some who hear him repent and believe the Gospel. They then desire him to watch over them, to build them up in the faith, and to guide their souls in the paths of righteousness. Here then is an independent congregation, subject to no pastor but their own, neither liable to be controlled in things spiritual by any other man or body of men whatsoever.

But soon after some from other parts, who are occasionally present while he speaks in the name of Him that sent him, beseech him to come over and help them also. Knowing it to be the will of God he consents (complies), yet not till he has conferred with the wisest and holiest of his congregation, and with their advice appointed one who has gifts and grace to watch over the flock till his return.

If it please God to raise another flock in the place, before he leaves them he does the same thing, appointing one whom God has fitted for the work to watch over these souls also. In like manner, in every place where it pleases God to gather a little flock by his word, he appoints one in his absence to take the oversight of the rest, and to assist them of the ability which God giveth. These are Deacons, or servants of the church, and look on their first pastor as their common father. And all these congregations regard him in the same light, and esteem him still as the shepherd of their souls.

These congregations are not strictly independent. They depend on one pastor, though not on each other.

As these congregations increase, and as the Deacons grow in years and grace, they need other subordinate Deacons or helpers; in respect of whom they may be called Presbyters, or Elders, as their father in the Lord may be called the Bishop or Overseer of them all."

2. Rupert E. Davies, "Episcopacy: Its History and Value," *The London Quarterly and Holborn Review,* no. 181 (1956): 86.

3. Lightfoot, *Philippians,* 196ff.

4. "At Jerusalem the position of James practically anticipated the form of the later episcopate, and was not without influence in promoting its universal extension." J. Armitage Robinson, *"The Primitive Ministry,"* in *Essays on The Early History of the Church and the Ministry,* Ed. H. B. Swete (1921), 88. Lightfoot is even more insistent on this point in *Philippians,* 197.

5. Lightfoot, *Philippians*, 208ff.

6. See *Trallians* 2.2, 7.2; *Magnesians* 2.1; *Ign. Ephesians* 2.2, 4.1; *Smyrnaeans* 8.1. (It is of interest that John Wesley included the Epistles of St. Ignatius in his *Christian Library*, vol. 1.)

7. *Ign. Ephes.* 4.1.

8. *Ign. Ephes.* 3.

9. *Ign. Ephes.* 20.

10. *Magnes.* 3.

11. *Trall.* 6.

12. *Philadephians* 3.

13. *Smyrnaeans* 8.2; *Phila.* 4.1.

14. *Smyrnaeans* 8.

15. *Ign. Ephes.* 3.

16. *Phila.* 3.

17. *Ign. Ephes.* 5.

18. *Magnes.* 7.1

19. *Smyrnaeans* 8.1.

20. *Smyrnaeans* 8.

21. *Smyrnaeans* 6.

22. *Smyrnaeans* 8.

23. Irenaeus, *Five Books of St. Irenaeus Against Heresies* (London: W. Smith, 1872), Books 3 and 4.

24. Cf. Lightfoot, *Philippians,* 228.

25. Cf. I Corinthians 16:15; 1:16.

26. I Clement 42-44.

27. *Ign. Romans* 4.

28. Fr. Gagarin, S. J., *The Russian Clergy* (reprint, New York: AMS Press, 1872).

29. A. G. Herbert, *Apostle and Bishop* (London: Faber and Faber, 1963), 16.

30. See John Wesley's statement in *Letters* 7:284: "For the *uninterrupted succession* I know to be a fable, which no man ever did or can prove" (italics his). This is the final clause of the *very sentence* in which he states that he is a "scriptural *episkopos.*" Yet his brother Charles to whom this letter is addressed remained unconvinced. Earlier, of course, John did espouse the teaching.

31. Cyril C. Richardson, ed., *Early Christian Fathers,* vol. 1 (Philadelphia: Westminster Press, 1953), 26.

32. Like a Jewish rabbi who was admitted to his office by the laying-on of the hands of three accredited teachers. "The bishop, sitting in his chair, is the descendent, by one line of descent, of the Jewish rabbi." Cf. Philip Carrington, *The Early Christian Church,* vol. 1. (Cambridge: University Press, 1957), 242-243.

33. Quoted *Schaff-Herzog Encyclopedia* 8:664.

34. Augustine *City of God* 19.19.

35. Joan Morris, *The Lady Was a Bishop* (New York: Macmillan, 1973), 3.

36. Ibid. 57.

37. *The Journal of the Rev. John Wesley, A. M.,* ed. Nehemiah Curnock, standard ed., 8 vols. (London: Epworth Press, 1938), 1:170.

39. Archbishop Soderblom felt that continuity was "in our Church perhaps purer and more unbroken than in the Church of England." Cf. Bengt Sundkler, *Nathan Soderblom* (Lund: Gleerups, 1968), 90. For his part Anglican Archbishop William Temple stated that "no particular interpretation is necessary."

III

HOW EPISCOPAL METHODISM BEGAN

Methodism can be said to have several beginnings. Some would see it as a recurrent form of Christianity, a renewal movement that has broken out repeatedly in the history of the church. According to Rupert E. Davies, Methodism bears these marks:

> A religion which prefers personal converse with God to institutional forms and authority; a concern to bring the truth to simple people; a stress on holiness; a reaffirmation of the doctrine of the Holy Spirit; a semi-lay Church Order; and all of this combined with orthodoxy.[1]

John Wesley would heartily concur.

Such a view may seem pretentious, but it does emphasize that what Wesleyanism stands for is no mere eighteenth-century innovation or aberration. It is a part of a tradition of the Church Universal.

Or Methodism may be seen as beginning at Epworth where John Wesley was born, fifteenth child of Samuel and Susanna Wesley. There he began his rigorous training—Thursday evening was his particular time—at his mother's knee. There he was at age five rescued from the rectory fire, "a brand plucked out of the burning." From Epworth, after Oxford, he served for two years as his father's curate in the nearby village of Wroote. In Epworth, too, he preached early in the revival using his father's tomb as his pulpit.

Or we could say that Methodism began in 1729 at Oxford University with the Holy Club where John and Charles Wesley met with George Whitefield and others to seek a more earnest Christianity through a group or society rooted in Bible study, serious devotions, and Christian service to the needy.* This experience as a devotional group propelled the three persons just named to Georgia (though Whitefield preceded the Wesleys there) where the brothers Wesley were to experience a somewhat abortive apostolic or missionary and pastoral ministry.

Georgia, too, was a distinctly Methodist beginning. There, as in the Holy Club, an effort was made

> (1) to advise the more serious among them to form themselves into a sort of *little society* [italics mine], and to meet once or twice a week, in order to reprove, instruct, and exhort one another. (2) To select out of these a smaller number for a more intimate union with each other.[2]

In both instances, at Oxford and in Georgia, we see familiar Methodist patterns which appear more clearly later on as bands, classes, and societies—in that ascending numerical order of size. Wesley referred to the Oxford (1729) and Savannah (1736) initiatives as the "first rise" and "second rise of Methodism."[3]

The "third rise"—another Methodist beginning—he attaches to a gathering of forty or fifty who in London agreed to meet together weekly beginning May 1738.[4] The

---

*It was in this very context that they were called, in derision, "Methodists."

Moravian influence is clear in the second and third rises of Methodism, and Peter Boehler was a cofounder with John Wesley of the London "society." This group later met in Fetter Lane, originally an Anglican society. There were many religious societies in the Church of England even before Wesley.

Soon afterward, following Aldersgate and upon George Whitefield's invitation, Wesley gave his attention to Bristol where other societies were established, finally centering in the "New Room in the Horsefair." After many trials the London and Bristol societies were linked as the "United Societies" in 1739.

The following year Fetter Lane experienced a division over the issue of what we would call "quietism," the Wesleyan portion joining with the "Foundery" society. The Foundery was Wesley's London headquarters just as the New Room was his Bristol headquarters. From these centers he spread his mission to other places, and other societies were planted. The various emerging societies were bound together by his overseership and by a common discipline expressed in the General Rules which Wesley had written out as a guide to Christian living. In view of our Methodist origin in societies, it is often observed that we are still struggling to become a church!

To afford supervisory and pastoral care to these scattered companies and to coordinate their work, he began his incessant itineration around England and Wales; then to Scotland and again and again to Ireland. Tirelessly he pursued his rounds, first of all by horseback and then by carriage fitted appropriately with a desk and bookcase. No detail seemed to escape his attention. When not able to be present in person, he exercised his care through constant correspondence. When excluded from Anglican pulpits he readily took to field preaching, a painful new departure at first; a method he had learned from Whitefield in Bristol and first practiced in April 1739. Vast crowds gathered when it was announced that John Wesley was to preach. There was reality, as well as legitimacy, to this fellow of Lincoln College's claim of the whole world being his parish.

Naturally he could not engage in all this by himself. His brother Charles was at the beginning his ally and, until his marriage, a constant associate in evangelism. He was likewise supported by a small company of Anglican clergymen who were sympathetic with his endeavors. But most of all he gathered and trained large numbers of lay preachers who were responsible to him and subject to his guidance and assignment.

It was in relation to these preachers that Wesley began to exercise what amounted to an episcopal office and continued this role until his life's end. We have seen that it was not without reason that he thought of himself as a "scriptural *episkopos*."

Of course, he was often under severe criticism for his supposed arbitrary use of authority. He was indeed sometimes called "Pope John." The Minutes of the 1766 Conference contain his response, for he did not just assume such power; rather he was *asked* to undertake leadership and guidance:

> But several gentlemen are much offended at my having so much power. My answer to them is this: I did not seek any part of this power. . . .
> But some of your Helpers say, *"This is shackling free-born Englishmen"* and demand a *free Conference*—that is a meeting of all, wherein all things shall be determined by most votes. I answer, it is possible after my death, something of this kind may take place, but not while I live. To *me* the preachers have engaged themselves to submit, to serve me as sons in the Gospel. . . . No one needs to submit to it, unless he will. . . . Every preacher and every member

may leave me when he pleases; but while he chooses to stay, it is on the same terms that he joined me at first.

But this is *arbitrary* power: this is no less than making yourself a Pope. If by arbitrary power you mean a power which I exercise singly without any colleagues therein, this is certainly true; but I see no hurt in it. *Arbitrary* in this sense is a very harmless word. If you mean *unjust, unreasonable,* or *tyrannical,* then it is not true. . . . Preaching twice or thrice a day is no burden to me at all: but the care of all the preachers and all the people is a burden indeed.[5]

Or again:

In November, 1738, several persons came to me in London, and desired me to advise and pray with them. I said, "If you will meet on Thursday night, I will help you as well as I can." More and more they desired to meet with me, till they were increased to many hundreds. The case was afterwards the same at Bristol, Kingswood, Newcastle, and many other parts of England, Scotland, and Ireland. It may be observed, the desire was on *their* part, not mine. My desire was to live and die in retirement. But I did not see that I could refuse them my help, and be guiltless before God.

Here commenced my power; namely, a power to appoint when, and where and how they should meet and to remove those, whose life showed they had no desire to flee from the wrath to come.[6]

Wesley stressed consistently that those preachers who related themselves to him must be directed by him in their work. The association was voluntary on their part; the alternative was to leave the work, a privilege of which a number availed themselves.

Apart from superintending the preachers in his own wide itineration, Wesley devised a conference of the preachers. The first one met in June 1744 at the Foundery in London. In attendance, all upon Wesley's own invitation, were regular Anglican clergymen as well as lay preachers of the connection (or connexion). They were concerned with matters of both doctrine and discipline. The Minutes of these sessions followed the familiar question-and-answer form, vestiges of which are still found in our present Annual Conference procedures. The proceedings of the first four conferences were printed as "doctrinal minutes," and in 1748 the cumulative "disciplinary minutes" were published. From time to time the Large Minutes were compiled. Typically there was open discussion, but the final decisions were made by Wesley himself. Thus he exercised his apostolic authority. This consultative body continued throughout his lifetime.

It is clear that John Wesley exercised the superintendent's role. The chief preacher of a given circuit was called an "assistant." Related to these were "helpers." The assistant roughly corresponded to presbyter or elder and the helper to deacon, though they were not ordained. Wesley's role corresponded to bishop.[7]

His overseership related not only to preachers but also to property; indeed, the two were related. The building of the New Room in Bristol almost immediately raised this issue. If a chapel were put under the authority of lay trustees, did this give them the right of determining who should preach there? Naturally they did insist on this right and, if assented to, would probably have destroyed Methodism as we know it. The issue was finally determined in Bristol by putting the property deed in Wesley's own hands.[8] Thereafter no chapel could be called "Methodist" unless complete control was lodged in the hands of the founder. He prepared a "Model Deed" in 1763 which provided that persons appointed by conference could use the premises as long as they faithfully preached Methodist doctrines.

This is in accord with Roman Catholic practice of property being vested in the "ordinary." In John Wesley's case he was not an officer in a church but in a society which doubtless softened the force of his status. In any event, he exercised the office of bishop among Methodists although he was not elected to it. The claim has often been made for him that "he was providentially appointed and spiritually ordained a bishop from his very relationship to his followers."[9] It is clear that he played this role in England for fifty years and among his American followers in one way or another for almost half as long. How this responsibility was to be continued after his death is our real concern here. To this we shall return after taking a look at Methodist beginnings in America.

American Beginnings

Since our theme is episcopacy, any narrative of general Methodist history must necessarily be brief. By any account the start of Methodism in the American colonies must emphasize lay initiatives. The short labors of the Wesley brothers in Georgia left no permanent deposit in America and the gains of George Whitefield, to the extent that they were permanent, registered mostly with the other churches already present in these colonies. Nevertheless the waves generated in England by our founder whose parish was the world were bound to be felt again on these shores.

Strangely enough the pioneer Methodist preachers came from Ireland. John Wesley himself did not preach on that island until 1747, but he was sufficiently encouraged by the response that he visited it twenty-one times in all. A small but vigorous body of Irish Methodists persists there in its own conference until the present time. It has been a principal source of missionaries to other parts of the globe, so much so that by the middle of the nineteenth century no fewer than five hundred Methodist preachers in the United States had been born in Ireland.

On one of his tours of Ireland, Wesley preached near the town of Drumsna. Members of the Strawbridge family were converted under Methodist preaching there, but there is no record that Wesley himself was the preacher. It was in Drumsna that Robert Strawbridge was born. He migrated to America about 1760 and finally settled at Sam's Creek, Maryland. He began preaching soon afterward, by about 1763. He caused to be built a log meeting house, probably in 1764. It was of this place that Asbury recorded in his *Journal* on May 1, 1801, "Here Mr. Strawbridge formed the first society in Maryland—and *America.*" This last word, which he italicized, would seem to confirm that Strawbridge's work antedated Philip Embury's in New York, but this is disputed. He must be credited with many "firsts" in his ministry and is sometimes regarded the "first Methodist Protestant."

In any event, at about the same time Philip Embury did organize in New York what some others regard the first Methodist society in America. A cousin of Barbara Heck, he was rebuked out of his lethargy by her in such a way that he began to preach again as he had done in Ireland. Shortly afterward Captain Thomas Webb, a British officer, joined the group. From this beginning developed the society that met in John Street Church, New York, built in 1768.

Captain Webb is also related to the start of Methodism on Long Island and in Philadelphia, among other places. He helped to establish the society in Philadelphia, and he preached in Old St. George's Church there, a property purchased from a Dutch Reformed body. Webb, an eloquent preacher, also had a part in launching Lovely Lane Chapel in Baltimore. Captain Webb preached in his regimentals, that is, in his "redcoat" uniform, a striking figure he must have made, bound to encourage attendance.

In 1768 a member of the New York society wrote to John Wesley pleading for more experienced preachers for the struggling groups of Methodists. It was in direct response to this appeal that the British Conference of 1769 sent two missionaries to the American colonies. They were Richard Boardman as "assistant" and Joseph Pilmore (a name spelled in various ways). They arrived in Philadelphia, where Pilmore began to preach, while Boardman proceeded to New York. Boardman was of frail health, which hampered his efforts, but Pilmore was especially earnest and effective. They both returned to England in 1774 on the eve of the War for Independence. Later in life Pilmore again returned to these shores but this time as an Episcopal clergyman. The two men, according to Jesse Lee, were the "first regular itinerant preachers" in America. It should be said that all who went as preachers to America volunteered. None was required to go.[10]

About the same time two unofficial missionaries arrived—Robert Williams and John King—But they were without credentials and came on their own initiative. In 1771, however, Wesley's next two missionaries were appointed by him and landed in the autumn of that year. They were Francis Asbury and Richard Wright.* Asbury was designated the following year as "assistant in America" in place of Boardman. He soon asked to be relieved of this office, but in any event he was superceded in June 1773 by Thomas Rankin, who arrived that year as Wesley's *general assistant,* a kind "suffragan bishop" to

---

*Two other unappointed volunteers, Joseph Yearby and William Glendenning, came over in 1772 and 1774 respectively. It should be remembered that Philip Otterbein and some native Americans who were to become preachers were already here.

Wesley. He was accompanied by George Shadford. These two were a study in contrasts: Rankin was a strict disciplinarian and experienced preacher, while Shadford was a sweet-spirited and well-beloved man. It was to Shadford that Wesley wrote his famous letter of March 1773: "I let you loose, George, on the great continent of America. Publish your message in the open face of the sun, and do all the good you can."

Returning to Rankin, we see that he lost no time in exercising his authority and called the first conference, which met on July 14, 1773, in St. George's, Philadelphia. By virtue of his appointment by John Wesley as general assistant, Rankin presided and appointed the preachers, then ten in number. If Wesley himself exercised the form of episcopal power in Great Britain, then in some rudimentary sense Rankin did so in the American colonies. Authority, relationships, doctrine, and discipline were all touched upon in the Philadelphia meeting whose proceedings are recorded in *Minutes of Some Conversations Between the Preachers in Connection with the Rev. Mr. John Wesley,* published in 1795:

The following queries were proposed to every preacher:

1. Ought not the authority of Mr. Wesley and that conference, to extend to the preachers and people in America, as well as in Great Britain and Ireland?

Answ. Yes.

2. Ought not the doctrine and discipline of the Methodists, as contained in the minutes, to be the sole rule of our conduct who labour, in the connection with Mr. Wesley, in America?

Answ. Yes.

3. If so, does it not follow, that if any preachers deviate from the minutes, we can have no fellowship with them till they change their conduct?

Answ. Yes.

The following rules were agreed to by all the preachers present:

1. Every preacher who acts in connection with Mr. Wesley and the brethren who labour in America, is strictly to avoid administering the ordinances of baptism and the Lord's supper.

2. All the people among whom we labour to be earnestly exhorted to attend the church and to receive the ordinances there; but in a particular manner to press the people in Maryland and Virginia, to the observance of this minute.

3. No person or persons to be admitted to our love-feasts oftener than twice or thrice, unless they become members; and none to be admitted to the society meetings more than thrice.

4. None of the preachers in America to reprint any of Mr. Wesley's books, without his authority (when it can be got) and the consent of their brethren.

5. Robert Williams to sell the books he has already printed, but to print no more, unless under the above restriction.

6. Every preacher who acts as an assistant, to send an account of the work once in six months to the general assistant.[11]

Note should be taken particularly of the restraining rules one and two concerning the ordinances or sacraments.

In 1774 two more missionaries were sent over: James Dempster and Martin Rodda. Neither made any great contribution to Methodism. In 1777 Rodda left the colonies, and in 1778 both Shadford and Rankin returned to England. Finally only Asbury was left, and even he was severely limited during a part of the Revolution. He was forced to seek sanctuary in the house of Judge Thomas White, Kent County, Delaware, from November 1778 to April 1780, leaving there only occasionally for short preaching forays.

The work advanced under great difficulty during the Revolution, but growth was not hindered. The 1773 Minutes recorded 1,160 members, but the number had grown by 1783, the year of the signing of the Treaty of Paris, to 13,740 members. The preachers in all categories had increased from ten in 1773 to eighty-two during the same decade. This was a remarkable achievement in light of the incredible difficulties that the war and many other limitations placed upon them. It is a wonder that the societies even survived let alone grew.

The Controversy over Sacraments

A particular crisis serves to illustrate the pressures under which the American societies had to exist. As we have observed, all the other English missionaries finally departed so that only Asbury remained and even he was essentially in hiding.

It was at this very time that a schism arose in Methodist ranks, especially in Virginia. It was over the administration of the sacraments. Already in Maryland Robert Strawbridge had followed the practices of baptizing and of administering the Lord's Supper. He did this out of what he considered to be necessity and assumed this authority stubbornly and deliberately as an unordained local preacher at the very beginning of his work. He doubtless did it also because of his Roman Catholic upbringing: to be deprived of the sacraments was for him unthinkable. This practice became a point of contention between him and Asbury. It must have been difficult for Asbury to deal with Strawbridge who was his senior by about twenty years. This was a matter already discussed at the 1773 Conference.

According to Asbury's *Journal* (July 14, 1773), it was agreed at the Philadelphia Conference that "no preacher in our connection shall be permitted to administer the ordinances at this time; except Mr. Strawbridge, and he under the particular direction of the assistant."[12] The Minutes themselves do not record this exception. Strawbridge never did accept the 1773 Conference rule with respect to the ordinances despite efforts to persuade him to do so.* Probably for this reason his name did not appear among the appointments for 1774. It is found again for a final time in 1775. Strawbridge, who continued to serve independently, died in 1781. After this pioneer's death a journal entry with reference to Robert Strawbridge does not show Asbury at his best, although he was very candid:

> I visited Bush chapel. The people here once left us to follow another; time was when the labors of their leader were made a blessing to them; but pride is a *busy* sin. He is now no more: upon the whole, I am inclined to think the Lord took him away in judgment, because he was in a way to do hurt to his cause; and that he saved him in mercy, because from his death-bed conversation he appears to have hope in his end.[13]

Others see Strawbridge's stand as a stalwart advocate for the people against outmoded ecclesiasticism.

The issue arising over the sacraments in Virginia and North Carolina was really of quite different focus. Strawbridge's stand could be seen as rejection of authority on the part of an individual. The latter development must be seen as complete rebellion and rejection of Methodist discipline by a sizable group of preachers; therefore, it would have been clear separation not only from the Anglican connection but from Methodism.

---

*Strawbridge was never in conscious "connexion with Mr. Wesley"—the distinctive mark of the Wesleyan Methodist.

Wesley's views were clear: that the preachers were to preach, not baptize and celebrate the Lord's Supper; that the adherents to the Methodist societies should have the sacraments from the Anglican clergy who were, of course, few in number. Moreover, he said that if Methodists leave the church, "I leave them." The conferences were consistent in upholding Wesley's standards and instructions. Many Methodist preachers and people were dissatisfied with this situation. Not all of the Anglican priests, even if they were nearby, were prepared to administer baptism and Holy Communion to Methodists. On their part, the Methodists were not happy at the prospect of the ordinances at the hands of those whom they sometimes regarded as worldly clergymen. Of course, if the sacraments had been seen as more instrumental, as means of grace, much of this struggle could have been lessened.

The Conference of 1779 met in two parts: one part on April 28 in Delaware where Asbury was in hiding, as it were. This conference voted strongly to continue the restraint. The same conference confirmed Asbury as Wesley's general assistant to which office Wesley himself had appointed him after Rankin's withdrawal.

The second part of the conference met on May 18 at Broken Back Church, Fluvanna County, Virginia. Here a majority of the preachers voted to do away with the restraining rules. They proceeded to set up a presbytery of four ministers: Philip Gatch, Reuben Ellis, Leroy Cole, and Thomas Foster. They were to ordain each other and then other preachers to administer the sacraments. Here was a clear breach of discipline.

Asbury proved his leadership capacity by skillfully restoring order. The northern group immediately reacted strongly and at the 1780 Conference resolved to regard their southern brethren no longer Methodists until they returned to discipline. Finally a compromise was reached so that both sides would suspend their actions until John Wesley could be consulted. Naturally he strongly supported Asbury's stand, and the crisis was averted. The war's approaching end and new issues had now to be addressed. Nevertheless, the sacramental issue did not go away. The members of the little Methodist societies were still like sheep without real shepherds.

Wesley's Ordinations

More than one hundred years ago the Reverend Theodore L. Flood and the Reverend (later Bishop) John W. Hamilton edited a volume on *Lives of Methodist Bishops.* They make the claim "that the office of a bishop in the Methodist Episcopal Church was providentially conferred upon, and assumed by, the father and founder of the Wesleyan Societies in England and America." They go on to say that the first preacher to exercise the office (Wesley) was not elected to it nor ordained to it in ordinary usage; the second to exercise episcopal powers (Coke) was also not elected to it but was ordained by the first. The third to exercise the office (Asbury) was elected by his peers and ordained by the second. They conclude, "But the Methodist Church has never offered an apology for the existence of her Episcopacy, and will allow no one to question the right of a single one of her bishops to exericse the duties of his office."[14] In the same context John Wesley is called the "fountain of our episcopal authority." These sentiments summarize the attitude to the office and its origin that has prevailed from *within* our tradition.

We have seen that American Methodism had grown to be numbered in thousands, yet most of these were without benefit of the sacraments. Many clergymen, as Tories, had fled the country prior to and during the Revolutionary

War. Most Methodists had never been baptized nor partaken of Communion though they often lived exemplary Christian lives, were active in their Christian societies, and were under rather strict discipline. The wonder is their patience and restraint. The deprivation of sacraments had the effect of making sacraments seem unimportant.

The English bishops had refused to send over enough ordained clergy or a bishop to care for this flock; in fact, they refused to ordain as bishop an Anglican who had been elected in America to the office of bishop. To go to England for orders was a perilous undertaking and virtually impossible during the war. The Bishop of London was technically charged with care for the colonies but after the American Revolution had no further authority in the States. An episcopal church without a bishop was an anomaly. It must be said that the influx of too many clergy of the Established Church would have aroused suspicion in some quarters, especially in Puritan New England. If a bishop had come, this suspicion would have been intensified.

Francis Asbury repeatedly appealed to Wesley to do something to remedy the situation.[15] His colleagues had for at least a decade been making the same plea. Asbury called for "proper persons," that is, those equipped for useful ministry and prepared to accept excessive hardship, as well as for some ordained persons to meet the sacramental needs. He also made it clear that he himself was ready to continue to serve and sacrifice. He even expressed the hope that Wesley himself would once again visit American shores:

> Dear sir, we are greatly in need of help. A minister, and such preachers as you can fully recommend, will be very acceptable; without your recommendation we shall receive none. But nothing is so pleasing to me, sir, as the thought of seeing you here: which is the ardent desire of thousands more in America.[16]

Though he could not consent to going to America himself, Wesley could not close his ears to American Methodists' call for help.

One can easily understand the difficult position in which Wesley found himself. He was a sacramentarian, a believer in frequent communion, but also he was a High Churchman who believed that only a regularly ordained clergyman ought to officiate at the Eucharist. Indeed, he said that he would rather murder than offend against this rule.[17] Methodist societies and chapels were for preaching; the church was for sacramental worship. Yet in England, but especially in the New World, people called Methodists, numbering thousands, were deprived of this ministry. His whole spirit was opposed to lay ministration of the ordinances, but to ordain them himself, when the bishops refused to, was tantamount to separation from the Established Church.

Moreover, John Wesley was growing older. He was surprised that he had lived so long. In 1753 he had despaired of life and even wrote his own epitaph.[18] Then in January 1773 he sought to recruit John Fletcher to be his successor, but Fletcher declined. Therefore, in 1784 he took three decisive steps which related to the continuation of his work following his death. Thomas Coke, who had had legal training, was his confidential advisor in all three developments. All three severely strained Wesley's relationship to the Church of England.

One had to do with the holding of property and the continuation of the societies in the Methodist connection after his death. From early days in Bristol, property was essentially vested in Wesley himself, as we have seen. After much testing and pondering a "deed poll" or legal "Deed of Declaration" was registered in the Court of Chancery. By it authority was lodged in a conference of one hundred men (about half the total number of preachers) known as the "Legal Hundred," to be a self-perpetuating body, originally chosen and appointed by Wesley. This corporate group became Wesley's successor. This caused pain and anger for some of those *not* chosen, but it gave a concrete form to the Conference and British Methodism was legally incorporated. The Conference also would perform collectively the function of *episkopé*.

In order to allay fears that this powerful body might be unfair in fulfilling its responsibilities, Wesley left a letter to be read at the first conference after his death.

> Chester, April 7, 1785
>
> My dear Brethren,—Some of our traveling preachers have expressed a fear that after my decease you would exclude them either from preaching in connexion with you or from some other privileges which they now enjoy. I know no other way to prevent any such inconvenience than to leave these my last words with you.
>
> I beseech you by the mercies of God that you never avail yourselves of the Deed of Declaration to assume any superiority over your brethren, but let all this go on among those itinerants who choose to remain together exactly in the same manner as when I was with you so far as circumstances will permit.
>
> In particular, I beseech you, if you ever loved me and if you now love God and your brethren, to have no respect of persons in stationing the preachers, in choosing children for Kingswood School, in disposing of the Yearly Contribution and the Preachers' Fund or any other public money. But do all things with a single eye, as I have done from the beginning. Go on thus, doing all things without prejudice or partiality, and God will be with you even to the end.[19]

The second major step in 1784 was his abridgment of *The Book of Common Prayer*, which was published as *The Sunday Service of the Methodists in North America*. He made few changes or additions; principally these were deletions. *The Sunday Service* included a full ordinal, one of the strongest indications that he intended a church to be established by American Methodists. He included also a revision of the Thirty-nine Articles, reduced in number to twenty-four. Here would seem to be another sign of separation which, of course, he never acknowledged.

The third major undertaking in 1784 was the most far-reaching one, that is, ordinations: first of all in response to the deeply felt need in America and then later in the British Isles themselves. His dilemma was a fierce one; either course he could take offended his High Churchmanship deeply: leave his people without sacraments or have an open break with the church. He solved the dilemma, for the Americans at any rate, by making provision for a threefold ministry of deacon, elder, and superintendent, thus effectively providing ministry for a *church* for Methodists there. Then he undertook the ordaining himself.

The account of the ordinations themselves can be given quite briefly as they are in the original references. On Tuesday, August 31, 1784, "Dr. Coke, Mr. Whatcoat, and Mr. Vasey came down from London (to Bristol) in order to embark for America."[20] The next day, Wednesday, September 1, the *Journal* records: "Being now clear in my own mind, I took a step I had long weighed in my mind and appointed Mr. Whatcoat and Mr. Vasey to go and serve the desolate sheep in America."[21] His diary of the same date uses "ordained" rather than "appointed." These ordinations took place at 4:00 A.M. in the home of Dr. John Castleman of 6 Dighton Street in Bristol.

On Thursday, September 2, Wesley's *Journal* entry is: "I added to them three more; which I verily believe, will be much to the glory of God." He apparently means here that he ordained Richard Whatcoat and Thomas Vasey elders, as he had ordained them deacons the day before, and "ordained Dr. Coke as a Superintendent, by the imposi-

tion of my hands, and prayer (being assisted by other
ordained ministers)." These other ministers were the
Reverend James Creighton, who had accompanied Coke
from London, and presumably Whatcoat and Vasey, now
newly ordained presbyters themselves. This occurred also
at about 4:00 A.M. Both Coke and Creighton had assisted
Wesley in the ordinations of Whatcoat and Vasey as a kind
of presbytery. He supplied them with written certificates.
Coke's had the following text:*

To all to whom these presents shall come, John Wesley,
late Fellow of Lincoln College in Oxford, Presbyter of the
Church of England, sendeth greeting.

Whereas many of the People in the Southern Provinces of
North America who desire to continue under my care, and
still adhere to the Doctrines and Discipline of the Church of
England, are greatly distrest for want of ministers to
administer the Sacraments of Baptism and the Lord's
Supper according to the usage of the said Church. And
whereas there does not appear to be any other way of
supplying them with ministers.

Know all men that I John Wesley think myself to be
providentially called at this time to set apart some persons
for the work of the ministry in America. And therefore
under the Protection of Almighty God, and with a single eye
to his glory, I have this day set apart as a Superintendent, by
the imposition of my hands and prayer (being assisted by
other ordained ministers) Thomas Coke, Doctor of Civil
Law, a Presbyter of the Church of England and man whom I
judge to be well qualified for that great work. And I do
hereby recommend him to all whom it may concern as a fit
person to preside over the Flock of Christ. In testimony
whereof I have hereunto set my hand and seal this second

---

*Original in Archives, Methodist Missionary Society, Marylebone St.
London. See Wesley, *Journal* 7:16.

day of September in the year of our Lord one thousand seven hundred and eighty-four.

John Wesley.

A few days later, September 9, he wrote a Preface to *The Sunday Service* which he had abridged the previous spring. The next day he wrote a letter to "Our Brethren in America." Equipped, then, with ordinations and certificates, with a Liturgy and a pastoral letter from the hands of the founder, the little company of three missionaries set sail for New York from Bristol on September 18, 1784. The text of the letter is as follows:

Bristol, September 10, 1784

1. By a very uncommon train of providences many of the Provinces of North America are totally disjoined from their Mother Country and erected into independent States. The English Government has no authority over them, either civil or ecclesiastical, any more than over the States of Holland. A civil authority is exercised over them, partly by the Congress, partly by the Provincial Assemblies. But no one either exercises or claims any ecclesiastical authority at all. In this peculiar situation some thousands of the inhabitants of these States desire my advice; and in compliance with their desire I have drawn up a little sketch.

2. Lord King's *Account of the Primitive Church* convinced me many years ago that bishops and presbyters are the same order, and consequently have the same right to ordain. For many years I have been importuned from time to time to exercise this right by ordaining part of our travelling preachers. But I have still refused not only for peace' sake, but because I was determined as little as possible to violate the established order of the National Church to which I belonged.

3. But the case is widely different between England and North America. Here there are bishops who have a legal

jurisdiction: in America there are none, neither any parish ministers. So that for some hundred miles together there is none either to baptize or to administer the Lord's supper. Here, therefore, my scruples are at an end; and I conceive myself at full liberty, as I violate no order and I invade no man's right by appointing and sending labourers into the harvest.

4. I have accordingly appointed Dr. Coke and Mr. Francis Asbury to be Joint Superintendents over our brethren in North America; as also Richard Whatcoat and Thomas Vasey to act as elders among them, by baptizing and administering the Lord's Supper. And I have prepared a Liturgy little differing from that of the Church of England (I think, the best constituted National Church in the world), which I advise all the travelling preachers to use on the Lord's Day in all the congregations, reading the Litany only on Wednesdays and Fridays and praying extempore on all other days. I also advise the elders to administer the Supper of the Lord on every Lord's Day.

5. If any one will point out a more rational and scriptural way of feeding and guiding those poor sheep in the wilderness, I will gladly embrace it. At present I cannot see any better method than that I have taken.

6. It has, indeed, been proposed to desire the English bishops to ordain part of our preachers for America. But to this I object; (1) I desired the Bishop of London to ordain only one, but could not prevail. (2) If they consented, we know the slowness of their proceedings; but the matter admits of no delay. (3) If they would ordain them now, they would likewise expect to govern them. And how grievously would this entangle us! (4) As our American brethren are now totally disentangled both from the State and from the English hierarchy, we dare not entangle them again either with the one or the other. They are now at full liberty simply to follow the Scriptures and the Primitive Church. And we judge it best that they should stand fast in that liberty wherewith God has so strangely made them free.[22]

As the letter states, Wesley had been importuned earlier to ordain, but he resisted this. At conference after conference this matter linked as it is with possible separation from the Church of England was discussed (for example, 1744, 1752, 1755, 1756, 1758, 1766, and so on). In 1775 Joseph Benson and John Fletcher strongly pressed the issue with Wesley, urging him to ask the Archbishop of Canterbury to allow such ordination, or for Wesley himself to "turn bishop" or to undertake presbyterial ordination.[23]

His appeals to Anglican bishops for relief he mentions in the letter above. The letter to the Bishop of London, Dr. Robert Lowth, was a highly worthy case for it was in support of ordination for John Hoskins, an effective missionary pioneer to Newfoundland. He argues the importance of spiritual and not mere intellectual equipment for ordinands, because a person might know something of Latin and Greek, but know "no more of saving souls than of catching whales."[24] This request was refused as was usually the case. Others had met a similar response both before and after this instance.

Then there was the case of the so-called Greek bishop, Erasmus by name. He appeared in London in 1763. Wesley took note of him, seemed satisfied as to his credentials,[25] and helped him. One of Wesley's preachers, John Jones, was ordained by this man, after Jones had checked his authenticity, this with Wesley's prior approval. Then several other preachers sought this route to ordination without approval and were repudiated by Wesley. The allegation, frequently made, that Wesley himself asked Erasmus to consecrate *him* a bishop appears to be utterly without substance.*

---

*See Asbury, *Letters,* 524, for a tangential reference.

Wesley was pushed by a variety of factors to undertake ordination himself. The pressure of need was clear. He knew himself to be a "scriptural *episkopos*" with authority to ordain. His reading of Lord Peter King Biship Stillingfleet had for years reinforced his conviction. In June 1780 he wrote his brother Charles: "I verily believe I have as good a right to ordain as to administer the Lord's supper." Then prudence overtook him and he added, "But I see abundant of reasons why I should not use that right, unless I was turned out of the Church."[26] He must have observed also that the Countess of Huntingdon's Connexion had sealed its secession from the Church of England by her registering her chapels as dissenting, and by two of her ministers withdrawing from the established church and, as a part of a presbytery, ordaining other preachers. For his part, Wesley sought, on the one hand, to prevent his preachers from becoming Independents after the manner of Fluvanna and, on the other, to prevent his risking separation by undertaking ordination himself.

The conference met in Leeds beginning on July 27, 1784. Wesley's intentions were not discussed with all the preachers but with a group of several confidants. They all opposed his ordaining. Fletcher made helpful suggestions, still advising Wesley to secure the ordinations from a bishop. Charles Wesley was not consulted, for his opposition was predictable. John Wesley had begun to talk with Thomas Coke about his dilemma in the autumn of 1783, and Coke, in turn, began hinting that he would soon leave for America. In later meetings, particularly one in February 1784, details appear to have matured. Two letters from Coke to Wesley during this period are also noteworthy. The first was written April 17, 1784:

Near Dublin, April 17, 1784.

Honored and very dear Sir: I intended to trouble you no more about my going to America; but your observations incline me to address you again on the subject.

If some one, in whom you could place the fullest confidence, and whom you think likely to have sufficient influence and prudence and delicacy of conduct for the purpose, were to go over and return, you would then have a source of sufficient information to determine on any points or propositions. I may be destitute of the last mentioned essential qualification (to the former I lay claim without reserve); otherwise my taking such a voyage might be expedient.

By this means you might have fuller information concerning the state of the country and the societies than epistolary correspondence can give you; and there might be a cement of union, remaining after your death, between the societies and preachers of the two countries. If the awful event of your decease should happen before my removal to the world of spirits, it is almost certain, that I should have business enough, of indispensable importance, on my hands in these kingdoms.

I am, dear sir, your most dutiful and most affectionate son,

Thomas Coke[27]

The second letter is even more direct:

9th August 1784

Honoured and dear Sir,

The more maturely I consider the subject, the more expedient it seems to me that the power of ordaining others should be received by me from you, by the imposition of your hands; and that you should lay hands on Brother Whatcoast and Brother Vasey, for the following reasons:—
1. It seems to me the most scriptural way, and most agreeable to the practice of the primitive churches. 2. I may want all the influence in America which you can throw into

my scale. Mr. Brackenbury informed me at Leeds that he saw a letter in London from Mr. Asbury, in which he observed "that he should not receive any person deputed by you to take any part of the superintendency of the work invested in him,"—or words that implied so much. I do not find the least degree of prejudice in my mind against Mr. Asbury; on the contrary, a very great love and esteem; and I am determined not to stir a finger without his consent, unless sheer necessity obliges me; but rather to lie at his feet in all things. But as the journey is long, and you cannot spare me often, and it is well to provide against all events, and an authority *formally* received from you will be fully admitted by the people, and my exercising the office of ordination without that formal authority may be disputed, if there be any opposition on any other account; I could therefore earnestly wish you would exercise that power in this instance, which I have not the shadow of a doubt but God hath invested you with for the good of the Connexion. I think you have tried me too often to doubt whether I will in any degree use the power you are pleased to invest me with further than I believe absolutely necessary for the prosperity of the work. . . . In short, it appears to me that everything should be prepared, and everything proper to be done, that can possibly be done, this side of the water. . . . In respect to Brother Rankin's argument, that you will escape a great deal of odium by omitting this, it is nothing. Either it will be known, or not known. If not known, then no odium will arise; but if known, you will be obliged to acknowledge that I acted under your direction, or suffer me to sink under the weight of my enemies, with perhaps your brother at the head of them. I shall entreat you to ponder these things.[28]

Coke was not without personal ambition and was certainly ready to serve Wesley as he moved forward to help the American brethren. Whatcoat and Vasey were selected by Wesley from among several who volunteered to go to America. There seems to have been very little reaction at the time from Anglican authority to these ordinations. Possibly they did not know of them or were simply apathetic. Charles Wesley, however, reacted vehemently and blamed John's decision on Coke's persuasiveness and upon his elder brother's old age, though there is evidence that at that time John Wesley was in particularly good health. Charles was so appalled that he responded by writing a number of satirical verses, such as the following ones which may be sung to the tune of "Old Hundredth":

Wesley himself and friends betrays,
  By his own good sense forsook,
While suddenly his hands he lays
  On the hot head of Coke.

Or again:

So easily are Bishops made
  By man's, or woman's whim?
Wesley his hands on Coke hath laid,
  But who laid hands on him?[29]

The brothers exchanged letters on the subject and agreed to disagree. It is John's letter of August 19, 1785, that makes reference to his being a "scriptural ἐπίσκοπος" and of *"uninterrupted succession"* being a fable. In this epistle, too, he makes the plaintive remark: "Perhaps, if you had kept close to me, I might have done better."[30]

His short letter to Charles, dated September 13, 1785, written from Bath, deserves to be reproduced entire:

Dear Brother,—I see no use of you and me disputing together; for neither of us is likely to convince the other. You say I separate from the Church; I say I do not. Then let it stand.

Your verse is a sad truth. I see fifty times more of England than you do, and I find few exceptions to it.

I believe Dr. Coke is as free from ambition as from covetousness. He has done nothing rashly that I know; but he has spoken rashly, which he retracted the moment I spoke to him of it. To publish as his present thoughts what he had before retracted was not fair play. He is now such a right to me as Thomas Walsh was. If you will not or cannot help me yourself, do not hinder those that can and will. I must and will save as many souls as I can while I live without being careful about what may *possibly be* when I die.

I pray do not confound the intellects of the people in London. You may thereby a little weaken my hands, but you will greatly weaken your own.—I am

Your affectionate Brother.[31]

Charles Wesley was certainly correct in one thing in his August 14, 1785, letter to his brother John: "When once you began ordaining in America, I knew, and you knew, that your preachers here would never rest till you ordained them."[32] John had indeed "crossed the Rubicon." The following year he ordained other presbyters for mission areas and for Scotland. This practice he continued intermittently into 1789, ordaining for Newfoundland, Nova Scotia, the West Indies, finally for England itself, for a total of some twenty-five ordinations. He even appears to have ordained another superintendent, Alexander Mather. After his death, however, the British Conference—thinking to leave the door open for reunion with the Church of England—did not begin the practice of ordaining by laying on hands until 1836, though preachers were received into "full connexion" by the imposition of hands.

The Christmas Conference

On September 18, 1784, Coke, Whatcoat, and Vasey set sail from Bristol to America. Theirs was a stormy voyage, but finally they arrived in New York on November 3 and sought out the brethren of John Street Church, especially the traveling preacher, John Dickens (or Dickins).

The next Sunday found them in Philadelphia where Bishop (or Superintendent) Coke preached twice in the morning for Dr. Samuel Magaw at St. Paul's Church, preaching on the witness of the Spirit. In the evening he was at St. George's among the Methodists. The next day they met another clergyman, Dr. (later Protestant Episcopal Bishop) William White, and Governor John Dickinson of Pennsylvania.

On borrowed horses they proceeded to Dover. Vasey seems to have remained behind as Coke and Whatcoat went on to Barratt's Chapel (built 1779), then "in the midst of a forest," where Coke preached on November 14 "to a noble congregation" of about five hundred people.[33] Afterward they administered Communion. "After the sermon," writes Coke, "a plain, robust man came up to me in the pulpit and kissed me: I thought it could be no other than Mr. *Asbury,* and I was not deceived."[34]

Meanwhile, Asbury's *Journal* entry of the same date records; "I came to Barratt's Chapel; here to my great joy, I met these dear men of God, Dr. Coke and Richard Whatcoat. We were greatly comforted together."[35] Asbury notes also his surprise at seeing Whatcoat, whom he had known before, assisting in the sacrament. He did not, of course, know of the ordinations two months earlier.*

At the time of their meeting Asbury was thirty-nine years old and had already labored for thirteen arduous

---

*By coincidence on the very day that Coke and Asbury met, Dr. Samuel Seabury of Connecticut was finally able to obtain consecration as bishop in Aberdeen, Scotland, by three nonjuring bishops of Aberdeen, Ross, and Moray. Incidentally, Seabury, like Coke, was consecrated in a private house.

years in America. Coke was two years younger. Although the two men were a study in contrasts in very many ways, they immediately struck up a warm and mutual friendship which was strained only occasionally during the years that were to follow. Coke wrote in his journal: "I exceedingly reverence Mr. Asbury; he has so much simplicity, . . . so much wisdom, . . . so much meekness and love, . . . so much command and authority, that he is exceedingly qualified for a primitive Bishop."[36] Meanwhile Francis Asbury, writing to his parents on December 6, 1784, said, "We are greatly rejoiced that if we are not worthy to have Mr. Wesley, (whom our Preachers and people venerate if possible, more than the Europeans) we are favoured with the man of his right hand, Dear Dr. Coke,—if only for a few months."[37]

In a sense, Asbury's ordinations might have taken place in Barratt's Chapel then and there (save for the absence of Thomas Vasey), for Coke was so authorized. But this would have been to reckon without Asbury's own views. As it happened a party, including eleven other American preachers, dined in the widow Barratt's home nearby. After dinner Asbury and Coke had a private conversation "concerning the future management of affairs in America." Asbury records his shock at what was proposed:

> It may be of God. My answer then was, if the preachers unanimously choose me, I shall not act in the capacity I have hitherto done by Mr. Wesley's appointment. The design of organizing the Methodists into an Independent Episcopal Church was opened to the preachers present, and it was agreed to call a general conference to meet at Baltimore the ensuing Christmas.[38]

This proved to be a decisive step. It certainly went against Wesley's intentions which apparently were to continue through the joint superintendents his own rather direct rule and then, according to the Deed of Declaration, through that of the British Conference. Asbury wanted the sanction of his brothers.*

Asbury knew from previous experience under Thomas Rankin that British control would only cause American resentment and would make his own position uncertain. If his sanction rested solely on Wesley, he would be subject to recall to England. Wesley had in October 1773 designated Asbury as his general assistant. The conferences of the spring of 1784 approved this "whilst he stands approved by Mr. Wesley." The American War of Independence, the sacramental controversy, and the very nature of American people reinforced this position. The proposal was therefore not an abrupt one but arose out of much seasoning and reasoning on his part. The outcome was that the superintendents should be answerable to an American body and episcopacy was to be from the very beginning basically of a constitutional nature and of necessity more democratic than autocratic. Here was the germ of a General Conference.

Then it was that Freeborn Garrettson was dispatched to the south "like an arrow"[39] to inform the preachers there of the Baltimore meeting. He did not reach them all, for he was "fond of preaching by the way," as Jesse Lee rather resentfully reports.[40] Lee himself heard of it too late, so that what with illness, distance, and uncertain weather he could not attend the general meeting.

In the interval Asbury arranged for a "familiarization

---

*Bishop Nolan B. Harmon, in an address to the Council of Bishops at Barratt's Chapel, April 27, 1984, expressed what happened in vivid terms: "At that moment the sovereignty in Methodism jumped the ocean and became firmly fixed on this side. Perhaps neither Wesley or Asbury realized it, but that is what happened by Asbury's stand."

tour" for Coke in Delaware, Maryland, and Virginia. He was led on this long journey by "Black Harry" Hosier whom he found an able preacher and an agreeable companion. Coke soon abandoned his robes and bands as inappropriate to preaching in the wilderness. Later on Asbury was also to try such a garb, but he, too, abandoned it. During this tour the little English superintendent baptized more people than he had done during his entire previous ministry. The experience meant that Coke did not come to Baltimore utterly unfamiliar with Americans and the conditions under which they lived. Meanwhile Whatcoat, and later Vasey, accompanied Asbury on a similar tour in western Maryland.

During his tour Asbury had time for reflection. "My soul is deeply engaged with God to know his will in this new business," he writes. November 26 was spent as "a day of fasting and prayer."

> The preachers and people seem to be much pleased with the projected plan; I myself am led to think it is of the Lord. I am not tickled with the honour to be gained—I see danger in the way. My soul waits upon God. O that he may lead us in the way we should go! Part of my time is, and must necessarily be, taken up with preparing for the conference.[41]

On November 30 he visited an Anglican clergyman, the Reverend Mason Locke Weems ("Parson Weems" of the George Washington and the cherry tree story), and had "an interesting conversation on the subject of the Episcopal mode of Church government."[42]Asbury had already for several years recorded his preference for the episcopal mode of ordinations.

On December 14 he met Coke again at Abingdon where "we talked of our concerns in great love."[43] On December

18 they came to Perry Hall mansion, the Gough home northeast of Baltimore where with other preachers he and Coke prepared for the conference. Still more preachers gathered in the vicinity of Baltimore and stayed with various Methodists. One young preacher, Thomas Haskins, records in his journal his doubts and fears about the steps soon to be taken, so that he, too, shared the uncertainty that doubtless many felt.

December 24, the day set for the opening of the conference, fell on a Friday. It was a cold and snowy day. The company from Perry Hall and elsewhere rode into Baltimore to Lovely Lane Chapel, then in sight of the Baltimore harbor. About sixty of the eighty-one preachers were present. No official minutes of the proceedings are available to us, but the journals of various participants are as well as the *Discipline* which the two general superintendents published in January 1785.

Coke presided and read and analyzed John Wesley's letter which has been called the "Magna Charta" of American episcopal Methodism, just as the Deed of Declaration was called the "Magna Charta" of British Methodism.[44] The debate that followed issued forth in an unanimous decision to form an independent episcopal church which would bear the name The Methodist Episcopal Church, with Wesley's liturgy, with three orders of ministry (deacon, elder, and superintendent), with the superintendent having a negative voice on all ordinations.[45] John Dickens offered the resolution to effect this, as reported by Thomas Ware.

Dr. Coke and Francis Asbury were both unanimously elected to the superintendency.[46] Then on Saturday, December 25, Asbury was ordained or "set apart" a deacon by Coke, assisted by Whatcoat and Vasey; on Sunday, December 26, they ordained him elder; and on Monday, December 27, he was set apart as superintendent.* In this last, at Asbury's request and with the conference's approval, Philip William Otterbein, Asbury's friend, assisted.

We have Coke's sermon preached at this ordination service on December 27.[47] It opens with a strong vindication of the action taken, that is, of establishing an independent episcopal church, and closes with the delineation of the character of a Christian bishop.

Asbury's further account of the conference is brief:

> Twelve elders were elected, and solemnly set apart to serve our societies in the United States, one for Antigua, and two for Nova Scotia. We spent the whole week in conference, debating freely, and determining all things by a majority of votes. The Doctor preaching every day at noon, and some one of the other preachers morning and evening. We were in great haste, and did much business in a little time.[48]

The further business had to do with determining details of church government. Just as nowadays General Conferences revise the *Discipline,* so in the Christmas Conference the Large Minutes Wesley had compiled from the conferences in England (to guide Methodism as a kind of cumulative constitution) were revised to suit American conditions. The catechetical series of eighty-one questions and answers make interesting reading.

---

*This rapid progress was nearly matched one hundred years later by evangelist William Taylor who was a lay delegate from the South India Conference to the 1884 General Conference of the Methodist Episcopal Church. Within twenty-four hours he was nominated, elected missionary bishop, ordained bishop, and assigned to Africa. Taylor had been ordained already as deacon and elder but had located; therefore, he could attend the General Conference as a lay delegate. Thomas Cranmer in his day outpaced them both by moving from layman to Archbishop of Canterbury.

Particularly notable are Questions Two, Three, and Four:

> Q. 2. What can be done in order to the future Union of the Methodists?
> A. During the Life of the Rev. Mr. Wesley, we acknowledge ourselves his Sons in the Gospel, ready in Matters belonging to Church-Government, to obey his Commands. And we do engage after his Death, to do every Thing that we judge consistent with the Cause of Religion in *America* and the political Interests of these States, to preserve and promote our Union with the Methodists in *Europe.*
>
> Q. 3. As the Ecclesiastical as well as Civil Affairs of these United States have passed through a very considerable Change by the Revolution, what Plan of Church-Government shall we hereafter pursue?
> A. We will form ourselves into an Episcopal Church under the Direction of Superintendents, Elders, Deacons and Helpers, according to the Forms of Ordination annexed to our Liturgy, and the Form of Discipline set forth in these Minutes.
>
> Q. 4. What may we reasonably believe to be God's Design in raising up the Preachers called *Methodists?*
> A. To reform the Continent, and to spread scriptural Holiness over these Lands.[49]

Thus they sanctioned a relationship with the Methodist founder, approved a form of ministry, and set a high missional goal for themselves.

With regard to Question Two, the answer was a pledge of loyalty to Mr. Wesley, the father of the Methodist family, as he was wont to say. The relationship came under some strain as events within a few years were to prove, and this action was altered; but the founder was respected and revered to the end. The relationship with Methodists of the

British Connexion was not particularly close during the nineteenth century, but with the Ecumenical Methodist Conference in 1881, now the World Methodist Council, and the approving of a Concordat of relationship with the British Conference as a part of the Constitution of The United Methodist Church in 1968, the spirit of this resolution has finally been fulfilled in the letter.

The answer to Question Three is a formal statement of and commitment to the kind of church American Methodists intended to be: "Episcopal," with three ordained offices of ministry (helpers became what later were called "local or lay preachers"), with appropriate ordinal and liturgy, as well as "Discipline." As the question itself states, the "Ecclesiastical" and "Civil Affairs" of the country have undergone changes, but come what may, this is what we choose.

Although Questions Two and Three are new and depart from the Large Minutes, Question Four is precisely the same as it was framed in 1763. The answer for British Methodism was: "To reform the Nation, particularly the Church; and to spread scriptural holiness over the land." This did not vary until in 1789 when Wesley added a prefix: "Not to form any new sect, but . . ." Wesley never wavered from this purpose. He must have been pleased to see his spiritual children express this aim in appropriately continental terms! This answer has often been more than a mere slogan with us, but oh! the struggles it has entailed!

Questions Twenty-six through Twenty-nine are pertinent to our theme:

Q. 26. What is the Office of·a *Superintendent?*

A. To ordain *Superintendents, Elders* and *Deacons;* to preside as a Moderator in our Conferences; to fix the Appointments of the Preachers for the several Circuits; and in the Intervals of the Conference, to change, receive or suspend Preachers, as Necessity may require; and to receive Appeals from the Preachers and People, and decide them.

N.B. No Person shall be ordained a *Superintendent, Elder* or *Deacon* without the Consent of a Majority of the Conference and the Consent and Imposition of Hands of a Superintendent; except in the Instance provided for the 29th Minute.

Q. 27. To whom is the *Superintendent* amenable for his Conduct?

A. To the Conference: who have Power to expel him for improper Conduct, if they see it necessary.

Q. 28. If the *Superintendent* ceases from Travelling at large among the People, shall he still exercise his Office in any Degree?

A. If he ceases from Travelling without the Consent of the Conference, he shall not thereafter exercise any ministerial Function whatsoever in our Church.

Q. 29. If by Death, Expulsion or otherwise there be no Superintendent remaining in our Church, what shall we do?

A. The Conference shall elect a Superintendent, and the Elders or any three of them shall ordain him according to our Liturgy.[50]

So it was that the organizers approved a constitutional superintendency. The specific responsibilities are ones Wesley himself had been fulfilling, and they are similar to what bishops have done historically. Particularly noteworthy is that the superintendent could not alone approve ordinations which required conference consent, but he could exercise veto. He was amenable to the conference and by its vote could be removed without what we should call "due process" or appeal. In case of necessity a newly elected bishop could be constituted by a presbytery of three, who would presumably act with authority similar to that which operated in Bristol on September 2, 1784, save for the presence of the apostolic figure of Wesley. Again, these provisions were all very intentional.

Bound with the Minutes were the Liturgy adopted by the conference, that is, Wesley's abridgement of the *Book of Common Prayer, The Sunday Service,* and his abbreviated twenty-four Articles of Religion, to which a twenty-fifth article was added, "Of Rulers of the United States of America." These constitute the principal doctrinal portion of the work of the conference. It should be noted that the earlier conference in April and May 1784 had affirmed the doctrine contained in the standard *Sermons, Notes Upon the New Testament,* and the Large Minutes.

To continue with reference to the completion of the Christmas Conference: on Friday the deacons who had been elected were ordained. On Saturday the college (Cokesbury) was discussed. On Sunday, January 2, 1785, the conference ended "in great peace and unanimity" with the ordination of ten elders and one deacon. Thus, nearly three years before the United States Constitutional Convention had convened, the first denomination in the United States, The Methodist Episcopal Church, was formally organized. Thomas Coke and Francis Asbury were, with the possible exception of Moravian bishops, the only bishops in the newly independent nation. Of course, Samuel Seabury, an American already consecrated in Scotland to be an Anglican or Protestant Episcopal bishop, was soon to return to his homeland.

The Meaning of All This

Having surveyed the field of the beginning of Methodism in England and particularly in America, the need for something to be done to fulfill the pastoral ministry in America, the Bristol ordinations by John Wesley, and the founding of The Methodist Episcopal Church, we must examine the meaning of these developments. What did Wesley intend by the ordinations? Did he intend to sanction an independent church separate from the Anglican? Did he intend ordination of Coke and Asbury for episcopacy? This raises also questions about the validity of what he did and the status of what resulted. The ground has been plowed over many times before, sometimes exhaustively, but possibly it may be examined once more in our context of the meaning and role of episcopacy in the Wesleyan tradition.

Simply stated, it is the judgment of this writer that, on balance, these questions must be given positive answers. This conclusion can be based in large part upon the documents that play a part in or lead up to the Christmas Conference.

First of all, Whatcoat and Vasey were ordained by Wesley (assisted by Thomas Coke and James Creighton) as *elders* "to feed the flock, and to administer Baptism and the Lord's Supper, according to the usage of the Church of England."[51] This was understood by the ordinands themselves and by others as being a presbyterial ordination, the three presbyters having formed a presbytery for the purpose.[52] Though valid in this sense, it was clearly irregular from the standpoint of the Church of England for three presbyters to ordain when only bishops had the power to ordain. Wesley felt under the pressure of necessity. He would hardly have engaged in an irregular and unusual procedure unless he *intended* to do what he did, which was to grant authorization to minister according to sacramental usages of the Church of England.

Second, the "setting apart" of Coke was a matter of a different magnitude: presbyters constituting a superintendent for a higher functional office. Wesley had fulfilled that office for England and America and had delegated it to

Coke for America only, an office essentially episcopal in nature.

When we examine Thomas Coke's certificate signed by John Wesley and setting him apart as superintendent (see pages 86 and 87), the following observations can be made:

1. In the greetings Wesley identifies himself as a presbyter of the Church of England. Upon this point Edgar W. Thompson, usually sympathetic, states that Wesley "rested on a bad title,"[53] in that, once again, he offends against canon law. But in the long perspective of primitive practice he was not on unstable ground; witness the ancient practice in Alexandria.

2. He then gives a kind of preamble stating his grounds for proceeding as he did:

   a. the needs of people in "the southern provinces of North America," that is, areas other than Canada which was still under England;

   b. response to those who "desire to continue under my care," who "still adhere to the doctrines and disciplines of the Church of England," and who "want ministers to administer sacraments . . . according to the usage of the said church";

   c. and finally because "there does not appear to be any other way of supplying them with ministers."

3. Because he feels himself "providentially called," he *sets apart* some persons for ministry in America. The words *set apart* are equivalent to *ordain,* a word he uses in his diary and allows to stand in the ordinal of his revised *Book of Common Prayer.*

4. He sets apart or ordains Thomas Coke, a presbyter of the Church of England, as a superintendent and does this in the historic way of laying on hands and prayer. This again appears *deliberate* by its very nature. Since Coke was already a presbyter, he must also have *intended* an office or an authority beyond that of presbyter.

5. He commends Coke to all as "a fit person to *preside over* the flock of Christ"—a clearly episcopal or overseer's role. The presbyters, by contrast, are to "*feed* the flock."

The point of all this is that the certificate is carefully and purposefully drafted in a specific manner, although Wesley does not use the title *bishop* but rather a synonym of Latin origin, *superintendent.*

Asbury's certificate is, in turn, signed by Coke as a presbyter of the Church of England and superintendent of The Methodist Episcopal Church in America.[54] In his case one certificate confers or confirms the offices of deacon, elder, and superintendent. It does not contain the preamble. Once again it uses *set apart,* and Francis Asbury is recommended "as a fit person to *preside over* the flock of Christ"—again a description of the episcopal office. In all three instances—deacon, elder, and superintendent—the offices are stated as being in The Methodist *Episcopal* Church, clearly descriptive of its chosen form of government.

Reference must be made to John Wesley's avoidance of the title *bishop* and preferring its synonym *superintendent.* He clearly approved the three orders of deacon, presbyter, and bishop, but just as clearly he opposed the notion of "divine right of episcopacy," a recent innovation in England.[55] Jeremy Taylor, for instance, wrote that "episcopacy is not only a divine institution, but the only order that derives immediately from Christ."[56] But Wesley did not agree with this, a large concession for "an High Churchman, the son of an High Churchman."[57] He did not like the trappings of the prelate and the princely bishop, for he had observed and experienced too much of that.

All of this Wesley had in mind when he wrote the "my dear Franky" letter to Asbury chiding him for adopting the title of bishop.[58] He had surely been delivered from any awe of bishops and from taking seriously the claims of a mechanical, tactile, "uninterrupted" apostolic succession. This he knew to be a "fable,"[59] a conclusion he was a long time coming to. For him episcopacy was not of the *esse* of the church. True apostolic succession was a matter of having an apostolic spirit. We must not lose sight of the fact that Wesley was convinced that ordination was not a sacrament; that no *man* could constitute any kind of minister; this was the work of the Holy Spirit.

Yet, as we have seen, he did not hesitate to think of himself as a kind of bishop, with his assistants who resembled elders and his helpers who were like deacons. John Wesley regarded himself as just as real, spiritual, and scriptural a bishop as the Archbishop of Canterbury. He was, indeed, a "superintending elder." His role was poles apart from what came to be called the "historic episcopate." In Georgia he was at least accused of calling himself "Ordinary"[60] and more than once in later life was described as papal in his conduct. He admitted his authority but "never was fond of it; it was rather a burden." He was sometimes called a "bishop" in England[61] and apparently considered at one time going himself to America to exercise the office of bishop, but apparently he sent Rankin instead.[62] He obviously exercised the office in actual practice, as we have noted more than once. Since he was founding father certain rights and responsibilites rested on him: he was "director" of the people called Methodists; he had authority to appoint the preachers, to remove and censure, to set up conferences, to hold deeds for property, to arrange for his successor. Indeed he held a lifelong monarchical role. He was an *extraordinarius* early aware that he was raised up by God for a special ministry thoroughly approved by its fruits.[63]

This may be an appropriate place to comment on two writers whose books had great influence on Wesley's thought regarding the ministry and its orders. One of these was Lord Peter King's *Account of the Primitive Church.* King wrote his book when a very young man of twenty-two years (and a Presbyterian), who was, by the way, destined to become Lord Chancellor of England. According to King, presbyters were inferior in degree but not in order; that is, bishops were charged with certain functions to which they had been elected and consecrated. Presbyters were capable of performing them, too, but not without the bishop's consent. Thus whatever a bishop could do, the presbyter *could* do but not necessarily *did* do.

King later on revised and even repudiated some of his earlier views. Moreover, he came to be embarrassed by Wesley's use of this book. Wesley nevertheless remained fixed in his understanding "that bishops and presbyters are (essentially) of one order" and consequently have the same inherent right to ordain.[64] This was not a conclusion arrived at suddenly in 1784; he had held it since 1746 when he first read the book by King on the way to Bristol. In 1789 he wrote revealingly, "When I said, 'I believe I am a scriptural bishop,' I spoke on Lord King's supposition that bishops and presbyters are essentially one order."[65]

The second writer was Samuel Stillingfleet, later Bishop of Worcester (1689). He also at the very early age of twenty-four wrote a book, *Irenicum,* published in 1659. As the title suggests, he wrote it to bring about peace in the internal church conflict then raging in England about church government. His thesis is that neither Jesus nor the apostles prescribed any particular form of church government; therefore, there might be a compromise between Episcopalians and Presbyterians. Bishops were sanctioned by the Scriptures but were not, in Stillingfleet's view, necessary. He distinguishes between the power of order to exercise ministry and sacraments, as presbyters do, and the power of jurisdiction which is in the hands of those appointed by the church to lead, such as bishops.

Stillingfleet, too, felt that *bishop* and *presbyter* were essentially synonymous terms and it was this overlap of roles that causes conflict and divisions. The one office finally emerged with superior rank over the other. Stillingfleet also tempered his views later in life, but Wesley's views were derived from his ideas as written in *Irenicum.*

Of the two writers, King was apparently the more influential with Wesley. He was as well more frequently quoted, even though Stillingfleet has the more comprehensive position and would seem more adequately to support Wesley's conclusions. He even sanctions presbyterial ordination in case of necessity. Stillingfleet also referred to the Alexandrian church's early custom, for some two hundred years, of the presbyters' choosing and ordaining their new bishop when the predecessor died. This was an appealing precedent for Wesley.

We return now to the third document to be considered in connection with the establishment of the Methodist Episcopal Church, namely, Wesley's letter under date of September 10, 1784, which Coke presented to the Christmas Conference (see pages 87, 88). Let us consider it paragraph by paragraph:

1. Wesley acknowledges the new situation created by the result of the American War of Independence. A new civil authority existed in America but no "ecclesiastical authority at all." His advice has been sought, and he has responded by having "drawn up a little sketch." This "little sketch" has been the source of much controversy. What was it? Was it this very letter and other accompanying papers? Or was the sketch lost? Or suppressed? Whether the sketch is inherent in other documents or a separate one, the recommendations Wesley made to American Methodists were no doubt influenced by the outline John Fletcher drew up and sent to Wesley at Leeds in 1775.[66]

Fletcher suggests, for instance, extracting portions of *The Book of Common Prayer* and "rectifying" the Thirty-nine Articles.

2. Lord King's book has convinced him that as a presbyter he has the right to ordain. He had refused to do so until now for the sake of peace and order. At the same time he is determined as little as possible to violate Anglican order.

3. The necessity in America gives him full liberty without scruples to proceed. He now deliberately chooses to exercise his right to ordain.

4. He announces his having set apart three men; his appointment of Coke and Asbury as "Joint Superintendents over our brethren in North America"; and by sending his revised Liturgy he enables and authorizes its use in ordaining others in a church similar to the Church of England, that is, an *episcopal* church.

5. He invites his critics to offer a better method, more rational and scriptural for "feeding and guiding" the flock, evidently a reference to the sacramental and pastoral care as well as oversight which were lacking.

6. If someone were to suggest that a "better method" would be to get English bishops to ordain, he states why that is now neither possible nor desirable. Therefore, American Methodists are at *full liberty* simply to follow the Scriptures and the primitive church, which he felt followed unadulterated Christianity. Clearly he releases any hold upon the American Methodists.

His intention is clear. He points to a bold way forward for them: to establish an autonomous structure. He stated later that he had taken an "extraordinary step in order to help them all he could. And I bless God it has had an admirable effect."[67] This positive assessment was written nearly two years later.

John Wesley offered a ministry, and the American body

sanctioned and accepted it. He offered them a Liturgy which they embodied in their first *Discipline*. He sent an abridgement of the Thirty-nine Articles, and they were accepted. He gave them full liberty, and they formed an *episcopal* church which should have pleased him. It was to have a *moderate* episcopacy—not a prelacy—which likewise should have pleased him despite his trouble with the designation *bishop*.

The superintendent was after the Anglican mold but stripped of ostentatious, princely, and worldly trappings. For the most part it was seen as an office and not specifically a separate order, though American Methodism has until the present, as we shall see, struggled to decide between the two. Episcopacy with us was not a downgrade in authority from the Anglican tradition; indeed, an itinerant, apostolic, episcopal role in many respects has more authority and was more effective than the Anglican model. It was an unique, practical, and functional episcopate, resting on the presbyterate but set apart by election and consecration to well-defined constitutional rights and responsibilities.

If American Methodists went beyond what Wesley had conceived, they were merely exercising the full liberty he offered them. What they did actually do was fully made known to him; the Minutes were printed on the press he used, and it was some years before he expressed any negative reaction, and that in a private letter to Francis Asbury.* American Methodists finally had become a

---

*One cannot fail to observe a kind of love-hate relationship between Wesley and Asbury, father and son. Perhaps this was because in many ways they were much alike. Stained glass windows in City Road Chapel, London, bear a silent testimony regarding their relationship: at one level are portrayed Elijah and Elisha and below them, Wesley and Asbury.

church; no longer were they "a Church, and no Church," as Asbury once mentioned.[68]

In light of everything we have considered we can say that what was done had the sanction of Scripture, Tradition, Reason and, in the end, Experience.

But ever the practical churchman, Wesley also rested his case on necessity, the "caring for the flock":

> Judging this to be a case of real necessity, I took a step which, for peace and quietness I had refrained from taking many years; I exercised that power which I am fully persuaded the great Shepherd and Bishop of the Church has given me. I appointed three of our laborers to go and help them, by not only preaching the word of God, but likewise administering the Lord's supper, and baptizing their children throughout that vast tract of land.[69]

The grounds of necessity find support from the practice of Alexandria, from Jerome, and also from no less an authority than Richard Hooker, Anglican scholar, who wrote long before Wesley's day:

> The whole Church visible being the true original subject of all power, it hath not ordinarily allowed any other than bishops alone to ordain; howbeit, as the ordinary course is ordinarily in all things to be observed, so it may be in some cases not unnecessary that we decline from the ordinary ways.
>
> Men may be extraordinarily, yet allowably, two ways admitted unto spiritual functions in the church. One is when God himself doth of himself raise up any whose labour he useth without requiring that men should authorize them. . . .
>
> Another extraordinary kind of vocation is when the exigence of necessity doth constrain to leave the usual ways of the church which otherwise we would willingly keep: where the church must needs have some ordained, and

neither hath nor can have possibly a bishop to ordain; in case of such necessity the ordinary institution of God hath given oftentimes, and may give, place.[70]

Support comes also from a Roman Catholic scholar writing long after Wesley's day, namely, Edward Schillebeeckx, in his study of ministerial leadership in the church:

This survey shows that as far as the New Testament is concerned the community has a right to a minister or ministers and to the celebration of the eucharist. This apostolic right has priority over the criteria for admission which the church can and may impose on its ministers (see already I Tim. 3:1–13). Of course some criteria are attached to the purpose and content of the ministry in the service of a community of God. However, the apostolic right of Christian communities may not be made null and void by the official church; this is itself bound by this apostolic right. Therefore if in changed circumstances there is a threat that a community may be without a minister or ministers (without priests), and if this situation becomes increasingly widespread, then criteria for admission which are not intrinsically necessary to the nature of the ministry and are also in fact a cause of the shortage of priests, must give way to the original, New Testament right of the community to leaders. In that case this apostolic right has priority over the church order which has in fact grown up and which in other circumstances may have been useful and healthy.[71]

Thus, born of necessity, episcopacy in the Wesleyan tradition, and indeed its ministry in general, rests upon a firm foundation, through the apostolic figure of John Wesley, an ordained presbyter of the Church of England, and finally, without pretense or apology, upon Jesus Christ himself.

Notes

1. Rupert E. Davies, *Methodism* (London: Pelican Books, 1963), 15-16.

2. Wesley, *Journal* 1:197-202.

3. Ibid. 1:198n.

4. *The Works of the Rev. John Wesley, A. M.,* ed. Thomas Jackson, 14 vols. (London: John Mason, 1856), 13:307.

5. 1766 Minutes, 60-62.

6. Ibid.

7. See John Bennet, 1745 Minutes, 24ff. See also Jesse Lee, *A Short History of the Methodists* (Baltimore: Magill and Clime, 1810), 41.

8. Wesley, *Journal* 2:197.

9. Theodore L. Flood and John W. Hamilton, eds., *Lives of Methodist Bishops* (New York: Phillips and Hunt, 1882), 11, 13. See also Francis J. McConnell, *John Wesley* (New York: Abingdon Press, 1939), 322-324.

10. Wesley, *Letters* 7:225.

11. *Minutes of Some Conversations Between the Preachers in Connection with the Rev. Mr. John Wesley* (Philadelphia, July 1773), 5-6.

12. Francis Asbury, *The Journal and Letters of Francis Asbury,* ed. Elmer T. Clark et al., 3 vols. (London: Epworth Press; Nashville: Abingdon Press, 1958), *Journal* 1:85.

13. Ibid., 410-11.

14. Flood and Hamilton, *Methodist Bishops,* 11-13.

15. Asbury, September 3, 1780 and September 20, 1783. *Letters,* 24-26; 29-31.

16. Ibid., March 20, 1784, p. 23. Cf. Wesley, *Journal* 7:23.

17. Wesley, September 3, 1756, *Letters* 3:186-88.

18. Charles Wesley, *Journal,* 2 vols. (1849; reprint, Grand Rapids, Mich.: Baker Book House, 1980), 2:96-97.

19. Wesley, *Letters* 7:266.

20. Wesley, *Journal* 7:15.

21. Ibid.

22. Wesley, *Letters,* 7:238-39.

23. Wesley, *Journal* 8:328ff.

24. Wesley, *Letters* 7:29-30; also 31, 169.

25. Recent examination would make it appear that Erasmus' credentials were not authentic. See George Tsoumas, *The Greek Orthodox Review,* Christmas issue no. 2 (1956), 62–73. See also R. P. Heitzenrater, *The Elusive Mr. Wesley,* 2 vols. (Nashville: Abingdon Press, 1984), 2:109-10.

26. Wesley, *Letters* 7:21.

27. John J. Tigert, *A Constitutional History of American Episcopal*

Methodism (Nashville: Publishing House of the Methodist Episcopal Church, South, 1908), 169.

28. John Vickers, *Thomas Coke* (London: Epworth Press, 1969), 77-78.

29. Frank Baker, ed., *Representative Verse of Charles Wesley* (Nashville: Abingdon Press, 1962), 367-68.

30. Wesley, *Letters* 7:284-85.

31. Ibid., 288-89.

32. Cited by editor in Wesley, *Letters* 7:284.

33. Coke preached on Christ "our wisdom, righteousness, sanctification and redemption" (I Cor. 1:30), a text frequently used by John Wesley in the early revival.

34. Thomas Coke, *Extracts of the Journals* (London: G. Paramore, 1793), 15-16.

35. Asbury, *Journal* 1:471.

36. Coke's journal, American ed. 244. Cited by Vickers, *Thomas Coke*, 82.

37. Asbury, *Letters*, 39.

38. Asbury, *Journal* 1:471-72.

39. Asbury later commented on the haste they all felt. *Journal* 1:471.

40. Lee, *Short History*, 93-94.

41. Asbury, *Journal* 1:472.

42. Ibid.

43. Ibid.

44. Tigert, *Constitutional History*, 197.

45. Thomas Haskins, *MSS* journal for December 24, 1784 (Library of Congress.)

46. Asbury, *Journal* 1:474. A single certificate covering all three ordinations is found on this page.

47. It was published at the "desire of the conference." Thomas Coke, *A Sermon* (New York: Mason and Lane, 1840).

48. Asbury, *Journal* 1:475-76.

49. Tigert, *Constitutional History*, 534-35.

50. Ibid., 548-59.

51. William Phoebus, ed., *Memoirs of the Rev. Richard Whatcoat* (New York: Joseph Allen, 1828), 18.

52. Handwritten letter under date 28 Nov. 1784, from Adam Fonerden, a local preacher in Baltimore, to Stephen Donaldson of Leesburg, Va. (Baltimore: Lovely Lane Museum of Baltimore Conference).

53. Edgar W. Thompson, *Wesley: Apostolic Man* (London: Epworth Press, 1957), 48.

54. Asbury, *Journal* 1:474.

55. Cf. 1747 Minutes.

56. A. J. Mason, *The Church of England and Episcopacy* (Cambridge: Cambridge University Press, 1914), 124-25.

57. Wesley, *Letters* 6:156.

58. Ibid. 8:91. Edgar Thompson thought this was merely an example of Wesley's humor!

59. Ibid. 7:284; see also Wesley, *Journal* 4:438.

60. Wesley, *Journal* 1:386.

61. Cf. Frank Baker, *John Wesley and the Church of England* (Nashville: Abingdon Press, 1970), 396.

62. See correspondence with Walter Sellen. *Letters* 5:303.

63. Wesley, *Letters* 1:322-23.

64. Wesley, *Journal* 3:232.

65. Wesley, *Letters* 8:143.

66. Cf. Wesley, *Journal* 8:328ff.

67. Wesley, *Letters* 7:333.

68. Asbury, *Letters,* 476-77.

69. Minutes of British Conference, 1786. Cited by Tigert, *Constitutional History,* 173.

70. Richard Hooker, *Works,* ed. John Keble, revised by R. W. Church and F. Paget, 3 vols. (Oxford: University Press, 1881), 3:231-32.

71. Edward Schillebeeckx, *Ministry* (New York: Crossroads, 1981), 37.

IV

SOME EPISODES IN THE DEVELOPMENT OF EPISCOPAL METHODISM

Abel Stevens claimed that The Methodist Episcopal Church, organized at the Christmas Conference, was the "real successor to the Anglican Church in America." Probably this is claiming a little too much. Though the Protestant Episcopal Church was not yet formally organized in 1784, there were many congregations in the United States in continuity with the Church of England of Colonial America, and these now had in Samuel Seabury a bishop, soon to return to American shores. Others have emphasized that American Methodists were not guilty of schism simply because there was not yet in existence in America any *organized* church from which to separate.* Soon afterward American Anglicans did move to organize the Protestant Episcopal Church, and they had formed a General Convention by 1789. The year before that the Presbyterians organized their General Assembly and others were to follow.

---

*Several times before 1792 exploration was made of possible reunion of Anglicans and Methodists, once *during* the Christmas Conference, but this came to nothing.

American Methodists were on their way. By the end of 1784 they had an ecclesial organization, the sacraments of baptism and the Lord's Supper, a Liturgy, a *Discipline,* a formulation of doctrine, a name, an organized ministry, a superintendency or episcopacy (their bishops not prelates but *primi inter pares*), and a company of devoted members. This was five years before the United States Constitution had been set in operation. The Methodist Episcopal Church was to grow up with the republic. It should be noted that our church's government was at the time vested entirely in the traveling preachers, in what H. Richard Niebuhr has called a "constitutional aristocracy."[1] The counsel of the laity was neither sought after nor received—this at what must now be reckoned a fearful cost.

The young church regarded that it had a superintendency or episcopacy not only synodally approved but of a nature sanctioned by the Scriptures and the primitive church, recommended to it by John Wesley who was indeed, humanly speaking, its "fountain." He "set apart" or ordained or consecrated Thomas Coke to the same office to be exercised in America. It was not of "an apostolic, uninterrupted succession" but in continuity of apostolic faith and faithfulness, in continuity with the church as a whole. Episcopacy was seen by most as an office and not an order, derived from the order of elder[2] but vested with superior jurisdictional or administrative authority sufficient for the execution of the responsibilties with which it was charged.

On his part Francis Asbury had no doubt of the legitimacy of his calling and ministry. He wrote long afterward (1805) when he was under fire in New York about the legitimacy of his episcopacy:

I will tell the world what I rest my authority upon. 1. Divine authority. 2. Seniority in America. 3. The election of the General Conference. 4. My ordination by Thomas Coke, William Philip Otterbein,* German Presbyterian minister, Richard Whatcoat, and Thomas Vasey. 5. Because the signs of an apostle have been seen in me.[3]

In his letter to the General Conference, 1808, Dr. Coke strongly affirmed the validity of Francis Asbury's consecration as a bishop.

Asbury lost no time in getting on with his apostolic tasks. Two days after the Christmas Conference closed he rode fifty miles through frost and snow to Fairfax, Virginia. A few days later we find him already using his newly granted authority to ordain and administer the two sacraments. For his part, in pursuit of his missionary interest, Bishop Coke went to Philadelphia and New York to raise money for Freeborn Garrettson and James Cromwell to travel to Nova Scotia to their appointed field of labor.

We look now at some length to episodes which have followed as they shed light on the development of episcopacy in our tradition. This focus should not, however, distort our view of the total and highly varied story of Methodism as it met the challenge of the frontier in America.

From "Superintendent" to "Bishop"

In January 1785 there were published *Minutes of Some Conversations between the Ministers and Preachers of The Methodist Episcopal Church at a General Conference Held at Baltimore.* Previously such Minutes were of "some conversations between the preachers in connection with

---

*Note that Asbury slipped in reversing the order of Otterbein's Christian names. Note also the omission of any reference to Wesley, to historic succession, or to the Church of England in whose membership he had been baptized and confirmed.

the Rev. Mr. John Wesley," and it was with the organizing of the church that the change in nomenclature was made.

In response to "Question 1: Who are the Superintendents of our Church?" the answer is given: "Thomas Coke, Francis Asbury." The next year, published under the designation, *Minutes of the General Conference of The Methodist Episcopal Church for the Year 1786,* the same question and answer are given. The earlier Christmas Conference was not really a *General* Conference as the term later came to be used.

The Minutes for 1787 contain a change:

Question 1: Who are the Superintendents of our church for the United States?
Answer: Thomas Coke (when present in the states) and Francis Asbury.

The next publication again changes its name to *Minutes taken at the General Conference of the Methodist Episcopal Church for the year 1788.* The question and answer appear the same as the previous year, save for the parenthesis concerning Dr. Coke. But Question One becomes: "Who are the *Bishops* of our church, for the United States?" (italics mine).*

In the year 1789 the words are: "Who are the persons that exercise the Episcopal Office in the Methodist Church in Europe and America?" The answer is "*John Wesley,* Thomas Coke, and Francis Asbury by regular order and succession" (italics mine).

---

*An even earlier reference to *bishop* was added in the 1788 *Discipline* as a footnote to Wesley's letter to the American brethren: "As the translators of our version of the Bible have used the English word bishop instead of superintendent, it has been thought by us that it would appear more scriptural to adopt their term bishop."

In 1790, however, the relevant questions are now *two* in number. The first is couched in a new way and is restricted to America.

Question 6: Who have been elected by the unanimous suffrages of the General Conference to superintend the Methodist Episcopal Church in America?
Answer: Thomas Coke, Francis Asbury.

The second repeats the single question of 1789:

Question 7: Who are the persons that exercise the Episcopal Office in the Methodist Church in Europe and America?
Answer: *John Wesley,* Thomas Coke and Francis Asbury, in regular order and succession (italics mine).

Meanwhile, apart from these Minutes, a *Discipline* was published in January 1785. Then in 1787 Bishop Asbury and John Dickins revised the 1785 *Discipline.* Instead of its having eighty-one continuous questions and answers, the questions were divided into thirty-one sections. This is sometimes called the "Bishops' Discipline" because in it the superintendents are for the first time called "bishops." The third question of the second section asked:

Question: Is there any other business to be done in the conference?
Answer: The electing and ordaining of Bishops, Elders and Deacons.[4]

The same usage is found in the third section, "On the Constituting of Bishops, and Their Duty."

This use of the title *bishop* naturally occasioned some question because the conference had not authorized such a change in advance. Lee observes: "Some of the preachers opposed the alteration, and wanted to retain the former title; but a majority of the preachers agreed to let the word *Bishop* remain."[5] If this use had been illegal, it was now legalized.

The reason for this was not mere pride on the part of Coke and Asbury. Possibly it was influenced by the arrival of Bishop Seabury back in the United States. Then, after all, it was a Methodist *Episcopal* Church. Some, however, have complained that this change confounded the issue. *Superintendent* does not convey connotations of princely pomp and grandeur as *bishop* inevitably did in European experience. It was as bishops that Coke and Asbury were graciously received by the newly inaugurated President George Washington in New York and delivered to him an "Address" in behalf of The Methodist Episcopal Church, dated May 29, 1789.[6] And it was to the *bishops* of the Methodist Episcopal Church that Washington replied.* The title was soon established firmly.

A Difference with John Wesley

On September 6, 1786, John Wesley wrote to Dr. Coke from London:

Dear Sir:—I desire that you would appoint a General Conference of all our preachers in the United States to meet at Baltimore on May 1, 1787, and that Mr. Richard Whatcoat may be appointed superintendent with Mr. Francis Asbury. I am, dear sir, your affectionate friend and brother, John Wesley,[7] [Note: *Mr.* Francis Asbury.]

---

*Bishops Coke and Asbury on May 26, 1785, dined in Mt. Vernon with George Washington "who received us very politely and gave us his opinion against slavery." Asbury, *Journal,* 1:489. On April 24, 1786, Asbury wrote Washington: "Give me leave to present you with one of our Prayer Books, and another to your lady."

Coke immediately dispatched this directive to the United States and invited the preachers to attend a General Conference.

When he learned of this, Asbury was not pleased with the mode of appointment, but he apparently did not question it because he wrote to Richard Whatcoat the following March 25 in these words:

> My dear Brother:—Hereby I inform you that Mr. Wesley has appointed you a joint Superintendent with me. I can, therefore, claim no superiority over you: the way will be for you to come after me through the whole continent if called, but through the States without all doubt. The best method will be to go out to the Ohio, upon a plan I have laid out for myself, and return to the Springs; there I will meet you and form a plan for our future work. The mode of appointment is not approved of, though many of us by no means object to the person. I am, with respect, Yours as ever, Francis Asbury.[8]

Did Asbury then suspect, however, that the preachers in general would react so stoutly against Wesley's directive? Probably so. For one thing they did not like the idea of his changing the date they had in 1786 set for the 1787 Conference.* Neither did they agree with Dr. Coke's insistence that they must accept Wesley's appointment of Whatcoat as a superintendent with Asbury. The preachers also refused to agree to a similar mandate from Wesley to elect Freeborn Garrettson as superintendent for Nova Scotia where he had rendered outstanding service. Garrettson himself was reluctant to accept further work there.

It should be said that at that time the conference was held in several sections, the same business dealt with in

---

*It had been set for Abingdon, Maryland, for July 24, 1787.

each section, and then the Minutes recorded in unitary fashion. The South Carolina Conference agreed with the appointment of Whatcoat, but the Virginia Conference strenuously opposed it in a fight led by James O'Kelly.

The Baltimore Conference *did* meet in Baltimore on May 1, 1787, as suggested. Not only did the preachers reject Wesley's proposals but rescinded their 1784 act of submission to the founder and dropped his name from the 1788 Minutes.

During all this Asbury apparently tried to keep a respectful distance from the conflict although he clearly saw the issue at stake: How can an independent church be maintained and at the same time be controlled from a distance? He saw, too, that Whatcoat's election might have been a prelude to an effort to bring about his own (Asbury's) recall to England. In the end Wesley's rule was rejected, and Asbury was blamed for this.* Lee reports that "we then wrote a long and loving letter to Mr. Wesley, and requested him to come over to America and visit his spiritual children."[9] It was a heavy blow to Wesley. He was sadly aggrieved by his name having been left out. As we have seen, in 1789 it was restored to the Minutes, but the "act of submission" was not restored. A part of the outcome was that a more vigorous episcopate was sustained in America and independence from the British Conference and John Wesley reinforced, though a vital linkage was broken.

The Role of Bishop Coke

The contribution that Bishop Coke made to American Methodism is by any accounting enormous. As Wesley's

---

*These events may account in part for the last letter Wesley wrote to Asbury, dated September 20, 1788, in which he complains about Francis's accepting the title *bishop.* Asbury spoke of the letter as "a bitter pill."

high commissioner he carried to these shores the various enabling instrumentalities for the new church. He had responsibilities in both England and the United States and missionary interests on other continents as well. As a result his visits were only intermittent to the American church. In all he made nine trips to this country, ranging in duration from about six weeks to about seven months.* It is not without good cause that he has been called the "foreign minister" of Methodism. He was a leading missionary and ecumenical statesman of his time.

Both Bishop Coke and Bishop Asbury contributed vastly to Methodism and the shaping of episcopacy. Some endeavor must be made to trace the tangled strands of their relationship. Both were able, strong, and sensitive persons. Clearly Asbury's commitment was entirely to the church in America, while Coke's attention and energies were divided. At times he seemed unsure where his primary loyalty lay. The latter never really escaped a certain suspicion in the eyes of independent Americans simply on the grounds of his being an Englishman. Some of Asbury's actions regarding him seem to stem from this fact.

Coke suffered from the debacle of 1787 regarding Wesley's directive concerning a General Conference. We have noted that his role as superintendent as listed in the Minutes of that year bears the parenthetical qualification, "when present in the States." This was dropped in the next Minutes. A more serious consequence was Coke's apparently voluntary undertaking not to use his episcopal powers when not in the United States:

---

*They were in 1784–85, 1787, 1789, 1791, 1792, 1796–97, 1797–98, 1800, and 1803–04. In at least one instance he made the Atlantic crossing from America in twenty-two days! He once made the westward passage in twenty-nine days.

I do solemnly engage by this instrument, that I never will, by virtue of my office as Superintendent of the Methodist Episcopal Church during my absence from the United States of America, exercise any government whatever in the said Methodist Church during my absence from the United States. And I do also engage that I will exercise no privilege in the said Church when present in the United States, except that of ordaining, according to the regulations and law already existing or hereafter to be made in the said Church, and that of presiding when present in Conference, and lastly that of traveling at large. Given under my hand, the second day of May, in the year 1787. Thomas Coke. Witnesses: John Tunnell, John Haggerty, Nelson Reed.[10]

In the minds of some, this action seriously undermined Coke's episcopal standing, particularly with respect to possibly introducing any further mandates by Wesley. It has been referred to as "an instrument of abdication"—an overstatement.[11]

Dr. Coke returned to the United States in 1789, for what proved to be discussions of "the Council," and again in 1791 when these discussions were continued. The earlier was the visit during which the two bishops carried Methodist felicitations to President Washington, a move for which Coke was severely criticized on both sides of the Atlantic, but for exactly contradictory reasons: in America because an *Englishman* was a representative to the United States president; in England because an Englishman was showing respect to an *American.*

From the latter trip Coke quickly returned to England upon hearing of the death of John Wesley, but not before he had indulged in two improprieties. One was his correspondence, under date of April 24, 1791, with Protestant Episcopal Bishop William White concerning reunion of Methodists and Episcopalians.[12] This he did without his colleague's prior knowledge. This effort at

Christian reconciliation was of no effect. The other incident was Coke's memorial sermon for Wesley delivered May 1, 1791, in Baltimore, on the text II Kings 2:12, "And Elisha saw it, and he cried, My father, my father, the chariot of Israel and the horsemen thereof." His none too subtle suggestion of his (Coke's) being Elisha to Wesley was not well received by Asbury who was present.[13] By the time Dr. Coke arrived in England it was too late for him to stand a chance of being appointed by the Conference as Wesley's successor, as he had hoped.

Coke came for his fifth visit to the United States, arriving just in time for the first regular General Conference in 1792, at which he presided during all the very tense deliberations. This was a brief sojourn, and he did not come again until the 1796 General Conference, where "strengthening the episcopacy"—that is, adding to the number of bishops—was discussed at length, because of Asbury's ill health. It was at this session that he recorded the following instrument:

> I offer myself to my American brethren entirely to their service, all I am and have, with my talents and labours in every respect, without any mental reservation whatsoever, to labour among them, and to assist Bishop Asbury; not to station the preachers at any time when he is present, but to exercise all episcopal duties, when I hold a Conference, in his absence and by his consent, and to visit the West Indies and France when there is an opening, and I can be spared.[14]

The General Conference accepted this offer and as a consequence did not elect any further bishops.

It should be noted that Coke's statement excepted stationing the preachers when Asbury was present—a future bone of contention. He agreed also to "assist Bishop Asbury," what he later termed a "coadjutor's" role. He did do this and relieved Asbury a great deal until he returned to England in February 1797 after assisting Asbury in producing an annotated *Discipline* which the General Conference had ordered. Coke did not agree to a plan drawn up by his colleague to implement their joint operation. He judged that Asbury would retain all the essential episcopal responsibilities except possibly preaching.[15] Asbury seemed always to be rather sure that Coke did not exercise too much episcopal authority.

As it turned out, Coke was not yet ready to fulfill his offer. For one thing the British Conference requested the American brethren to release him from his commitment, for it, too, wanted his services. At the same time a serious schism in the West Indies required his urgent attention there.[16] Coke paid a very short visit (his seventh) to the States in the autumn of 1797.

When he visited the Virginia Conference, it undertook to respond through Asbury to the British Conference's appeal which Coke brought. Asbury pleaded shortage of personnel and an inability until the next General Conference (1800) to reply officially. Meanwhile, in view of his own weakness, Bishop Asbury adopted the practice of an experienced elder's traveling with him, for example, Jesse Lee, William McKendree, Nicholas Snethen, or later on, Henry Boehm.

Coke came back to the United States (his eighth visit) for the 1800 General Conference at which Whatcoat was elected, presumably relieving pressure upon Francis Asbury. The two older bishops still could not agree on a mutually acceptable division of labor and authority. Coke was permitted by the General Conference to accept assignments in England and Ireland. While there he served as either secretary or president of the British Conference and presided at the Irish Conference yearly.*

---

*Asbury at this time felt under pressure and in 1800 spoke of resigning. See Lee, *Short History*, 265; and Asbury, *Letters*, 392.

In November 1803 Thomas Coke came to America for the last time and stayed through the 1804 General Conference. This time he reports that he had closed his affairs at home and had brought all his baggage to the States. He itinerated extensively and presided at the General Conference. He was still not consulted on the stationing of preachers nor even given a copy of their stations. He rightfully complained: "Every Bishop ought to have a right to give his judgment on every point, or he is but the shadow of a Bishop."[17] So it was that he returned to England. As late as 1806 Bishop Coke was still pleading to return to America, but there was no real response to his pleas. Asbury did continue to write to him in a very brotherly fashion.[18] Asbury's standpoint may be seen in the following words from a letter written earlier to George Roberts on January 11, 1804:

> From what I can judge the British Conference will be half undone if he is absent, they have and will have wave after wave. Therefore I hope the General Conference will permit the Doctor to go without any difficulties. I am deeply sensible that neither Dr. Coke nor any other person can render me any essential services in the Annual Conferences, more than the members of said conferences can do, unless they will take the whole work out of my hands.[19]

Asbury can be seen either as power-hungry or as quite right in view of the best interests of the church which could not prosper under intermittent supervision. Perhaps both of these factors were present. After all, during his nine visits, spread over twenty years, Coke spent a total of only about three years in the United States. His two marriages, both ending in the death of his greatly loved spouses, would have made episcopal itineration exceedingly difficult for him.

Beginning in 1808 and thereafter till his death, his name appeared in the American Minutes with this notation:

Dr. Coke, at the request of the British Conference, and by consent of our General Conference, resides in Europe: he is not to exercise the office of Superintendent among us in the United States, until he be recalled by the General Conference, or by all the Annual Conferences respectively.

Throughout their period of service together Coke was acknowledged to be the senior bishop. In documents signed by both men Coke's name appears first. Asbury usually surrendered the chair to his colleague who presided at every general gathering of the preachers from 1784 through 1804. Coke's contributions to American Methodism were not small. He was one of its founders; he was largely responsible for the device of the General Conference; he originated the Trust Clause, a model deed which has proved of immense practical value in maintaining a connectional and itinerant system; he was generous and farsighted in caring for the physical welfare of the preachers, their widows and orphans; he was the progenitor of an authentic missionary vision among us.

Both men had weaknesses as well as strengths. Each one must frequently have expressed attitudes or taken positions highly disturbing to the other. But they respected each other till the end. From Asbury we learn what itinerant ministry, especially itinerant general superintendency, can be and do. From Coke we learn that episcopacy must rightly be possessed of a missionary vision.

The Council

We have seen that at the beginning it was very difficult to coordinate and correlate the growing work of the church. Even the Minutes reflect this. The conferences, although held sequentially in several sections, were reported as one. Any new rule had to be approved by successive action by all the conferences or by a majority vote of all the preachers. As the number of conferences multiplied this became very burdensome. There were eleven conferences in 1789, and of course, they were very widespread. Reaching an agreement among them all was exceedingly toilsome for the bishop. Thus this initial provision for overall governance soon collapsed under its own weight.

Neither Asbury nor Coke possessed the organizing genius of a Wesley. Asbury devised a plan for a Council with which Coke initially agreed. Later Coke changed his mind about it. Asbury records in his *Journal,* "I was closely employed in making my plan."[20] He saw this plan as an alternative to a *general* conference which would be expensive and would keep the preachers from their tasks for prolonged periods. It was called a Council[21] of no fewer than nine members, including the bishops and presiding elders. The bishops would call it to meet "at such times and places as they shall judge expedient." It was to have had wide powers with respect to the unity of the church, its worship, doctrine, and discipline and was "authorized to mature anything for the good of the Church, and for promoting and improving our colleges and plan of education." Asbury apparently meant by it to share the executive power; instead, he was perceived as attempting to concentrate power in the bishops' hands and thus combine legislative and executive functions.

The plan was finally, though not readily, approved. There were two meetings beginning December 1, 1789, and again December 1, 1790, with a third session set for 1792 which never met. Lee records Minutes for both sessions. It was doomed from the start for it was ill-conceived and essentially inoperative. Each proposal would have required unanimous approval by the Council and subsequent confirmation by the conferences. It was unrepresentative, cumbersome, and divisive. It was what we should call "elitist," made up entirely of bishops and those they appointed. Coke, O'Kelly, Lee, and Ware united in a successful effort to bring about its demise.

The Council would have proposed policy for *later* agreement of the preachers; a General Conference would act to bring about *prior agreement* on policy to be pursued by the church. The outcome was a victory for the preachers over the administrative authority, a successful resistance to executive power. Now the stage was set for a real General Conference as an instrument through which the preachers could legislate. The idea of a Council was dropped, and Asbury had to accept this with as much grace as possible.

General Conference

The Christmas Conference has often been called a "General Conference," but ordinarily it is not classed as one. It was an unique organizing convention of lay preachers which created the denomination. We have emphasized that Wesley did not expect any such American conference to be held at all; perhaps he expected the British Conference to fill the legislative need of the American church. The 1786 Minutes also speak of these successive conferences being "General Conferences" though the Minutes were a cumulative compilation of actions taken by multiple conferences held in sequence and not records of *single* sessions. In them collectively the Christmas Conference had placed the continuing legislative governance of the church.

Again, Wesley had asked that Coke summon a "General Conference" in 1787; but this was not of a nature that gatherings of such designation were to become. Some unitary device for the expression of general consensus of the preachers was necessary. The several conferences meeting in sequential concert proved cumbersome and ineffective, though by their concerted action they initiated and changed legislation. The Council was rejected as a failure and a fiasco and finally was superseded by the 1792 General Conference. The various conferences (sixteen in all) agreed during the course of 1792 to authorize an assembling of *all* the traveling preachers in full connection in a General Conference to be convened November 1, 1792. This was a *real* General Conference and, according to Jesse Lee and Francis Asbury, the *first* one. All along the decisive legislative power rested in the totality of the preachers, and therefore they *could* and did authorize a General Conference as a more efficient means of discharging their power than a Council could have been.

It was precisely the persons who successfully opposed the Council who must be given credit with the idea of holding a General Conference, namely, Thomas Coke, James O'Kelly, and Jesse Lee.[22] Lee was, in fact, rebuked by the Council for making the proposal. O'Kelly was present at the first council meeting but refused to attend the second one, having become persuaded that the more democratic approach of a General Conference involving all the preachers was vastly to be preferred over a small nonrepresentative body. Apparently he communicated with Dr. Coke about this and obtained his support—as he indicates in a letter to O'Kelly under date of May 4, 1791.[23] Bishop Asbury was never enthusiastic about General Conferences. He stubbornly resisted their creation and development in spite of the fact that it was at his insistence that the Christmas Conference was held. They were costly in time and money as well as risky as he saw them. On occasion he complains about General Conferences not being very effective.[24]

The first General Conference of The Methodist Episcopal Church, then, met in Baltimore on November 1, 1792.
Bishop Coke arrived suddenly and unexpectedly just the
night before and was welcomed heartily. The preachers
also came in great numbers. As Lee says:

> Our preachers who had been received into full connection,
> came together from all parts of the United States where we
> had any circuits formed, with an expectation that something
> of great importance would take place in the connection in
> consequence of that conference. The preachers generally
> thought that in all probability there would never be another
> conference of that kind, at which all the preachers in
> connection might attend. The work was spreading through
> all the United States, and the different territories, and was
> likely to increase more and more, so that it was generally
> thought that this conference would adopt some permanent
> regulations, which would prevent the preachers in future
> from coming together in a general conference. This
> persuasion brought out more of the preachers than
> otherwise would have attended.[25]

By his preaching and by his calm presiding, Dr. Coke
contributed much to the deliberations. For his part, he was
impressed with the vigor and caliber of the debates.

The conference busied itself with agreeing upon
its rules of procedure which are not very unfamiliar
even with respect to current practices. Any preacher
could propose a motion; accepting a new rule or
abolishing an old one required a two-thirds vote, but to
alter or amend only a majority. One solid matter was
decided: the General Conference should convene every
four years.

The deliberations were then dominated by the debate
occasioned by the resolution introduced on the second day
by James O'Kelly:

> After the bishop appoints the preachers at conference to their several circuits, if any one think himself injured by the appointment, he shall have liberty to appeal to the conference and state his objections; and if the conference approve his objections, the bishop shall appoint him to another circuit.[26]

Asbury was ill at the time and, of course, was himself the focus of much of the debate. He spent much time in his room. He did, however, send the conference the following letter:

> My Dear Brethren: Let my absence give you no pain—Dr. Coke presides. I am happily excused from assisting to make laws by which myself am to be governed; I have only to obey and execute. I am happy in the consideration that I never stationed a preacher through enmity or as a punishment. I have acted for the glory of God, the good of the people, and to promote the usefulness of the preachers. Are you sure, that, if you please yourselves, the people will be as fully satisfied? They often say, "Let us have such a preacher;" and sometimes, "we will not have such a preacher—we will sooner pay him to stay at home." Perhaps I must say, "His appeal forced him upon you." I am one, ye are many. I am as willing to serve you as ever. I want not to sit in any man's way. I scorn to solicit votes. I am a very trembling, poor creature to hear praise or dispraise. Speak your minds freely; but remember, you are only making laws for the present time. It may be that as in some other things, so in this, a future day may give you further light. I am yours, etc. Francis Asbury.[27]

The story of the debate on O'Kelly's resolution that ensued has been told many times; it raged on for three days, often with considerable heat. The conference was sharply divided on the issue. As discussion continued John Dickins proposed that the motion be divided: *that* the bishop should appoint was finally approved without opposition; but that the preacher who felt injured should have the right of appeal put the debate back where it started. The motion originally entered on Friday continued in discussion all that day and the next. There was a rule allowing each person to speak three times on each motion, and with the dividing of the question it was possible to speak three times on each part. So the debate dragged on.

On Sunday there was time for passions to subside; at services both Coke and O'Kelly preached. But the debate began anew on Monday morning. An extra session was held Monday evening at "Mr. Otterbein's church" where on the final vote the motion was lost "by a large majority."*

James O'Kelly proved a poor loser, for at this stage he and some other preachers allied with him, including young William McKendree, withdrew from the conference session. Thus ended this vigorous contest over episcopal authority. It would not be the last attempt to challenge it. Observers felt that if its partisans had carried on the debate in better spirit the effort might well have succeeded. As it was, O'Kelly was seen by most as a troublemaker bent on disrupting the unity of the church. Nevertheless, Bishop Asbury writes that the "conference ended in peace."[28]

Ever since John Wesley called the first conference in 1744 the Methodist movement has had two controlling factors: a conference, and an appointing or overseeing role. Of course, one could press the point that at the beginning, since Wesley's conference had only a consultative function, there was only one controlling factor. In

---

*It is seldom noted that one reason the O'Kelly motion was lost was that an appeal by *one* of the preachers against an appointment immediately made all the other preachers uneasy. "Could the appellant want my place?" One appeal could potentially hold up every appointment.

America the superintendent was the appointing authority, and the conference was the legislative authority. Someone has suggested that after Wesley, Methodists in England had a conference without a ministry and in the beginning America had a ministry and no conference. Now the latter situation was clearly corrected: it had both.

The General Conference was firmly established as the legal and legislative authority of Methodism, and the superintending and appointing authority was made clearly answerable to it. The one meant that the issues could be calmly debated; the other meant that policies and decisions could be promptly executed. John J. Tigert has concluded of the General Conference that "as a mass convention of the entire travelling ministry its powers were general, supreme and final."[29] This was realized in the 1792 meeting. Thereafter, American Methodism was a connectional system with a supervisory authority, the bishops.

Having been sustained in strength by the outcome of the debate, at the same General Conference in large measure the nature of the episcopacy was also fixed more firmly. At the same time it must be noted that the powers of the General Conference during the period 1792–1808 were such that the episcopacy itself or any detail relating to it or any other aspect of the governance of Methodism from 1784 on could have been altered or destroyed by a majority vote of that body, for in it full authority resided. It did not, in fact, actually use any of these sweeping powers. The episcopacy then had no firm warrant or constitutional guarantee. It did have, as it were, a vote of confidence by the preachers in 1792.[30] Executive power was vested in the bishops *ad interim;* legislative authority it kept to itself;*

---

*It should be noted, however, that until 1808—and sometimes beyond that date—bishops could and did on occasion make motions, debate, and vote, because they, too, were traveling preachers.

judicial review had not yet become an urgent issue, but at this stage it rested in the General Conference though it might be exercised in some degree by the bishops. In other words, a system of authentic "checks and balances" had not yet been instituted.

In a section of the 1792 *Discipline* captioned "Of the Election and Consecration of Bishops, and of their Duty," the General Conference also made it clear that in the future, bishops should be constituted "by the election of the general conference and the laying on of the hands of three bishops, or at least of one bishop and two elders." Moreover, the bishop was made amenable for his conduct to the "general conference, who have power to expel him for improper conduct, if they see necessary." A procedure for trying "an immoral bishop, in the interval of the general conference" was also authorized.*

Finally, the duties of bishops were defined:

1. To preside in our conferences.
2. To fix the appointments of the preachers for the several circuits.
3. In the intervals of the conferences, to change, receive, or suspend preachers, as necessity may require.
4. To travel through the connection at large.
5. To oversee the spiritual and temporal business of the societies.
6. To ordain bishops, elders and deacons.

It is clear that these duties are here very broadly defined and encompassed a number of other responsibilities that had to be addressed by episcopal authority and experience

---

*Far from being "beyond reach," a bishop accused of an offense could be suspended until the next General Conference by a two-thirds vote of nine preachers (seven elders and two deacons). The General Conference could then depose the bishop *without* trial.

as the bishops traveled through the connection. They did some things according to unwritten law and tradition. In addition, they appointed the presiding elders (a designation first used in the 1792 *Discipline*), and of course, much more was to be heard of this later on.

The O'Kelly Schism

We have seen that James O'Kelly's resolution was decisively defeated in Baltimore. The next day he and a few followers, including William McKendree, left their seats in the General Conference and a few days later returned in anger to Virginia. There they continued their struggle and in time caused a considerable defection from the Methodists, first called "Republican Methodists" and finally "Christians." Asbury was able to win back young McKendree by treating him with exceeding kindness and inviting him to travel with him. McKendree was to be criticized severely for this later on. Only one traveling elder was finally lost, but a number of local preachers continued to follow O'Kelly. Some of the congregations also returned to the Methodist fold, but undoubtedly there was considerable erosion which did "serious injury to the cause of God," as Coke reported.

In some respects this development is reminiscent of the Strawbridge-Fluvanna resistance to authority. Indeed, O'Kelly, who had arrived from Ireland in 1778 and was already a preacher by the following year, was at the Fluvanna Conference, though there is no evidence of his having been involved in the ordinations there. He was a very able man, articulate but irascible and consumed by personal ambition, as sometimes both Coke and Asbury were. He was ordained deacon and elder at the Christmas Conference and moved into what amounted to the "presiding eldership," a role he pursued with strict discipline.

We have seen how he opposed the Council, but he continued to carry on a kind of running battle with what he perceived as Bishop Asbury's arbitrary authoritarianism.

Not all the controversy was carried on in good spirit. O'Kelly maintained that he had been driven out by Asbury, that The Methodist Episcopal Church was unscriptural, oppressive, and undemocratic. He was deeply influenced by literature of his time on natural rights of men and by anti-Catholic and anti-British writings.[31] He called Asbury a "pope" and loved to cast aspersions upon him: "Seeing he remaineth a High Priest over the Methodist Episcopal Church."[32] Jesse Lee gives a fairly complete account of the controversy and speaks of how the O'Kellyites abhorred the name of *bishop*.[33] On his part, Asbury observes in a letter to Thomas Morrell, "I believe now nothing short of being an episcopos was his first aim."[34] The *Discipline* of 1798 was annotated by Coke and Asbury largely to answer O'Kelly's charges. But the charges were hurled by O'Kelly for years in a series of polemical writings and then answered effectively by Nicholas Snethen, Asbury's "silver trumpet," himself later to become a leader in the Methodist reform movement.

Mention should be made here of a lesser defection at about the same time by some followers of William Hammett in and around Charleston, South Carolina. Hammett was ordained by Wesley in 1786 and sent with Coke for missionary service in Nova Scotia. Bad weather diverted their ship to the West Indies where for a period he was a very effective missionary. When in 1791 he became ill, Coke brought him to Charleston. There some Methodists were charmed by this preacher of the British Connexion, and resisting Asbury's authority, they insisted on his being appointed their pastor. He proved a thorn in the side of both bishops, falsely accusing them of the grossest offenses. This led to a split in the church, an abortive effort on Hammett's part to form a "Primitive Methodist Church." This came to nothing, and after Hammett's death the flock returned to the fold.

Another Schism

The first schism from The Methodist Episcopal Church was occasioned by dispute over episcopal authority, although after the event many other, sometimes carping, criticisms were voiced by the opposition. The second schism was over racial discrimination with some admixture of resistance to the bishop and especially lack of imagination on the part of the majority group.

Black people were present and involved in Methodist beginnings in both Maryland and New York.[35] Asbury had a particular interest in evangelism among them and was impressed by their piety and zeal.[36] Both Asbury and Coke traveled with Harry Hosier (or Hoosier), himself an extremely gifted preacher. Both Hosier and Richard Allen were present at the Christmas Conference. Bishop Asbury ordained Richard Allen in 1799, the first black preacher to enter the full-time Methodist itinerant ministry.

Allen was born a slave, was instrumental in leading his master to conversion and then was allowed to purchase his own freedom. Settling in Philadelphia he attended St. George's Church along with a number of other black members. Then in 1786 the blacks were directed to the balcony of the church for seating; they were also refused Communion with the white members. As a result the black members withdrew in a body and established what became known as Bethel Church (Mother Bethel).*

---

*There was trouble over the deed for this church, for the black members by sad experience resisted the usual Trust Clause, which would have meant loss of voice in appointment of their pastor.

Black members in other places experienced similar discrimination. Therefore, in April 1816 a convention was called in Philadelphia which resulted in the organization of a separate denomination, The African Methodist Episcopal Church. Richard Allen was elected and consecrated its first bishop.[37]* Particularly after Asbury's death thousands of black members left The Methodist Episcopal Church to join this newly formed church. It has grown to be the largest of the black Methodist bodies in the United States. It has numbered some very able bishops in its ranks.

The African Methodist Episcopal *Discipline* now contains the following statement:

On the matter of Episcopacy, the following concepts are clear:

1. The Bishop is to be the symbol of unity in the Church.

2. The Bishop should see himself as overseer, watchman, shepherd.

3. The Episcopacy must be understood as an office and not an order.

4. The Bishop is to be considered as first among equals (Primus Inter Pares).

5. The Bishop's role is that of chief-pastor.

6. The Bishop is to be the representation of both order and servant-life.[38]

Of special interest also is a formal statement disavowing apostolic succession.[39]

Meanwhile a similar movement among other black Methodists began in New York City in Zion Chapel (Mother Zion) and Asbury Chapel. It stemmed not so much from protest as expediency. At first it sought to be a

---

*The second bishop was Morris Brown who was for a time "assistant bishop" to Richard Allen. For a time such an office was provided for in the African Methodist Episcopal *Discipline*.

possible black jurisdiction within The Methodist Episcopal Church. In July 1820, however, it became a separate entity known originally as The African Methodist Episcopal Church in America, later adding the suffix Zion, after the name of its "mother church." The first bishop was James Varick, elected at age twenty-four! At the beginning their practice was to elect term bishops, subject to reelection.[40]

We consider out of historical order The Colored (now Christian) Methodist Episcopal Church, established in 1870 by Negro members of The Methodist Episcopal Church, South. These members had petitioned the General Conference of that body for a separate organization to be achieved in a constitutional manner. This was approved, and the first two bishops elected were William H. Miles and R. H. Vanderhorst.[41] Currently the Christian Methodist Episcopal and African Methodist Episcopal Zion churches are engaged in serious conversations looking forward to organic union at an early date.

It must be observed that all three of these kindred Methodist bodies have a strong understanding of and tradition of the office of bishops. It has not been eroded in them nearly to the degree that this has happened in the parent denomination.

All along a number of black members remained within the parent church. Their great contribution there lies beyond the scope of this study but must gratefully be acknowledged.

Toward a Delegated General Conference

With the steady growth of The Methodist Episcopal Church a General Conference seating *all* of the traveling preachers became increasingly cumbersome. It also involved considerable expense and lengthy absence of the preachers from their posts as they traveled back and forth to the sessions. Thus a move toward a *delegated* General Conference was gradually launched. It will be recalled that Jesse Lee had suggested such a representative conference as early as 1791.*

At the 1796 General Conference no new bishop was elected, for, as we have seen, Coke agreed to join Asbury in order to "strengthen the episcopacy." The same session saw the creation of six yearly or *Annual* Conferences to replace what formerly were known as "District Conferences" of no clearly defined boundaries which were called in considerable numbers at the bishop's discretion and at locations suited to the members' convenience.[42] The six Annual Conferences were New England, Philadelphia, Baltimore, Virginia, South Carolina, and Western.** An important authority was vested in the bishops: of creating other Annual Conferences if they deemed this necessary.*** As has already been stated, the General Conference authorized the two bishops to issue the *Discipline* with notes, and in this they did not neglect the opportunity to deal at length with episcopacy.[43]

There was then discussion as to whether or not a further bishop when elected should possess the same powers as his predecessors or serve under their direction. In 1797 Asbury had explored the possibility of there being two grades of bishops. Nevertheless, an important decision was made by the General Conference that bishops should "be on an equal footing, and be joint superintendents."[44] In spite of this, later on Asbury frequently referred to himself as the senior bishop and McKendree as the junior bishop.

---

*See Asbury, *Journal* 1:687.

**The Western Conference originally included Buffalo, New York, and Natchez, Mississippi!

***When the bishops actually exercised this power in 1810 with respect to the Genesee Conference, a considerable furor was created.

At the 1800 General Conference Bishop Asbury offered to resign but was urged to continue.[45] The session was marked by the election of Richard Whatcoat as a third bishop. He was a saintly, sweet-spirited man with some High Church leaning in regard to the bishopric. The election was by a narrow margin on the second ballot. On the first ballot he was tied with Jesse Lee. One cannot but surmise what the future might have been had the latter been elected. Lee was of sterner stuff, somewhat of the mold of a McKendree.

The conference displayed genuine evangelistic fervor but was otherwise not very productive in a practical sense, according to Asbury's observation. Approval was given to the organization of the New York Conference. At this session also the idea of a delegated General Conference was raised but not approved. At the 1800 session,* as at its predecessor, the appointed presiding eldership was called into question—without success.[46]

The fourth General Conference met in Baltimore in May 1804 and was the last one at which Bishop Coke presided. All three bishops were present. The *Discipline* was divided into two portions, temporal and spiritual, as Asbury had suggested. The attitude was favorable toward a delegated General Conference, but no practical steps were undertaken to sanction it. Lee reports what he regards as an unsuccessful and unwise experiment of opening the galleries for nonmembers to observe the debate.[47] It was legislated that appointment of preachers at any one station should not exceed two years: the bishops appointed but the General Conference determined for what duration. Once again an effort was made to do away with the presiding elder or make the office elective. Again, it failed.

---

*At this General Conference a regular plan was approved for the support of bishops. See Lee, *Short History*, 264.

It was at the 1808 session of the General Conference that the long-sought delegated General Conference was finally debated and approved. Bishop Asbury alone was in the chair, since Bishop Whatcoat had died July 5, 1806. At this conference Asbury's younger colleague, William McKendree, was elected. This is the last such conference reported by Jesse Lee in his *Short History;* he calls it the *last* General Conference, that is, the last one at which *all* traveling elders of four years' service were automatically members.[48] Somehow Bishop Asbury must not have grasped completely the far-reaching meaning of the work of this conference. His *Journal* entry for May 6, 1808, states rather blandly:

> We have done very little except making the rule for representation hereafter, one member to the General Conference for every five members of the annual conferences; and the electing dear brother William M'Kendree *assistant bishop:* the burden is now borne by two pairs of shoulders instead of one; the care is cast upon two hearts and heads (italics mine).[49]

Actually the 1808 Conference was crucial, for it gave Methodism what was finally declared to be its Constitution. Henry Boehm observes that "previous to the session of this conference the Church had been like our nation under the *articles of confederation.*"[50] We have seen that between 1792 and through 1808 the General Conference had complete and unlimited power over the church because it rested upon the combined suffrage of *all* traveling elders. This was in 1808 conveyed by them to ensuing delegated General Conferences but limited and restricted in such a way as to protect the rights of all and preserve the unity and government of the denomination. The legislation which enabled this is called our Constitution. All following General Conferences are creatures of the one held in 1808.

The process which accomplished this will be told in only the severest outline, for it has often been told before. It was not achieved by a single, well-rounded document such as the United States Constitution produced by the Constitutional Convention in 1787. Rather, it involved the formulation of and debate about a rather simple and straightforward enabling as well as limiting resolution, and its eventual approval by the conference.

In 1806 the New York and Baltimore conferences had approved a memorial which would have authorized a delegated conference of seven members from each Annual Conference to meet in Baltimore on July 4, 1807, to elect superintendents and for no other purpose.[51] This was approved also by the New England, Western, and South Carolina conferences but defeated by Virginia where it was seen as a breach of rules as well as dangerous and destructive to the welfare of the church. (If approved, this petition would have sanctioned an electoral college to elect bishops.) It is generally understood that what was intended was the election of one "localized" bishop for each Annual Conference. If this had succeeded, it would have instituted a diocesan episcopacy and would have destroyed the general superintendency.

A slightly different memorial proposing equal representation of the several Annual Conferences at a General Conference was formulated the following year by the New York Conference. This, too, was supported by some of the other Annual Conferences; it failed of the necessary approval by all of them; and then it was moved on the floor of the 1808 Conference. When considering this, the body demonstrated its desire for further definition of rules "to regulate the General Conferences." This resulted in the appointment of a Committee of Fourteen—the ablest members of the conference—to draw up such regulations. A subcommittee for drafting, made up of Joshua Soule (then age twenty-seven), Ezekiel Cooper, and Philip Bruce, was then formed. Bruce was a kind of silent partner; for Cooper, episcopacy was an abstraction with content to be defined by circumstance; for Soule, it was a concrete plan of itinerant general superintendency. Both Soule and Cooper drafted a statement, but Soule's prevailed and was recommended to the conference as a whole. It was further debated on the floor. Surprisingly, Jesse Lee, the first proponent of a delegated General Conference, opposed it on the grounds that the proposals abridged the rights of the Annual Conferences.

The debate was interrupted to consider a further proposal by Ezekiel Cooper to *elect* presiding elders by the Annual Conference. This perennial issue was thoroughly aired and finally defeated rather soundly.

The proposals of the Committee of Fourteen, that is, the Restrictive Rules, were again taken up, and after lengthy debate they too were defeated. This development disheartened the representatives of smaller and more distant conferences who had felt outnumbered all along. Faced with imminent disunity and fragmentation of the church, the majority party found a way to reconsider the main motion. It was amended to allow the Annual Conferences to choose the one-in-five preachers as delegates to the General Conference either on the basis of seniority or by choice by ballot. After further amendment the proposals, essentially as drafted by Joshua Soule, were approved. Unity was preserved, and The Methodist Episcopal Church had its Constitution. A delegated body of ministers was thus vested with full legislative authority save for six restraining rules. All power not reserved for the Annual Conference was granted to the General Conference.

Whether or not the 1808 General Conference was

actually a constitution-making body was to be a subject for debate for many decades to come. Long debated, too, was the question of whether or not the comprehensive resolution was or was not a real constitution.*

The action is recorded in the 1808 *Discipline:*

Question 2: Who shall compose the General Conference, and what are the regulations and powers belonging to it?

Answer 1: The General Conference shall be composed of one member for every five members of each Annual Conference, to be appointed either by seniority or choice, at the discretion of such Annual Conference; yet so that such representatives shall have traveled at least four full calendar years from the time that they are received on trial by an Annual Conference, and are in full connection at the time of holding the Conference.

2. The General Conference shall meet on the first day of May, in the year of our Lord 1812, in the city of New York, and thenceforward on the first day of May once in four years, perpetually, in such place or places as shall be fixed on by the General Conference from time to time. But the general superintendents, with or by the advice of all the Annual Conferences, or, if there be no general superintendent, all the Annual Conferences respectively, shall have power to call a General Conference, if they judge it necessary, at any time.

3. At all times when the General Conferences meet, it shall take two-thirds of the representatives of all the Annual Conferences to make a quorum for transacting business.

4. One of the general superintendents shall preside in the General Conference; but in case no general superintendent

---

*Some observers have pointed out that this was not ratified by the Annual Conference. The answer would appear to be that all Annual Conference members with four years in the traveling ministry were *eligible* to be present at the General Conference itself and could have exercised their suffrage there.

be present, the General Conference shall choose a president *pro tempore.*

5. The General Conference shall have full powers to make rules and regulations for our Church, under the following limitations and restrictions, viz.:

1. The General Conference shall not revoke, alter, or change our Articles of Religion, nor establish any new standards or rules of doctrine contrary to our present existing and established standards of doctrine.

2. They shall now allow of more than one representative for every five members of the Annual Conference, nor allow of a less number than one for every seven.

3. They shall not change or alter any part or rule of our government, so as to do away episcopacy or destroy the plan of our itinerant general superintendency.

4. They shall not revoke or change the General Rules of the United Societies.

5. They shall not do away the privileges of our ministers or preachers of trial by a committee, and of an appeal. Neither shall they do away the privileges of our members of trial before the society or by a committee, and of an appeal.

6. They shall not appropriate the produce of the Book Concern, nor of the Chartered Fund, to any purpose other than for the benefit of the traveling, supernumerary, superannuated, and worn-out preachers, their wives, widows, and children.

Provided, nevertheless, that upon the joint recommendation of all the Annual Conferences, then a majority of two-thirds of the General Conference succeeding shall suffice to alter any of the above restrictions.[52]

For our purposes it should be observed that this action did guarantee and protect (at least from simple legislative change) an episcopacy of a nature similar to that which had emerged and had been sanctioned in the experience of the church since 1784, though clearly answerable to the General Conference. This is the force of the Third

Restrictive Rule. The same authority that approved this safeguard placed the General Conference under constitutional restraint. Both creations—governing conference and episcopal leaders—were responsible in the final analysis to the whole body of preachers and, much later, to the whole body of the church.

Under such powers and restraints the first delegated General Conference met four years later in New York City under the guidance of the presidents, Bishops Asbury and McKendree. For the first time an Episcopal Address was delivered by Bishop McKendree, and it was referred to an appropriate committee of the General Conference.[53] Another innovation by the junior bishop was the instituting of a conference cabinet of the presiding elders of the several conferences to advise the bishop.[54] There was real truth in the statement that in Bishop McKendree "Asbury faced his match."

The General Conference of 1816 met for the first time without Francis Asbury who had died a few weeks before on March 31. Bishop McKendree's hands were strengthened by election to the episcopacy of Enoch George and Robert R. Roberts. Added to the bishops' responsibilities was the devising of a course of study for the preachers: a natural role for bishops as theirs has always been seen as a teaching office. On the other hand, yet another effort was made to have the Annual Conferences elect the presiding elder upon the nomination by the bishop of three candidates, but this failed of enough support.

I am indebted to a young scholar of the Baltimore Conference, the Reverend Emora T. Brannan, for pointing out a significant element at the 1816 General Conference which might easily pass unnoticed.* It has to

---

*See "The Presiding Elder Question" (Ph.D. diss., Duke University, 1974), 8-9.

do with the essential mission of Methodism. As early as 1763 in the Large Minutes and again at the Christmas Conference, the same question was asked and, with only changes appropriate to the different political setting, was given the same answer:

Question 4: What may we reasonably believe to be God's Design in raising up the Preachers called *Methodists?*
Answer: To reform the Continent, and to spread scriptural Holiness over these lands.

Yet in Bishop McKendree's Episcopal Address in 1816 we find him saying: "We believe God's design in raising up preachers called Methodists in America, was to reform the continent by spreading scriptural holiness over these lands." The connective "and" had become the preposition "by"; and in so doing the twofold mission of the church became a unitary churchly mission!

With the death of Asbury the church and its episcopal office came to the end of an era. What we would call a "power vacuum" obviously existed. Would an effort be made to seize it? Bishop Asbury was literally and figuratively seen as a father in the faith, but what of the brethren? Methodism began to take a new turn, and upon this we shall touch in the next section which sets the stage for much more to come.

The Presiding Elder Question

One might almost say the presiding elder question was a question before there were presiding elders. John Wesley's general assistants, Rankin and Asbury, in the 1770s and 1780s for all intents and purposes functioned as "presiding elders" or "suffragan bishops," save for the fact that they were at that time still unordained. As authority figures their powers were open to question and resistance whether by Robert Strawbridge or the Fluvanna group. Again, the elders ordained at the Christmas Conference were really presiding elders. In the 1785 Minutes their names appear at the head of a group of other preachers whom they supervised on the circuits.

The designation *presiding elder* first appears in 1789 in connection with the Council of which they were defined as members. It found its way officially into the *Discipline* of 1792. In that same edition we find:

Question 1. By whom are the presiding elders to be chosen?

Answer: By the bishop.

Their duties are then defined:

1. To travel through his appointed district.
2. In the absence of the bishop to take charge of all the elders. . . .
3. To change, receive, or suspend preachers . . . during the intervals of the conferences. . . .
4. . . . to preside in the conferences. . . .
5. To be present, as far as possible, at all the quarterly meetings. . . .
6. To oversee the spiritual and temporal business . . . in his district.
7. . . . that . . . our discipline be enforced in his district.
8. To attend the bishop when present . . . (and) give him when absent all necessary information.

They were not to be appointed to the same district for more than four successive years.

Thus the presiding elder was essentially an assistant bishop. Abel Stevens said that the bishop was the "right hand" of the Methodist *Discipline* and the presiding elder the "left hand." Asbury saw this officer as the "eyes and ears of the bishop." He was for order, good order "like a well-disciplined army." Asbury wrote,

> If a bishop, at any distance where a mail can go, has consequential business to the whole Conference, he has only to communicate to one man; he to write to the other presiding elders; they to communicate to the men who have charge of stations and circuits; the work is done.[55]

The bishop did not want the presiding elder to be elected precisely because this effectiveness would be lost and the chain corrupted by "the poison of electioneering."[56] Some observers of the Evangelical United Brethren Church, which had this elective system, would bear out this fear as well founded. "The superintendency and presiding elders keep the whole body in harmony."[57] In view of this, Bishop Asbury saw any tampering with this office as an erosion of episcopal power and efficiency. The plan of itineracy, basic to American Methodism, required an episcopacy with sufficient authority to make the system work.

On the other hand, it was precisely because of this concentration of power that it was challenged for decades. Even down to the present day when the office of district superintendency would be perceived as more democratic and humane than it was in the early nineteenth century, this question still raises its head.* A convenient way of "getting at" the authority of the bishop was to challenge his prerogative of appointing the presiding elder.

Thus the office was first placed in the *Discipline* in 1792. In 1796 it was not attacked, though Coke and Asbury

---

*Freeborn Garrettson, writing home from the 1820 General Conference, said: "We have harmony among us; but we have not yet come to the disputed point, which we have to contest every General Conference."

mounted a vigorous defense of it in their annotated *Discipline* of 1798, prompted in considerable measure by the O'Kelly defection. This reads with great interest.[58] They argue that every episcopal church has the office of presiding elder by whatever name: for instance, the Anglican archdeacon or rural dean. We have seen, however that the office was under assault at every General Conference from 1800 to 1820. At this last session the proponents of election won. The rule was then suspended in 1820 because of a constitutional challenge, as it was again in 1824 and finally "put to rest" in 1828. Or was it?

The presiding elder question has particularly to do with the period beginning with the 1820 Conference and ending with the 1824 Conference, including especially the interval between them. The tangled story of this episode has been told many times, from many perspectives, for it was a highly divisive and partisan issue. Stripped to bare essentials it tells of the development of a liberal wing of the church ("The Reformers"), who desired changes with respect to the appointment of this officer, and the conservatives who wanted no change and who saw such change as destructive of the very foundation of the Methodist system. The lines were clearly drawn. The matter came to sharp focus at the 1820 General Conference. A comparatively mild compromise "solution" was put forward: that when a presiding elder was to be chosen, the bishop would nominate three persons for the office, one of whom would then be elected by ballot without debate by the Annual Conference. He might also remove a presiding elder and fill an interim vacancy. This resolution, after lengthy and acrimonious debate, passed by a vote of sixty-one to twenty-five.

At this point Joshua Soule, who had been elected bishop nearly a week before but had not yet been consecrated, arose and announced that he would not enter upon the work of an itinerant general superintendent "impaired" as it was by such a constitutional breach. By this he meant that the General Conference had exceeded its constitutional authority by enacting a rule that offended against the Third Restrictive Rule which forbade changing or altering "any part or rule of our government so as to do away episcopacy, or destroy the plan of our itinerant general superintendency." In other words, since at the time of the "Constitution's" enactment in 1808 the appointment of presiding elder was in the hands of bishops and in Soule's view an integral part of our appointment system for our itinerant ministry, it could not be changed by mere legislation. Bishop-elect Soule had actually drafted the Constitution, and his view had at the very least to be heard with respect. The fat was now in the fire.

Soule held his ground and was supported in his constitutional protest by Bishops McKendree and Roberts. Bishop George sided with the liberal opposition. Some have surmised collusion among them, or at least between the first two. In a formal statement to the conference, Bishop McKendree declared the resolution unconstitutional.[59] Even though the General Conference then suspended its earlier enactment for presiding elders to be nominated and elected, Soule was not consecrated, having declined the office. The matter was held over till the 1824 General Conference. Meanwhile it was a sharp issue for discussion by the Annual Conferences and by the church at large.

The quadrennium 1820–1824 was indeed stormy. Beginning in 1821 Bishop McKendree saw fit to place the issue before the Annual Conferences. Since he was deeply convinced that a constitutional and not a merely prudential principle was at stake, he deemed it appropriate to submit it to the whole body of traveling elders who as members of the various conferences were the final arbiters of such matters. He did this by a closely argued *Address*. His points were that for the presiding elders to be elected was tantamount to transferring to the preachers the executive power that was rightfully the province of the bishops; that to do so would injure or destroy the itinerant plan; that to ignore one breach of the Constitution was to jeopardize everyone's protection under the same Constitution. McKendree argued that the delegated General Conference is made up of two parts: the representatives of the Annual Conferences and the bishops. Both are answerable to the preachers collectively: the "General Superintendents serve as watchmen to guard the Annual Conferences against attacks on their constitutional right."

Seven of the then existing twelve conferences did declare that the 1820 rule violated the Third Restrictive Rule but were willing to amend the Constitution to make this legal. The other five conferences were not even willing to admit that a constitutional principle was at stake and decided that the General Conference was perfectly competent to *legislate* such a rule change. Since a constitutional remedy required concurrence of all twelve conferences, their negative vote or failure to vote defeated even their own purpose.

One hardly needs to report that this caused much acrimonious debate and was highly productive of ill feeling. The bishops differed sharply among themselves as to the merits of the issue as well as with respect to the appropriate course to effect a remedy. In the 1824 General Conference it was agreed, by a very narrow margin, that the rule to make presiding elders elective was unconstitutional. In 1828 the rule was "rescinded and made void." At the 1824 Conference, however, Joshua Soule and Elijah Hedding were elected bishops (Soule for the second time) and preserved a balance acceptable to the various regional interests. Unfortunately the whole struggle took on a sectional aspect; the South and West against the North and

East—a pattern that developed more and more acutely until 1844.

The contest between the liberals and conservatives subsided for a time as they united their energies to try to meet another crisis as they saw it: the challenge of lay representation. Faced with a third issue, common to them both, the erstwhile contenders joined forces for a time. In other words, they relied on expediency rather than on a genuine resolution of their conflict. The presiding elder issue subsided but was to rear its head again years later. A dreadful price was exacted in the form of yet other schisms in 1828–30, in 1842, and finally in 1844. From this distance it is hard to grasp why such matters could be debated so heatedly. But these controversies overlay even deeper issues. Bishop McKendree and later Bishop Soule saw a legitimate principle at stake which concerned the role of episcopacy and finally the welfare of the whole church as an effective agent of mission. McKendree likened his situation to that of Samuel, prophet and judge of Israel, who faced rebellion by those who wanted to do what was "right in their own eyes."[60]

We are trying to follow a very tangled web indeed as it respects the meaning and role of episcopacy. One needs to raise one's head occasionally and view the larger landscape. In most ways the prospect was pleasing. The church was growing in breadth and depth. Revival fires broke out in many places; souls were saved. Renewed men and women were provoked to all manner of good works—individually and institutionally—as they prayed and rejoiced in serving the Lord.

Methodist Reform and The Methodist Protestant Church[61]

We have seen how persistent was the effort to elect presiding elders by the Annual Conference members and the resultant debate when this was denied. This move was accompanied by agitation for representation and rights for the local preachers and for the laity. Many saw or experienced Methodism as having an autocratic, almost monarchical, system of government. Thus an intermittent and then persistent stream of protest runs through our early history: Robert Strawbridge, the Fluvanna incident, the O'Kelly schism, the presiding elder question, the movement for reform. There was a definite democratic or populist strain in our past which insisted on being heard. Looking back, we have many reasons to be grateful for this part of our heritage.

This latent strain of protest came strongly to the surface in the actions of the 1820 General Conference. This was accentuated in the following quadrennium as the issues were discussed at the Annual Conference and local levels. The lines began to be drawn very sharply. On the one hand, the liberals included Nicholas Snethen, Asbury's "silver trumpet" and one-time defender against the verbal assaults of O'Kelly; Alexander McCaine, secretary but nonmember of the 1820 General Conference; Asa Shinn; Samuel R. Jennings, physician, educator, and lay preacher; and William S. Stockton, prominent layman and editor. These men were frequently joined by others, particularly in the early days of the struggle, some of whom later stayed with the mother church. Very often in order to prevent reprisals they wrote under pseudonyms; McCaine was "Martin Luther, Jr. or Nehemiah," Henry B. Bascom was "Eusebius," Asa Shinn was "Bartimeus," Ezekiel Cooper was "A Methodist" or "Philo Episcopous," and so on. The reformers deeply resented those who switched loyalties as McKendree (once pro-O'Kelly), John Emory, Nathan Bangs, Dr. Thomas E. Bond, Beverly Waugh, or Timothy Merritt had done. Ranged against the Reformers were such persons as William Winans, William Capers, S. G.

Roszel, Alfred Brunson, and Joshua Wells, in addition to the bishops and those who switched sides.

A terrible running battle was engaged in, not only on the floor of conferences but especially in the church press and sometimes in the secular press. The *Methodist Magazine,* edited by Nathan Bangs, generally closed its columns to the Reformers. Therefore another magazine, *The Wesleyan Repository,* was established as an organ of the movement for reform. *The Christian Advocate and Journal* of New York was another periodical that proved a vehicle to defend the status quo. Still another reform periodical first published in 1824 was *Mutual Rights.* Thus there was no lack of forums for discussion. A blast at episcopacy, Alexander McCaine's book, *History and Mystery of Methodist Episcopacy,* appeared in 1827, so the battle heated as it went along. This called forth John Emory's *Defense of "Our Fathers."* McCaine returned with *Defense of the Truth.* The polemics were indeed fierce and iconoclastic but usually not directed in the manner of personal assault.

Part of the struggle was against episcopacy which was seen as deliberately foisted on the new church created in haste in 1784 and in defiance of Wesley. The Asburian episcopacy was the target of the most excessive criticism for his alleged arbitrary and autocratic government of the church. Even when a certain parental affection attaches to Wesley and Asbury, none at all is reserved for McKendree and Soule. The former were exceedingly paternalistic, but with them paternalism was redeemed somewhat by bonds of filial affection; assumed paternalism, as in the case of the latter, is bound to be tyrannical, it was said.

Edward J. Drinkhouse, M.D.—a Methodist Protestant apologist and polemicist—saw the Deed of Declaration as the cardinal error in British Methodism and the founding of The Methodist Episcopal Church as the cardinal error in

American Methodism.[62] Had Drinkhouse really thought through the consequences in both cases if our forefathers had acted differently? The Reformers often complained that the so-called constitution claimed by Soule for the 1808 actions was no constitution at all. They also insisted that the episcopacy was in the understanding of Asburians a *third order* and not just an office.* The Reformers insisted on curbing episcopal authority and increasing that of the General Conference.

In spite of these matters the real focus of the Reformers was lay representation. The most persistent champion of this cause was Nicholas Snethen.[63] He was encouraged by Ezekiel Cooper and others. It was insisted that it was a church for ministry and not a ministry for the church. Yet in the beginning there was a ministry before a laity, a ministry—indeed a lay ministry for the most part—calling together a laity into societies.

An effort was mounted to grant laity equal representation in Annual and General Conferences. A memorial to effect this was introduced in the General Conference of 1824 but was sidetracked. Jeffersonian and Jacksonian principles of democracy had a powerful effect on this emphasis. A totally clerical church government seemed to fly in the face of the whole American republican experiment. Methodism as a movement of societies was a preaching order, not too different from Roman Catholic notions; but as a church on the American scene a place had to be made for laity. Actually this had to wait for several more decades. Years later Bishop James H. Straughn

---

*This writer has concluded that in our tradition it is an office and not an order, but it must be admitted that earlier views were, to say the least, ambiguous. Some clearly believed in three orders. The trend latterly is to see only two orders, and overall this view clearly prevails. Bishops are not "elevated," but elected and "set apart."

stated that not protest against excesses of bishops but nonrepresentation for the laity was the issue that caused the separation of Methodist Protestants.[64]

Schism was once again the costly price that had to be paid for failure of authority to respond to the insistent needs of those who felt exploited and unrepresented in the councils of the Methodists. After the 1824 General Conference, and especially after the 1828 General Conference, events moved swiftly. In an increasing number of instances rebellious Reformers were suspended or expelled from the church. First of all, there were established "Associated Methodist Churches," followed by organizing conventions convened at Baltimore in 1828, then in November 1830 for what was to emerge as The Methodist Protestant Church. It had a well-defined written constitution. It had no bishops and no presiding elders; laymen were given equal representation at Annual and General Conferences. It was a connectional body with a Methodist doctrinal base. There was a president who made appointments, reviewed by a committee of the conference.* There was thus an effort made to correct the "evils" the Reformers had opposed. It did not make provision against slavery, and this was later to plague the new body, which also split for some years over that issue. The main body of Methodism once again suffered sorely in numbers lost and in the quality of the leaders who felt obliged to defect from the ranks of the mother church.

In 1843 another schism occurred with the organization of The Wesleyan Methodist Church of the United States of

---

*In fact each Methodist Protestant Annual Conference decided how it would make appointments. Some conferences "let its president be the *committee*" for this purpose. There was the right of appeal which was almost never used. The late Bishop James H. Straughn observed only one such appeal while he was president of the church.

America. Its leadership became disenchanted because of inaction over the issue of slavery. This separate body of ministers and laity was formed by the Reverend Orange Scott, evangelist and abolitionist, and others into a new denomination, "free from episcopacy and slavery, and embracing a system of itineracy under proper limitations and restrictions."[65] For a time there was a considerable defection from Methodist Episcopal ranks of both ministers and members. Later some returned.

A Divided Church

The turmoil that accompanied the growth of Methodism during the first sixty years of its life seems almost to make our more recent history peaceful by comparison. In spite of everything the church did grow, and a truly triumphant story can be told of this.

The events related to the General Conference of 1844 did not result so much in a schism *from* but a schism *of* episcopal Methodism, a division that was to last for nearly one hundred years. This manifestly did not take place in isolation from the divisive trends developing rapidly in the nation. The fact is that the straining and snapping of churchly bonds, North and South, were a prelude to the tragic political and military battles that were to follow. Bishop Nolan B. Harmon states that "in the debates of 1844 the historian can hear the guns of Gettysburg."

The General Conferences that followed 1828 not only did not respond adequately to polity pressures from within the constituency but also failed to take very decisive action on the contemporary social issues, notably slavery. John Emory pointed out that in the 1798 *Discipline,* Bishops Coke and Asbury did not comment on the Section on Slavery.The reasons usually offered for this failure had to do with preserving the unity of Methodism, not notably successful.

Yet the denomination put great weight on success in church growth and in pursuing its mission of spreading scriptural holiness. Its judgments were often based on the pragmatic, not to say the expedient, and not always on high principle. It was also anxious to maintain a sectional balance in its leadership. From an initially strong position with respect to opposition to slavery, its witness in this respect gradually became mostly a spent force, its position more and more lethargic in pursuit of the exceeding sinfulness of slavery. We have seen some of the erosion of membership that resulted; at times the church even found itself defending slavery.[66]

The matter was, however, in one way or another on the agenda of each successive General Conference. From reading the record of the General Conferences, one gains the impression that there was a reluctance to deal firmly with the issue; the hope was that the problem would "go away," as one might say nowadays. For example, in the General Conference of 1840 it was decided that although bishops could at Annual Conferences decide questions of law, with an appeal to the General Conference, the *application* of the law rested with the conferences—which might simply ignore the decision.[67]

At this same conference Bishop Hedding broke a precedent that had prevailed until that time. While Bishop Andrew at this session had followed the custom of the bishop's voting to break a tie vote, his colleague Hedding on another occasion refused to follow the custom. He had already reached his position on this matter as early as 1837.[68] He explained from the chair that originally "bishops could speak and vote on all subjects": They were traveling preachers, all of whom could participate freely. In fact they did make motions, debate, and vote through 1808. Beginning in 1812 the General Conference was made up of delegates from the Annual Conferences, and bishops were not delegates. Even so, some bishops introduced resolutions until 1844. Then Bishop Hedding further elaborated that the Speaker of the House of Representatives in the United States could vote because he was a member of that body, and the vice president of the United States could vote in a tie because the Constitution of the United States authorized it. Not so with bishops. Since 1844 bishops have not resolved tie votes at General Conference.[69] A bishop at its sessions is a moderator. He can decide questions of order, under appeal by the body, but he cannot decide questions of law as he can at Annual Conferences, for the lawmaking body itself is in session at a General Conference.

The 1844 General Conference meeting May 1 in New York City was the longest such conference and presumably the most momentous ever held. Its story has been told many times and will not be retold extensively here.[70] The delegates were strong and able, representative of all sections of the country and of the issues involved; few extremists were present. Efforts have been made to declare that the issue in 1844 was not slavery and, if it were, that this was a political, civic, and economic problem not a moral one. Rather, it is asserted that the issue at stake was a constitutional one: the authority of bishops *versus* the power of the General Conference. The weight must surely come down on the side of slavery's being the divisive issue.[71] Both the issues were present; both—whether slavery or constitutionality—involved the episcopacy. Each aspect played into the other and precipitated a crisis. The bonds of unity could no longer stand the strains of a double stress.

The conference moved into its work slowly to allow the members to become well acquainted with one another. The Episcopal Address delivered by Bishop Soule did not deal with slavery but polity.

Then attention turned to the appeal of a Baltimore Conference member, Francis A. Harding, against his suspension by the Baltimore Conference for holding slaves acquired by marriage. The appeal was not approved; his suspension was affirmed by decisive vote.

Then the similar case of Bishop James O. Andrew was considered. He, too, was involuntarily a slaveholder through marriage and lived in the state of Georgia where slaves could not be freed. First of all, the so-called Griffith proposal was put forward: that Bishop Andrew be "affectionately requested" to resign.[72] This request, mild-mannered enough in its phrasing, if passed by the General Conference, would have been tantamount to a *demand* for resignation. This raised the constitutional issue. It was softened even further by a substitute motion (the so-called Finley resolution), which read:

> Whereas, the Discipline of our church forbids the doing anything calculated to destroy our itinerant general superintendency, and whereas Bishop Andrew has become connected with slavery by marriage and otherwise, and this act having drawn after it circumstances which in the estimation of the General Conference will greatly embarrass the exercise of his office as an itinerant general Superintendent, if not in some places entirely prevent it; therefore,
>
> Resolved, That it is the sense of this General Conference that he desist from the exercise of this office so long as this impediment remains.[73]

The constitutional aspect of the matter remained. Both of these resolutions were debated for days on end; finally on June 1 the Finley resolution was passed one hundred ten to sixty-eight, by what was practically a sectional vote.

On May 30, 1844, a last-ditch effort at reconciliation had been made by the bishops (all except Andrew himself) to recommend that the matter be carried over until the ensuing General Conference, with Andrew to be assigned meanwhile to conferences where his leadership was acceptable.[74] Bishop Hedding, however, broke ranks and reversed his initial agreement to this solution. This measure which was narrowly defeated might have prevailed if Hedding had not withdrawn support. This was the crisis point of the conference.

It is difficult to realize at our distance from the reality of events that both sides desired to take home nothing short of a victory. In other words, even if the unity of the church could have been saved by some measure devised at the center, disunity and defection would have been inevitable back home regardless of geographical section. To force Andrew's resignation would have provoked secession by the Southern conferences; to fail to act would have led to even further defections in the North toward The Wesleyan Methodist Church. Finally, an initially friendly division of the church seemed to be the only avenue that remained open. Neither side could claim victory, and both sides must share the shame and consequences of separation.

The Southern delegates regarded the Finley resolution as an "extra-judicial act." A few days later, on June 5, they presented to the conference a "Declaration" which read in part:

> That the continued agitation on the subject of slavery and abolition in a portion of the church; the frequent action on that subject in the General Conference; and especially the extra-judicial proceedings against Bishop Andrew, which resulted, on Saturday last, in the virtual suspension of him from his office as Superintendent, must produce a state of things in the South which renders a continuance of the jurisdiction of this General Conference over these Conferences inconsistent with the success of the ministry in the slave-holding states.[75]

The following day a "Protest" was presented, signed by nearly all the Southern delegates:

By pressing the issue in question, therefore, the majority virtually dissolve the government of the Methodist Episcopal Church, because in every constitutional aspect it is sundered by so crippling a coordinate branch of it as to destroy the itinerant general suprintendency altogether.[76]

In response to specific queries from the bishops as to how to administer details concerning Bishop Andrew's status, a three-part resolution was moved for adoption:

1. Resolved, As the sense of this Conference, that Bishop Andrew's name stand in the Minutes, Hymnbook, and Discipline, as formerly.
2. Resolved, That the rule in relation to the support of a Bishop, and his family, applies to Bishop Andrew.
3. Resolved, That whether in any, and if any, in what work, Bishop Andrew be employed, is to be determined by his own decision and action, in relation to the previous action of this Conference in his case.[77]

These were all approved but by votes that reflected sectional lines of decision.

Furthermore, a detailed "Plan of Separation"[78] was devised to stand ready for use "in the event of separation." This was in response to the "Declaration." It was passed by large majorities. Finally a resolution giving a factual account of conference actions and proceedings on the Bishop Andrew case was approved for the record. This was a response to the "Protest."

There proved to be, as we have seen, very little actually said or done directly about slavery, though it was in the background all the time, with constitutional matters kept to the foreground. Southerners did not attempt to defend it; it was an evil but one they felt they had to live with. Indeed, the discussion of constitutionality was a way of speaking in somewhat cloaked fashion about slaveholding, just as it had done for some years. This kept the debate on more comfortable ground for both parties.

What, briefly stated, *was* the constitutional issue in 1844? It had to do with episcopal status, power, and prerogative versus the authority of the General Conference. From the perspective of the South, Methodist episcopacy clearly predated the General Conference. Methodist polity had two collateral poles of powers: one executive and the other legislative. The bishops and General Conference were coordinate. Soule called episcopacy a distinct department of government of the church. The episcopacy since 1808 had been protected by the Third Restrictive Rule cited above (p. 151). To challenge the general superintendency was to offend against this rule. This was the basic debate which raged from 1820 to 1828.

Bishop Soule had essentially written the Constitution; he had with Bishop McKendree "successfully" defended it, at great cost. He gave the Episcopal Address in 1844 and stood like a rock, still defending the position he had taken years before. From this standpoint, the actions proposed and then taken with respect to Bishop Andrew were unconstitutional. If Andrew had offended legally or morally, then "due process" should have been used against him. This view requires admission that ultimate authority lies not in the General Conference but in the Annual Conferences that originally delegated power to the quadrennial conference.

In the North and East, as contrasted with the South and West, Methodist ministers and members of successive General Conferences tended to sit rather looser to constitutional matters. This is seen in their failure to support Bishop McKendree as he pleaded for support for the suspended resolutions of 1820. The General Conference was seen as supreme and the bishops merely executive officers of it. On the floor of the 1844 General Conference, the Reverend Leonidas L. Hamline[79] delivered an eloquent address stating the case (some would say vastly overstating the case) for this view. This effort undoubtedly contributed to his election as bishop at the same session. He was joined by others who went even further than he did in favor of unilateral authority in Methodism, that is, the power of the General Conference. To the partisans of this standpoint bishops are the creation of General Conference. They pleaded that in it all legislative, executive, and even judicial authority finally rests. It was against this kind of thinking that the debaters from the South directed their fire and the "Protest." It was this, the General Conference side, that prevailed by sheer weight of votes. To Southern members this essentially destroyed general superintendency.[80]

The deed was done. The delegates and bishops scattered. Representatives of thirteen Southern conferences, in accordance with the General Conference Plan of Separation, met in Louisville in May 1845 in an organizing convention which established The Methodist Episcopal Church, South. The following summer they held their first General Conference in Petersburg, Virginia. Bishops Soule and Andrew went with this church, while Bishops Hedding, Waugh, Morris, and newly elected Hamline and Janes went with the Northern branch. American Methodism was divided into six parts: The Methodist Episcopal Church; The Methodist Episcopal Church, South; The African Methodist Episcopal Church; The African Methodist Episcopal Zion Church; The Methodist Protestant Church; and The Wesleyan Methodist Church. Episcopacy was involved in one way or another in the genesis of every one of them. The years 1939 and 1968 were still a long way away.

From 1844 to 1939

The story of ninety-five years of separation is a long and complicated one, inharmonious at first and latterly more fraternal in nature. Only a few of the developments that related to episcopacy in The Methodist Episcopal Church and The Methodist Episcopal Church, South, will be listed. The two divided, but the sister churches developed episcopacy along astonishingly similar lines. Of course, each maintained and reinforced the positions regarding the episcopal office that they had set forth so strongly in the debates of the 1844 session. Nevertheless, at the time of reunion in 1939 the episcopacies of the two related traditions were amazingly alike, and very little adjustment needed to be made to fit them into one continuing office. For example, both continued the custom of Episcopal Addresses and cabinets of district superintendents or presiding elders as The Methodist Episcopal Church, South, continued to call them until 1939. By and large episcopacy in the South was more powerful and more revered than in the North; it followed more closely the Asburian-McKendree style. There did develop what was called the "Bourbon bishop" in the Southern church, but there were also some stalwart and often stubborn bishops in the North as well. Nevertheless it became a maxim that The Methodist Episcopal Church was not governed *by* bishops but *with* bishops.

Frequently cited in this respect is the resignation of Bishop Hamline in 1852. His stated reason was health, though he lived on for thirteen years; perhaps he was simply demonstrating what he had pleaded for in 1844: that the bishop was merely an officer of the General Conference. That body accepted his resignation. There was thought to be no indelible quality to his office. Election, not consecration, was decisive and determinative in American Methodism: no small consideration for our ecclesiology as compared to other episcopal communions.

The Methodist Episcopal General Conferences of 1820 and 1824 had both concluded that they alone could not determine the constitutionality of their own acts. Reference had to be made to the Annual Conferences for their vote so that together the General Conference and the body of preachers came to a constitutional decision. The Southern church met this problem directly, as we shall see shortly. The Methodist Episcopal Church did not do so and wrestled with this issue in a variety of ways throughout the period 1844 to 1939, mainly through a Committee on Judiciary in which bishops had no part. This was, of course, consistent with views that prevailed in 1844.

Beginning in 1856 the General Conference of The Methodist Episcopal Church became concerned about usages regarding episcopacy as reflected in the ritual. Finally in 1864 the word *ordain* with respect to bishops was changed to *consecrate*.[81]

The Methodist Episcopal General Conference of 1884 passed this resolution: "Resolved, That we re-affirm the doctrine of the fathers of our Church, that the bishopric is not an order but an office, and that in orders a bishop is merely an elder or presbyter."[82] This point was further driven home by a rubric added to the consecration service in 1884: "This service is not to be understood as an ordination to a higher order in the Christian ministry, beyond and above that of elders or presbyters, but as a solemn and fitting consecration for the special and most sacred duties of superintendency in the Church."[83]

It has already been pointed out that Methodism has been ambiguous regarding the issue of episcopacy's being an office or an order. The earlier view leaned to order, the latter to office; neither conclusion was unanimous. *Ordain* suggests "order." The change of the word to *consecrate* has helped to eliminate that suggestion. It should be noted that in the event of a bishop's being tried, it would be by elders—his peers in order.

At the 1884 General Conference session of The Methodist Episcopal Church it was also driven home that bishops could speak at General Conference by invitation and consent of the body not by right.[84]

Of great significance was the development of *lay* delegates to the General Conference, which meant that thereafter they helped to elect bishops and, at a slower pace, lay membership of Annual Conferences.[85] The struggle for this was long and sometimes bitter. When it was achieved, one of the points of protest of the Methodist Protestants had been met. We would take this for granted now, but it was a radical step at the time, for conferences were made up of preachers even though most of them in *primitive* Methodism were *lay* preachers. Approval to seat delegates was given by the Northern church in 1868, and they were first seated in 1872—two from each Annual Conference. Women came later (1888). Ministers and laity both sat and voted as one body in the General Conferences but *could* vote by orders, that is, ministers and laity voting separately. The same session (1872) finally arranged for a judicial procedure for the trial of bishops who until then theoretically could have been peremptorily dismissed by the General Conference!

Along the way other developments may be noted. From time to time the old issue of election or confirmation of presiding elders (they became district superintendents in 1908 in The Methodist Episcopal Church) would reappear, in 1932, for instance. So also would the proposal for term or tenured episcopacy (1852, 1872, 1888, 1920, 1928). In 1900 an effort was made to strike out all reference to "bishop" in the *Discipline* and replace it by "general superintendent"; this failed.

In 1908 also the General Conference approved a Social Creed, this in no small measure by the effort and leadership of liberal bishops. At the same session approval was given for election of bishops by Central (or overseas) Conferences. The trend toward "localization" of bishops began to manifest itself in the 1880s, but this will be discussed in the next chapter.

Turning now to The Methodist Episcopal Church, South, we may note somewhat similar developments.[86] The 1846 General Conference kept exactly the same section on episcopacy as was written in 1844.

Of greatest importance was the practice in The Methodist Episcopal Church, South, of giving the bishops a so-called veto on legislation deemed by them to be unconstitutional. *Veto* is not the right word; *check* or *suspensive veto* would be better. This power was present even before 1844, though not undisputed. In 1854 the General Conference of the Southern church authorized the bishops to interpose their objections to any legislation they felt was unconstitutional. This was first of all done legislatively, not constitutionally. During the interim 1870 to 1874 it was then referred to the Annual Conferences—"the whole body of travelling preachers"— for their judgment. This authorization itself became *constitutional* later for it was passed by a two-thirds vote of the General Conference and by a three-fourths cumulative vote by the preachers in the Annual Conferences; there were only nine votes against the motion. Bishop Soule's view had always been that judicial power belonged to the Annual Conferences or preachers collectively with bishops as their agents. It was seen as a safeguard and protection of the body of the church. But it could also be seen as arbitrary or at least so perceived. So it was that a separate arm, a Judicial Council, was established in 1934.[87] One of its first acts was to decide that the proposed Plan of Union was indeed constitutional.

The Southern church followed the Northern branch in changing the word *ordination* of bishops to *consecration*. Earlier in 1866, two years before the Northern branch, it afforded equal *lay* representation at the General Conference *and* Annual Conference, and this was implemented in 1870.

Atticus G. Haygood was elected bishop in 1882 but did not accept. True to Southern views of the matter, he did not resign but "declined to accept."[88] He *did* accept when elected again in 1890. Term episcopacy was proposed in 1922 and again in 1934 but was rejected by the General Conference both times. In 1934 Bishop John M. Moore delivered the Episcopal Address and made a strong plea for episcopacy as a third *order*. The episcopacy was no prelacy, no divine right, but as a College of Bishops, a coordinate part of the government of the church.

Reunion

In 1939 the severed family of episcopal Methodism became one again in a renewed entity, The Methodist Church, with *Episcopal* dropped out of the name.* The two episcopal traditions fit almost exactly together. The Methodist Protestants had a term president but according to Bishop Straughn's testimony he marched from Methodist Protestant presidency to Methodist episcopacy without missing a step. In 1939 the bishops of the two episcopal Methodisms and the president of the Methodist Protestants celebrated a feast of commemoration and then a joyful reunion.

For the first time ours was a specifically defined constitutional episcopacy "of like plan, powers, privileges,

---

*The *Christian Century* commented that "the Methodists adopted the pat and sufficient name, The Methodist Church."

and duties as now exist in The Methodist Episcopal Church and The Methodist Episcopal Church, South."[89] A Council of Bishops[90] was also provided for in the Constitution. Restrictive Rule Three, now numbered Two, continued. Bishops were no longer elected by the General Conference, which remained supreme, but by the Jurisdictional and Central Conferences. This was feared likely to breed a new sectionalism. The creation of a segregated Central Jurisdiction caused much pain and embarrassment, but if there is any virtue at all in necessity, it at least gave the church an authentic moral issue within its structure to wrestle with for the next thirty years.

During the subsequent years the episcopacy of our church has not been allowed to stand still. It has been challenged to lead and on its own initiative has led crusades for a New World Order; to address racism with a program: a New Church for a New World; and much more. It has comprehended something of the global reality of our time by its overseas visitation program for bishops. It has been studied *twice* by quadrennial commissions (1960–64 and 1972–76).[91] A proposal for term episcopacy has once again been raised and defeated (1976). Retirement age for bishops has been lowered twice. The limit of tenure of a bishop in any one area has been lowered twice: first to twelve years and then to eight years (aside from the most exceptional circumstance). A further union has taken place, with the Evangelical United Brethren Church in 1968, and as a result, there has been another new name: The United Methodist Church with episcopacy "like" its predecessors.* The Restrictive Rule regarding general

---

*See addendum to this chapter on bishops of the Evangelical United Brethren heritage. See also *Nineteen Bishops of the Evangelical United Brethren Church* (Nashville: Parthenon Press, 1974) by Bishop Paul W. Milhouse.

superintendency remains with a subtle change: "do away episcopacy" becomes "do away *with* episcopacy." There is a difference![92] A woman—the very first in a major denomination—was elected in 1980. Two more women were elected bishops in 1984, a year that also saw our first bishop of Hispanic background elected. A strong episcopacy—a racially inclusive one—remains in place today.

This account of episodes in the development of episcopal Methodism has become quite extended though intentionally no effort has been made to go into details of more recent development. That account will be implicit in the remaining chapters. Behind the story that has been told stand the figures of real persons who for two hundred years, not without faults and stumbling, have been faithful to their calling and have loved and served both the church and her Lord. Many of their names and faces will come to the minds of interested readers, and they will have abundant cause to be grateful to God!

Addendum to Chapter IV
Episcopacy in the Evangelical United Brethren Tradition

In this narrative mention has been made of the strands of United Methodist history that came from the Evangelical United Brethren heritage. These have not been dealt with in any extended or comprehensive fashion. No effort has been made, for instance, to integrate this history with that of episcopacy stemming from Methodism's Christmas Conference. Therefore, a brief addendum is inserted at this point.

Episcopacy among the Evangelicals and the United Brethren was essentially Wesleyan in its nature, by deliberate choice. A short history of these two related movements will make this clear, for they were related to each other and both were from their beginnings associated with Methodism in America.

The United Brethren story is tied to the personality and ministry of Philip William Otterbein. Born of a minister's family in Dillenberg, Germany, June 3, 1726, he was well educated in nearby Herborn and ordained a minister in the Reformed Church in 1749. Soon afterward he volunteered for missionary service in America. He arrived here on July 28, 1752, and was made pastor of a Reformed church in Lancaster, Pennsylvania. This was followed by pastorates near Reading, Pennsylvania; then Frederick, Maryland; then York, Pennsylvania; and finally in Baltimore.

In 1767 at a famous "great" meeting in Isaac Long's barn, near Lancaster, Otterbein heard a Mennonite bishop, Martin Boehm, preach. So impressed was he by the message that he went forward and embraced Boehm, remarking, "Wir sind Brüder" (hence, "United Brethren"). Between them they shared the Reformed pietist and Anabaptist pietist streams of tradition that proved to have a natural affinity for pietism of the Wesleyan variety. Both men were deeply influenced by Methodism and its preachers. We have already seen how Francis Asbury desired Otterbein to participate in his ordination at the Christmas Conference. Asbury termed Otterbein "the German apostle to America."[93]

Otterbein had himself experienced a new spiritual awakening soon after arrival on these shores and gradually gathered around himself groups of other spiritually quickened laity. These were sometimes called "Otterbein's People."

Martin Boehm, born in Pennsylvania in 1725, was likewise aroused by the inner needs of people and felt a strong call to preach the good news. He offered God's mercy to the needy and neglected people in Pennsylvania, Maryland, and Virginia, particularly those who were

German-speaking. To equip himself for this undertaking, he intensively studied John Wesley's sermons and other writings. He, too, was a friend of Asbury, and Henry Boehm, Martin's son, was a traveling companion of the pioneer Methodist bishop.

These two men, Philip Otterbein and Martin Boehm, and two others, George A. Geeting (or Guething) and Christian Newcomer, were responsible for summoning great meetings or conferences in 1789 at Baltimore and in 1791 in York County, Pennsylvania, which were preludes to more formal organizational sessions of what was to become a new denomination. Finally at a meeting in Frederick, Maryland, on September 25, 1800, they organized the "United Brethren in Christ." This was a grouping of societies, and they were at first as reluctant to apply the designation of *church* to their organization as John Wesley had been with regard to his societies. At this session Otterbein and Boehm were elected superintendents or bishops, though the latter title was not employed officially until 1813, the year after Martin Boehm's death. They were both reelected bishop in 1805.

Christian Newcomer was elected a bishop of the United Brethren in 1813. Later that year Bishop Otterbein died. By June 6, 1815, the United Brethren completed their formal organization. Their first General Conference approved a *Discipline* and an episcopal form of government. The designation of *bishop* became fixed, for it was after all scriptural. The United Brethren agreed that by *bishop* "we mean an officer in the church for the time being who is elected from among the Elders of the Church."[94]

Meanwhile, Jacob Albright began his movement. He, too, was born in Pennsylvania and was originally a member of the Lutheran church. He served in the Revolutionary War as a drummer boy, participating in the battles of Brandywine and Germantown. Afterward he settled down as a farmer in Lancaster County. Following a personal tragedy he was soundly converted, joined a Methodist class meeting, and began to preach, having been licensed by the Methodists in 1796. For such association with Methodists he was dismissed from the Lutheran congregation, just as Martin Boehm had been excommunicated by the Mennonites. Then Albright's absence from Methodist class meetings because of his preaching trips caused his name to be dropped from *their* rolls as well!

By 1800 Jacob Albright was organizing into classes those who had responded to his message. These became known as "Albright's People." On November 3, 1803, seventeen persons gathered together as the first council of the movement. Then in 1807, "five itinerant preachers, three local preachers, and twenty class leaders and exhorters" organized themselves as the "Newly Formed Methodist Conference." (It was German-speaking.) Albright advised them to establish an episcopal form of government. They authorized him to compile a *Discipline* reflecting their agreement with him, and they elected him their first bishop.

Jacob Albright died the following year, and a colleague, George Miller, completed the *Discipline*. The work continued and Annual Conferences met. In 1816 the first General Conference was held. It adopted "The Evangelical Association" as the official name for their body.

Their *Discipline* provided for the office of bishop, but from the death of Albright in 1808 until 1839 no bishop was actually elected. In that year John Seybert was chosen as the second bishop of the Association. In the long interval episcopacy was much discussed, a four-year term approved, reelection limited to four more years was sanctioned, but as stated, for thirty years there was no election!

After that, episcopal leaders for the Evangelical Association were elected every four years. They even approved, very much later (in 1931), more than two four-year terms but only when it was supported by a two-thirds vote of the General Conference.

We have mentioned the reluctance of these two bodies to call themselves "churches." They, like the primitive Methodists, saw themselves as *ecclesiolae in ecclesia.* Both were originally German-speaking, sometimes called "German Methodists." Gradually they accommodated to the use of English. Slowly the United Brethren in Christ became known as the *Church* of the United Brethren in Christ, but the Evangelical Association became the Evangelical *Church* only in 1922.

Both bodies along the way explored possible union with other churches, for example, with The Methodist Episcopal Church, The Methodist Protestant Church, the Congregational Church, and others. Both experienced schism within their ranks; both achieved family reunions. The two churches joined together in 1946 to become the Evangelical United Brethren Church and twenty-two years later united with The Methodist Church to establish The United Methodist Church. Such, in all too brief statement, is the story of these two kindred churches.

The Plan of Union (1968) and the new Constitution called for

a continuance of an episcopacy in The United Methodist Church of like plan, powers, privileges, and duties as now exist in The Methodist Church and in The Evangelical United Brethren Church in all those matters in which they agree and may be considered identical: and the differences between these historic episcopacies are deemed to be reconciled and harmonized by and in this Plan of Union and Constitution of The United Methodist Church and actions taken pursuant thereto so that a unified superintendency and episcopacy is hereby created and established of, in, and by those who now are and shall be bishops of The United Methodist Church; and the said episcopacy shall have such further powers, privileges, and duties as are herein set forth.[95]

The concept and role of bishop were essentially the same in the two churches united in 1968. This is true also of the predecessor churches which in 1946 became the Evangelical United Brethren Church. All shared an itinerant system of ministry and a presiding eldership or district/conference superintendency. The principal difference was that in the United Brethren and Evangelical heritages, there was an episcopal term of four years but with the possibility of reelection. In practice reelection of bishops was almost invariable, and at the time of union there was no limit to the number of times a bishop could be reelected, subject to an age limitation of election by seventy-two. Furthermore, there was an elective presiding eldership (conference superintendency). This was originally on the nomination of the bishop who could also fill an interim vacancy in the conference superintendency.

If a bishop were not reelected, he originally posed a problem, for a bishop ceased to be an Annual Conference member. This was later corrected by allowing such membership to be reclaimed by a bishop who was not reelected or did not choose to be. Furthermore, if a bishop were reelected after an interval of one or more quadrenniums in which he had not served as bishop, reconsecration was not required. Following three four-year terms one could become a bishop emeritus after retirement. Such a bishop could be recalled to active duty. Earlier practice among the United Brethren was to *ordain* bishops; later they were consecrated. Among the Evangelicals they were never ordained but installed.

The Evangelical United Brethren tradition was for one

order of ordained ministry: that of elder. Bishops were of the order of elder. As in the Methodist tradition episcopacy was regarded an office not an order, not a rank but a duty. It was of election by the General Conference, not by divine right.

In these traditions bishops were likewise general superintendents serving the whole church rather than diocesan officials. An area system developed slowly with the United Brethren just as in Methodism. Areas were adopted by the Evangelical Church only in 1931.

Bishops were members of *all* general agencies, except Publication, where only two were members and the others advisory. Bishops were members of General Conference with right of speech and vote. Bishops emeriti were advisory members of agencies and the General Conference.

Corporately the bishops formed a Board of Bishops with duties similar to the College of Bishops (M.E., South) or Board of Bishops (M.E.) of episcopal Methodism, and the Council of Bishops of The Methodist Church after 1939. The Board of Bishops met at regular intervals. It supervised the spiritual and temporal interests of the church; it prepared and presented an episcopal message to the General Conference; it also was charged with planning General Conference sessions.

The bishops' responsibilities collectively were to review the total work of the denomination; to make recommendations to various church agencies; to interpret the law and discipline of the church. In these latter cases their decisions were binding pending appeal to the next ensuing General Conference. The Board of Bishops could declare an "emergency" under certain circumstances, in which case the denomination's General Council of Administration could act for the church in the emergency. As in Methodist practice, bishops were amenable to the General Conference. Bishops could be elected by mail vote.

Individually bishops attended Annual Conferences and presided. They could not vote except to break a tie. They could nominate for election and appoint conference superintendents to their tasks. They ordained, assisted by two elders. They traveled throughout the church and saw to it that the church functioned according to the Word of God. They watched over the flock of Christ.

Clearly bishops' powers and duties were similar to those that developed within episcopal Methodism. They enjoyed similar authority and privileges, honor and respect. Nevertheless it is also true that bishops in the Evangelical United Brethren heritage had somewhat *less* authority than their Methodist counterparts exercised, although in individual instances this has been difficult to discern. This was offset by the role Evangelical United Brethren bishops played as voting members of the General Conference and in general administration agencies. The two strands of episcopal experience were brought together readily. In the present *Discipline* of The United Methodist Church, the historical listing of bishops is entirely integrated in the order of their election—of whatever particular origin.

Notes

1. H. Richard Niebuhr, *The Social Sources of Denominationalism* (New York: Henry Holt and Co., 1929), 173.

2. Long afterward Bishop M. Merrill wrote, "All the special powers of the episcopal office came to it by the delegation from the Eldership." *A Digest of Methodist Law* (Cincinnati: Methodist Book Concern, 1912), 81.

Once while presiding over the Indiana Conference Bishop Levi Scott prefaced the reading the appointments by saying, "Brother Presbyters, I rise as a presbyter-Bishop to give you your work for a year." Cited by James M. Buckley, *Constitutional and Parliamentary History of the Methodist Episcopal Church* (New York: Eaton & Mains, 1912), 190.

3. Asbury, *Journal* 2:469-70. Asbury must have taken his office quite seriously. In January 1785 he appeared in "full canonicals, gown, cassock, and bands"—natural for one brought up in the Church of

England. But he soon put this garb aside as Coke had also as he moved along the frontier.

4. Cited by Lee, *Short History,* 128.

5. Ibid. Asbury states in his *Journal* 1:312: "I believe the Episcopal mode of Ordination to be more proper than that of Presbyters; but I wish there were primitive qualifications in all who handle sacred things" (September 10, 1779).

6. Asbury, *Letters,* 70-72.

7. Wesley, *Letters,* 7:339.

8. Asbury, *Letters,* 49.

9. Lee, *Short History,* 127. But see Wesley, *Letters* 8:183.

10. Cited by Tigert, *Constitutional History,* 227. See also Lee, *Short History,* 125.

11. Cf. Asbury, *Letters,* 50, 54.

12. Cf. ibid., 94–98. He had similar correspondence with Bishop Seabury, dated May 14, 1791, and in 1790 with Wilberforce.

13. Asbury, *Journal* 1:673. Coke's sermon "mentioned some things which gave offence." Coke later on admitted to Asbury his imprudence on this occasion. Cf. Asbury, *Letters,* 101–102.

14. Cf. Lee, *Short History,* 248.

15. Cf. Asbury, *Letters,* 334-39. Almost exactly the same letter is in the Ezekiel Cooper collection at Garrett-Evangelical Theological Seminary, Evanston, Illinois.

16. Cf. letter to Ezekiel Cooper dated April 21, 1798. Collection of Cooper papers in Garrett-Evangelical Seminary. Coke wrote almost exactly the same text to Whatcoat on the same day. As the Cooper collection shows, Coke could afford secretarial help and frequently the same text appears in various styles of handwriting, though signed by Coke. This long letter gives the most coherent account from Coke's viewpoint of his perception of his offer to be a full-time bishop in the United States.

17. Asbury, *Letters,* 337.

18. Cf. letters dated May 7, 1806, and July 17, 1806, ibid., 341, 349.

19. Ibid., 274.

20. Asbury, *Journal* 1:592.

21. Cf. Lee's rather full account of the Council, *Short History,* 149ff.

22. Lee even suggested to Asbury the idea of a *delegated* General Conference. See Asbury, *Journal* 1:687.

23. Asbury, *Letters,* 99. See also Coke's letter to the General Conference of 1808, dated January 29, 1808, ibid., 382-84.

24. Ibid., 264-65.

25. Lee, *Short History,* 176-77.

26. Ibid., 178.

27. Asbury, *Letters,* 112-13.

28. Asbury, *Journal,* 1:735.

29. Tigert, *Constitutional History*, 263.

30. Ibid., 273-74.

31. Cf. Charles F. Kilgore, *The James O'Kelly Schism in the Methodist Episcopal Church* (Mexico City: Casa Unida de Publicaciones, 1963), 63-64.

32. James O'Kelly, *The Author's Apology for Protesting Against the Methodist Episcopal Government* (Richmond: John Dixon, 1798), 21.

33. Lee, *Short History*, 204.

34. Asbury, *Letters*, 113.

35. See Joseph Pilmoor's Journal, (The Historical Center Library, Old St. George's Philadelphia), passim.

36. See Asbury, *Journal* 1:222, 402, et al.; 2:44, 65; and *Letters*, 15 et al.

37. Cf. Richard Allen, *The Life Experiences and Gospel Labors of the Rt. Rev. Richard Allen, Written by Himself,* intro. by George A. Singleton (Nashville: Abingdon Press, 1960). See also H. M. Turner, *Methodist Polity* (Northbrook, Ill.: Metro Books, Inc., 1972).

38. *The Book of Discipline* of The African Methodist Episcopal Church, 41st rev. ed. (Nashville: A.M.E. Sunday School Union, 1976), 12.

39. Ibid., 29-30.

40. Cf. *The Doctrines and Discipline of The African Methodist Episcopal Zion Church* (Charlotte: A.M.E.Z. Publishing House, 1978). See also J. W. Hand, *One Hundred Years of Zion Methodism* (Charlotte: A.M.E.Z. Publishing House, 1895).

41. Cf. *The Doctrines and Discipline of the Christian Methodist Episcopal Church* (Memphis: C.M.E.C. Publishing House, 1974).

42. Lee, *Short History*, 233-34.

43. See the *Doctrines and Discipline of The Methodist Episcopal Church in America,* with explanatory notes by Thomas Coke and Francis Asbury, 1798.

44. Lee, *Short History*, 265. See also Asbury, *Letters*, 392.

45. Ibid., 266. See also Buckley, *Constitutional and Parliamentary History*, 201; and Asbury, *Letters*, 164.

46. Asbury, *Journal* 2:103.

47. Lee, *Short History*, 300. A strange conclusion by today's standards.

48. Ibid., 186, 347.

49. Asbury, *Journal* 2:569.

50. Henry Boehm, *Reminiscences* (New York: Nelson & Phillips, 1875), 181.

51. Lee, *Short History*, 344-45.

52. *Discipline*, 1808, pp. 14-16.

53. This was the occasion when the aged Asbury intervened: "This is a new thing. I never did business in this way, and why is this new thing

introduced?" McKendree replied, "You are our *father*, we are your sons; you never had need of it. I am only a *brother*, and have need of it."

54. Cf. Robert Paine, *Life and Times of William M'Kendree*, 2 vols. (Nashville: Southern Methodist Publishing House, 1869), 1:260-61.

55. Asbury, *Letters*, 196, 549 et al., 544.

56. Ibid., 438.

57. Ibid., 463.

58. Annotated *Discipline*, 1798, pp. 47-53.

59. Paine, *William M'Kendree*, 1:314-15.

60. Many writers deal with the presiding elder question. See especially Emora T. Brannan, "The Presiding Elder Question" (Ph.D. diss., Duke University, 1974).

61. The most comprehensive review of this whole movement is Edward J. Drinkhouse, *History of Methodist Reform*, 2 vols. (Pittsburgh: Board of Publication of the Methodist Protestant Church, 1899). This is exhaustive but calm in stating the case for the Reformers. John Emory's Defense of "Our Fathers" is good on the other side. Harlan L. Feeman's *Francis Asbury's Silver Trumpet* is interesting. T. H. Colhouer's *Non-episcopal Methodism* also strongly argues the Methodist Protestant case. The very last paragraph of the last Appendix of Vol. I of Drinkhouse is typical of some of the writing: "If the President of the United States (Bishop) were elected by Congress for life, and if the President appointed the governors of states (Presiding Elders), and if the governors recommended to the President the appointment of county sheriffs (pastors), and if the sheriffs appointed or nominated the county commissioners (Quarterly Conference), and if the legislature (Annual Conference) were composed of the sheriffs and governor and elected one-half of the members of Congress (General Conference), and a convention (Electoral Conference) of delegates chosen by the county commissioners elected the other half of the members of Congress, we would have a civil government exactly like the government of the Methodist Episcopal Church. But no one would call this a representative government." (Written by T. H. Lewis.)

62. Cf. Drinkhouse, (Pittsburgh: Methodist Protestant Publishing House, 1892). *Methodist Reform*, 1:9. See also D. S. Stephen, *Wesley and Episcopacy*.

63. See also *Essays on Lay Representation* (Baltimore: John J. Harrod, 1835), v.

64. See James H. Straughn, essay in W. K. Anderson's *Methodism*, (Nashville: Methodist Publishing House, 1947), 251.

65. Ira Ford McLeister, *History of the Wesleyan Methodist Church of America* (Syracuse: Wesleyan Methodist Publishing Assoc., 1934).

66. A charge cited by abolitionist L. C. Matlack in Wade C. Barclay,

History of Methodist Missions (New York: Board of Missions, the Methodist Church, 1950), 2:105.

67. Cf. General Conference *Journal*, 1840, 120-21. The Episcopal Address at this conference would further reinforce this perspective: they recommended "no new . . . legislation . . . on slavery." The Address did, however, speak extensively on bishops' powers and their amenability to the General Conference.

68. D. W. Clark, *Life and Times of Rev. Elijah Hedding* (New York: Carlton & Phillips, 1855), 514. In 1837 Hedding declared, "I am superintendent—jointly with my colleagues—of the whole church; I am required to oversee the spiritual business of the whole; I am related alike to all the conferences; therefore, I ought not to do anything in one conference which I know has a tendency to injure another."

Incidentally, in 1820 Bishop Roberts twice declined to vote to break a tie on constitutional grounds. Cf. Brannan, "Presiding Elder Question," 280.

69. Ibid., 556-57.

70. Cf. John N. Norwood, *The Schism in the Methodist Episcopal Church, 1844: A Study of Slavery and Ecclesiastical Politics* (Alfred, N. Y.: Alfred University Press, 1923). Also Tigert, *Constitutional History*, 435-59.

71. See John Norwood, *Schism in M.E.C.:* Frederick A. Norwood, *The Story of American Methodism* (Nashville: Abingdon Press, 1974), 199-205; *The History of American Methodism*, vol. 2, essay by Norman W. Spellman, p. 65; Brannan, "Presiding Elder Question," 331. See also Donald G. Mathews, *Slavery and Methodism* (Princeton, N.J.: Princeton University Press, 1965), 250N.

72. General Conference, *Journal*, 1844, 64.

73. Ibid., 65-66.

74. Ibid., 76.

75. Ibid., 109.

76. Ibid., 111.

77. Ibid., 118.

78. Ibid., 135-37.

79. For his address and others, see *Report of Debates in the General Conference of The Methodist Episcopal Church, Held in the City of New York* (New York: Lane & Tippett, 1844).

80. See Tigert, *Constitutional History*, 371-80.

81. General Conference, *Journal*, 1864, 471.

82. General Conference, *Journal*, 1884, 207.

83. Ibid., 267.

84. *Daily Christian Advocate*, 1884, 179.

85. Cf. John A. Wright, *People and Preachers in The Methodist Episcopal Church* (Philadelphia: J. B. Lippincott, 1886), passim.

86. An interesting account of episcopacy in Southern Methodism,

especially in the later period, is found in Robert W. Sledge, *Hands on the Ark* (Lake Junaluska, N.C.: Commission on Archives and History, 1975).

87. Ibid. 201-203.

88. *Daily Christian Advocate* (Methodist Episcopal, South, General Conference, 1882), 6.

89. *Discipline* of The Methodist Church, 1939, par. 34.

90. On the Council of Bishops, see Roy H. Short, *History of the Council of Bishops of The United Methodist Church, 1939–1979* (Nashville: Abingdon Press, 1980).

91. Details of interviews with bishops in both these studies are closed during their lifetimes, otherwise a major source for such an essay as this. But resultant legislative changes appear in the *Disciplines* of 1964 and 1976, respectively.

92. The somewhat quaint expression, "do away," suggests erosion, whittling away; whereas "do away with" suggests dispensing with entirely. Ezekiel Cooper commented on "do away." He suggests it means "episcopacy shall not be annihilated, abolished and made extinct . . . if modified, changed, improved, altered or amended, it shall remain and not . . . made rid of." Garrett-Evangelical Library Collection, Letter "G," MSS 14, n.d.

93. Asbury, *Letters,* 479.

94. 1815 *Minutes.*

95. The United Methodist Church, *Discipline,* 1968, p. 29.

V

GENERAL SUPERINTENDENTS—THE OTHER NAME FOR BISHOPS

In what has gone before, a sketch has been given of the roots of episcopacy in the Wesleyan tradition in Scripture and in the stream of general church history. The beginnings of episcopal Methodism in America have been set forth, and the issues related closely to our episcopal polity outlined. No effort has been made to deal with these complicated strands in exhaustive fashion. Nevertheless the main trends and events which have helped to shape the office as we grasp it and exercise it have been touched upon. Detailed historical and biographical analysis is beyond the intention of this volume. Of great importance in this tradition is the emphasis upon general superintendency, and we now turn to this aspect of the subject.

Bishops in the Wesleyan tradition are general superintendents. That is their other name. But the two designations are not precisely synonymous. *General superintendent* has churchwide overtones and reflects the manifold administrative and temporal duties required of our chief pastors; *bishop* accents their more specifically ecclesiastical and spiritual duties. *General superintendent* does not arouse connotations of pomp and privilege to the same degree as *bishop* may. By either title the bishop or general superintendent has at church conference sessions been presiding officer and in the interim chief executive officer.

Among United Methodists bishops are general officers related to the whole church. One of their basic duties is, and has been from the beginning, "to travel through the connection at large." They are general pastors. It is sometimes said of them that each bishop is one of the pastors of every single congregation of our entire connectional system.

Our episcopacy is specifically an itinerant general superintendency, a description as well as a designation of the unique role of bishops in Methodism. It is this aspect of the office in particular that is protected in the Constitution of our church by the Third Restrictive Rule: "The General Conference shall not change or alter any part or rule of our government so as to do away with episcopacy or destroy the plan of our itinerant general superintendency."[1] The words are carefully chosen, and one might say that every word has a very particular meaning in relation to the episcopal office among us.

The usage itself, "general superintendency," appears for the first time in 1808 in this very formulation. It is a *joint* itinerant general superintendency, that is, *one* superintendency for the whole church, shared equally by all the bishops.

John Wesley himself was the very model of an itinerant general superintendent. His incessant travels about the British Isles testify to this. Moreover, the work he did while traveling—preaching, presiding at conferences, appointing the preachers, planning, corresponding, counseling, disciplining, defending the gospel—is what general superintendents are supposed to do. He was involved in everything pertaining to the Methodist societies and was the symbolic and actual head of all the people called

Methodists. In helping him his general assistants came to do what presiding elders or district superintendents do. Wesley thought that it was a shame for any Methodist preacher to confine himself to one place, for he was a debtor to all the world.

Likewise, Thomas Coke did the work of a general superintendent, but neither in exactly the same way as Wesley did before him nor as Asbury did. His itineration was usually over a far-flung, almost global, circuit.

Francis Asbury was the general superintendent *par excellence*. He constantly traveled throughout the connection at large,* which was his responsibility and his burden. The hardships and dangers he endured in his exhausting efforts can scarcely be grasped by us nowadays.

If "the bishop cease from travelling at large among the people," so went the *Discipline,* "he shall not hereafter exercise *any ministerial function whatsoever* in our church"[2] (italics mine). The 1808 *Discipline* qualified this by inserting, "without the consent of the General Conference." Later still it was further softened by allowing a bishop who resigned to become an elder again in an Annual Conference, but this was demanding discipline! It was Coke's eventual failure to travel in the United States that prompted the General Conference of 1808, for practical purposes, to apply this rule to him.

Itinerant general superintendency is an apostolic task after the Pauline model. Asbury repeatedly called Wesley "an apostolic man" and also thought of himself as possessing "the signs of an apostle."[3] So he traveled without ceasing. In so doing during his lifetime he undoubtedly saw more of his fellow citizens and was seen

---

*There is an often overlooked human dimension to Asbury: sometimes he mentions his horses by name. Jane and Foxx were two of them.

by more of them than any other American of his period. He also acquired an intimate and unparalleled knowledge of every aspect of American Methodism. Methodist people usually like to see a bishop—a symbol of unity and authority. Every bishop can testify, however, to having heard scores of times: "You are the first bishop ever to visit our church!" This is usually not the case! Memories are short.

Other bishops continued this responsibility in emulation of Asbury, for they also belonged to the whole church. Just as is our practice even to the present, traveling elders cease to be members of a local church—even the one to which they are appointed pastors—but become instead a member of an Annual Conference; so bishops cease to be members of either local churches or Annual Conferences. They belong to the whole church.

Bishop Whatcoat, to the limit of his strength, followed the Asburian pattern of travel. Indeed he itinerated with Asbury. So did William McKendree until Francis's death—often in peril from storms and floods, from piercing winds and searing heat, not to mention the hazards of highwaymen or of warring Indians. Much the same can be said of Joshua Soule (though he toured very little in the North) who wrote, "I have occupied the humblest cabin, scarcely supplied with the necessaries of life. I have slept on the earth with a bearskin for my couch and the heavens for my protection. I have bedded on snow from three to four feet deep with the heavens spread over me."[4] This was what was expected of general superintendents in the service of God and to all the people.*

In our time bishops are assigned residential responsibility

---

*Yet Bishop George wrote to Bishop McKendree that he did not have the strength "to undertake a continental superintendency." Cited by Tigert, *Constitutional History,* 396.

in a particular area. But they are not diocesan officers. They are still general officers charged with the "general oversight and promotion of the temporal and spiritual interests of the whole Church."* They cannot fulfill their responsibilities exactly as the pioneer bishops did, but they remain general superintendents with supervisory duties laid upon them for the whole connection.[5]

Dr. Thomas B. Neely (later bishop) has stated this succinctly:

> The work of the bishop was to be general rather than local; he was not to be limited to a fixed locality, but was to itinerate over and for the Church generally; he was to be a superintendent for the Church generally, a general and not a local superintendent; and to generally superintend he was to itinerate, to travel officially, through and for the General Church. This was the kind of episcopacy that was incorporated in the Constitution of the Church and placed beyond the power of the General Conference to destroy or modify directly or indirectly.[6]

Why General Superintendency?

The question may well be raised as it often has been: *Why* have an episcopacy or general superintendency? For one thing, an *episcopal* form of government was deliberately chosen in 1784. But the answer to such a question leads us directly to an understanding of our basic mission. The classic articulation of that mission is: "To reform the Continent, and to spread scriptural Holiness over these lands." The mission envisaged a broad perspective, "from sea to sea," as Coke used to put it. This statement of what

---

*This view goes back at least to Ignatius and Cyprian. See *Sacramentum Mundi* (New York: Herder and Herder, 1968), 1:222, 227.

we believe to be God's design for us has been, and often needs to be, reinterpreted to relate specifically to given periods. The answer also has to do with how we organize to pursue this mission. For us this involves an itinerant conception of ministry; the deployment of such a ministry; and the authority by which it is deployed: an episcopacy.

All of this adds up to what Coke and Asbury call, in the annotated *Discipline* of 1798, "our grand plan."[7] This system or plan involves a rather special vocabulary of peculiarly Methodist usage; it combines laws, practices, traditions, and customs that have been regarded as almost sacred by Methodist adherents. This plan has remained astonishingly intact in its broad character down to the present day.

Not surprisingly the plan derives basically from John Wesley. It begins with a ministry of which the Wesley brothers were the first ordained participants but especially with John Wesley. As the movement increased in England and America there were related to him mainly lay preachers—general assistants, assistants, helpers, and class leaders. These all came to have their counterparts in The Methodist Episcopal Church in descending scale of office: bishop, presiding elder, elders, deacons, local preachers (some of whom were also ordained), and class leaders. All of these were equipped with authority adequate for the discharge of the service assigned to them.

Actually the direction of flow in the development of ministry was the other way; they arose from the ranks. As societies multiplied, preachers and conferences increased in number, and conferences were developed (from 1744 in England and from 1773 in America). In time these became in the United States a variety of conferences: General Conference; yearly or Annual Conferences; District Conferences (original name for Annual Conferences but later it was used essentially for what nowadays we call

"District Conferences"); Quarterly Conferences (now Charge Conferences) at the local level—a chain of interlinking and mutually supporting bodies. So it was that the "plan" involved a mission, a ministry, and organizational structure. It was what might be called "a pastoral, regulatory, and supervisory pyramid" to enable the mission.

Itinerancy

The capstone, the most essential ingredient to this system of plan, was its itinerancy—its traveling ministry. This was the *sine qua non* that lent coherence to the whole connection and conference structure. Of this Asbury and Coke wrote,

> All the different orders which compose our conferences are employed in the *travelling line;* and our local preachers are, *in some degree,* travelling preachers. Every thing is kept moving as far as possible; and we will be bold to say, that, next to the grace of God, there is nothing *like this* for keeping the whole body alive from the centre to the circumference on every hand.[8]

Of this characteristic Thomas Ware observed that "we were all missionaries."[9] They were truly a pilgrim band. This was completely in accord with Wesley's own views, for as Nicholas Snethen once stated, "there was nothing in this world he so much dreaded as a preacher who was not always in motion."[10] The ministers were *itinerant* in that they were frequently appointed to new fields and then they itinerated *within* their new circuits. The preachers generally traveled around their circuits once a quarter, with the fifth Sunday off for special preaching because it did not fit the regular schedule. The lengthy intervals between the visits of the circuit rider necessitated the laity's exercising *their* ministry as exhorters or class leaders which they did very well. As the preachers became more settled and localized, the lay class leaders were essentially displaced, and the class meeting gradually died.

The Church of the United Brethren in Christ used the same plan: "The itinerant method of ministerial supply, the episcopacy, the sub-episcopacy, or presiding eldership, quadrennial, annual and quarterly conferences, all are common to both churches."[11]

Why did they engage in an itinerant ministry; why such frequent changes? They had their answers: they went where the people were; theirs was an aggressive proclamation following the primitive example; it gave a certain independence to the ministry, avoiding bondage to local views; it made for a fair distribution of available talent; it contributed to unity and also afforded at least some pastoral care; it was economical under frontier conditions; it answered needs of both pastors and people; it was, they felt, the method of Jesus, the first apostles, and Paul—all itinerant preachers.

There was a price to pay in hardship and health. Many died young; some could not stand the pace. Marriage usually meant location or else even more hardships for families. For his part Asbury preferred celibates; sometimes it was involuntary celibacy—marrying an itinerant preacher was not an attractive prospect for most women.[12]

Not all approved of the plan, of course. Even in his day Joseph Pilmore had his doubts about it, thinking it wasteful of effort and relatively fruitless. Thomas Coke, too, had misgivings. But they both continued to itinerate. Some of the "Reformers" also wrote against the extreme privation that the itinerancy at times imposed. Naturally there were strengths involved in a more settled ministry, not to mention its greater comforts.

Nevertheless, the itinerant system continued and continues to this day, although it has been altered according to circumstance, tempered and humanized along the way. The preachers itinerated and so did the bishops as part of an itinerant ministry. They were convinced that a traveling ministry required a traveling superintendency. They managed somehow to mingle shepherding with their visitations.

Bishop Asbury said in his "valedictory" message, "We . . . try sacredly to maintain our traveling plan and support a true missionary apostolic church."[13] Later he continued with an historical observation: "There were no local bishops until the second century." Then, addressing his colleague William McKendree to whom he was writing: "My dear Bishop, it is the traveling apostolic order and ministry that is found in our very constitution." In the same context he warned "against the growing evil of locality in bishops, elders, preachers, or Conferences. Locality is essential to cities and towns, but traveling is as essential to the country."[14] Bishop McKendree surely agreed for he, too, was thoroughly committed to the "itinerant plan of preaching the Gospel."[15]

Our question raised earlier was: Why have an episcopacy or general superintendency? The "grand plan" of Methodism requires it and sees it necessary for effective mission. All that is written above is involved in the Third Restrictive Rule. Episcopacy is an essential "part or rule of *our* government" as United Methodists, just as a system of conferences, ministerial orders, and appropriate lay roles are also a part.

Therefore, according to this constitutional provision, "The General Conference (by simple legislative action) shall not change or alter any part or rule of our government so as to *do away* with episcopacy or destroy the *plan* of (not dogma or assumption such as divine right) *our* (our own peculiar history and understanding, experience, custom, usage, and model relating to the episcopal office; as opposed, say, to a view such as apostolic succession) *itinerant* (not merely limited, localized, or diocesan) *general* (churchwide) *superintendency* (executive supervision)." (all parentheses and italics mine).

The Appointive Process

But that is not all. An itinerant ministry by its very nature involves appointment or assignment of the traveling members to their tasks. This, in turn, involves an appointing authority that is acquainted as widely as possible with the entire field of work. Such an appointing authority would be one, therefore, that would be charged with the responsibility of *episkopé*—the function of oversight. That function is for us cared for by bishops or general superintendents.

This is why we may say they are essential to effective itinerancy. This is also why Francis Asbury supported the idea of episcopacy, not as an end in itself but to make itinerancy possible. His principal emphasis and aim was to preserve itinerancy, and the general superintendency was almost incidental to that end. Here we have from one man a twofold and, in the eyes of some, a contradictory contribution: by his insistence upon participation of the preachers in shaping the nature of our church, we have what has become its chief legislative court, the General Conference; and by his persistence in itinerant superintendency, we have the unique shape that characterizes Methodist episcopacy.

In no sense is episcopacy among us more unique than precisely in the duty and authority "to fix (set, settle) the Appointments of the Preachers"[16] (parenthesis mine). This makes the bishop in Methodism *sui generis,* at least in Protestantism. Church history has seen nothing else quite like this. No other church had ever attempted such as system on such a scale. A new pattern called for new authority. This enabled also a balance of "supply and demand"; the surplus of ministers in one conference could be transferred to another or sent as missionaries to the far frontier.

Coke and Asbury raise this question: "But why . . . does the general conference lodge the power of stationing the preachers in the episcopacy? We answer, On account of their entire confidence in it."[17] They continue by claiming that this work is done without tyranny or partiality and with a broad knowledge of the whole church and its needs.* Asbury, too, was a man under orders both human and divine. Human nature and human frailty are such that it can scarcely be claimed that in every instance this impartiality prevailed, but this has been the standard. Anyone who has ever held the office could testify to the conscientiousness with which this demanding task has been discharged.

In any event, it has been the testimony of the bishops who have most deeply reflected on the matter that general superintendency is essentially necessary to make an itinerant ministry effective.[18] Since the time of Bishop McKendree this duty has been fulfilled with the advice of a cabinet of presiding elders or district superintendents. (Can it be that McKendree was in part prompted to inaugurate the cabinet by the lingering memory of the right of appeal voiced in 1792 by his erstwhile friend and mentor, James O'Kelly?)

The power and authority of stationing the preachers is the focal point of the Methodist conception of episcopacy. This method of matching pastors with churches has been

---

*"Local men have local ideas," said Asbury.

much criticized and much misunderstood. Without question instances of abuse can be cited; certainly instances of faulty judgment can be found. Yet it is not a role assumed by an arbitrary autocrat. He or she is elected to the office, and the bishop remains accountable at many levels and is also under authority as well as being subject to appointment.

Bishop Nolan B. Harmon has rightly stated,

> The itinerant system requires three things:
>
> 1. That the congregations give up their right to choose their ministers.
>
> 2. That the preachers give up their right to select their own fields of labor.
>
> 3. That the appointment be made by a competent, impartial, untrammeled authority (the bishop), whose powers and duties must be outlined carefully and ordered by the whole church.[19]

Such a system requires an episcopacy strong enough to deal with all three factors. When engaged in this responsibility, the bishop is acting also as general superintendent and acts on behalf of the whole church and its ministry and laity. For all are bound in a covenant before God of mutual responsibility and commitment. The whole ministerial body is under covenant with one another and the church to go where sent. The congregation covenants to receive the minister sent. The nature of such a covenant clearly needs to be understood by ministers and their families. Boards of Ordained Ministry, bishops, and cabinets as well as seminaries must continue to emphasize this.

Upon joining the conference the candidates for ministry accept the conditions of fulfilling it and subscribe publicly to the *Discipline* and polity of The United Methodist

Church. The bishop has in his or her time made similar vows and is bound by the same covenant. These vows are further confirmed at services of ordination both as deacon and elder and on the bishop's part in consecration to the episcopal office.

The Constitution of our church since 1968 has stipulated: "The bishops shall appoint, after consultation with the district superintendent, ministers to the charges."[20] Upon this provision and related legislation but especially on the basis of solemn covenant the appointment becomes possible. Anyone who has served on a cabinet will know with what care, consideration, and compassion this is done.

We have seen repeated efforts to erode the necessary authority of general superintendents that makes this system effective. A whittling away at the episcopacy continues. The *Discipline* makes clear that episcopacy is itself intended to be a regulated and accountable body. At times the other agencies at the general church level or Annual Conference level would make inroads on the functions entrusted to the bishops. Or ministers themselves find reasons to resist the appointive process to which they are pledged. In this process it is not bishops who suffer but the whole body of our church.

When complaints are raised against the appointment system, notice is not taken of the drawbacks related to the "call system." For example, one may not be "called." Moreover, the advantages of the itinerant appointive system may be lost sight of. Here are just a few of them.

1. It is *a* principal guarantee of the freedom of the pulpit. This implies a supportive role on the part of the appointive authority when this freedom is exercised responsibly.

2. It affords a ready way to deal fairly with both pastor and congregation when genuine problems of "incompati-

bility" arise between them. This implies that it should not be used arbitrarily and under pressure, but an appointment *can* be terminated or changed with relative ease and dispatch, if necessary.

3. It is well suited to missional requirements; that is, a pastor's talents *can* be and more often than not are matched with the congregation's needs.

4. It offers promise of our moving as a denomination toward becoming a more racially inclusive fellowship. This implies a highly intentional use of the appointive system on the part of all partners in the convenant to achieve this end.

The 1976 General Conference approved extensive guidelines for consultation during the appointive process. This was further extended in the 1980 sessions (*Discipline,* pars. 527-31). The bishops are committed to such consultation. Well before 1976, appropriate consultation was practiced in many episcopal areas, and in January 1976 the Council of Bishops as a whole agreed to guidelines to be used in all areas. This has complicated the process but not to a degree that is incompatible with a viable itinerant system. Those most in a position to judge would agree that this trend cannot be pressed much further without serious damage to a plan that has served Methodism well for more than two centuries and still shows promise for the future.[21]

General Superintendency Observed

We have moved far ahead to the present in regard to the appointment aspect of general superintendency. We go back now to look at how the office actually operated at the genesis of American Methodism.

When Francis Asbury *alone* exercised the episcopal office, he *was* the general superintendency. This he did between 1784 and 1800, except for the three years altogether when Thomas Coke was in this country, and again between the time of Richard Whatcoat's death in 1806 and the 1808 General Conference.

It was, as we have observed, Asbury's custom even when Coke was here to keep much of the work in his own hands, despite the fact that they were *joint* superintendents. They did travel together to most of the conferences and as senior bishop Coke usually presided, but the stationing of preachers Asbury kept largely to himself. He and Bishop Whatcoat also traveled together "in partnership"; the senior bishop presided as a rule. Although they consulted on appointments, the decisions were made by Asbury. Whatcoat was essentially an assistant bishop.

After 1808 the "senior" Bishop Asbury and the "junior" Bishop McKendree itinerated together to all of the conferences except when the former's health prevented it. By 1811 he had resigned the chair to his younger colleague and in 1815, the year before his death, entrusted to him also the stationing of the preachers. It should be said that because of their schedule of travel the bishops always set the time of Annual Conferences and the conference itself the *place;* this practice continues until today.

Recall that the problem was how to administer *one* office with more than one incumbent. As bishops became more numerous, this obviously became more complicated. One possible way was to divide the conferences and then alternate in visitation. This is just what Bishop Coke proposed in 1805 and 1806, but his colleague did not agree to this.[22]

The year 1816 saw the election of Enoch George and Robert R. Roberts. There were now three general superintendents. They devised a plan of supervision that involved dividing administration of the conferences among the bishops and then alternating annually. The bishop who presided at a given conference had continuing administrative responsibility for it during the year that followed. All bishops were to attend each conference when possible, assisting the one presiding when their counsel was needed.[23] The two younger bishops did not like this pattern very much, and it was gradually abandoned as impractical. But it is important to note that whether one bishop or three were present, the entire episcopal responsibility and authority were present, for the office was joint and coequal. *Bishops,* not *a* bishop, are administrative and executive heads of the church.*

As the church continued to grow, the episcopacy was further strengthened in 1824 by the election of Joshua Soule and Elijah Hedding. Now *five* bishops shared *one* general superintendency. The number of conferences increased, and it was not feasible for the five to travel together. The principle of alternation in presiding at the conferences also began to break down. Bishop Soule, who once on principle did not wish to be less than a general superintendent, in practice itinerated almost exclusively in the Southern and Western conferences and only once in 1831 traveled to his native New England. Bishop Hedding also nearly always restricted his traveling to the North and East. So it was that the general superintendency, if not localized, became sectionalized. Moreover, as we have already noted, sectional views of episcopacy emerged, and the stage was set for the events of 1844.

Contradictions

We have given a brief account of how the bishops endeavored to fulfill the responsibility of the general superintendency during the first sixty years of episcopal Methodism. There was far more to this office than can be

---

*On this see Bishop James A. Straughn in W. K. Anderson's *Methodism* (Nashville: Methodist Publishing House, 1947), 255.

comprehended merely by the physical *presence* of all the bishops—at least at times—in all of the Annual Conferences. This proved impossible. There are other enduring dimensions: one office of general oversight is shared by a number of persons; collectively they are charged with the temporal and spiritual interests of the whole church; each and all of them are bishops of the entire church and pastors of all the parts; wherever one bishop is, the whole of episcopacy is there in his or her person; general superintendency is a powerful symbol of the unity of the church; this symbol can become a reality as bishops travel throughout the connection. This may seem to be a bit neat and subtle, but it is a part of our heritage that needs to be grasped and maintained.

There have been, however, a number of contradictions which tend to work against this conception. They need now to be examined.

1. *Missionary Bishops*

Our earliest bishops were missionaries: John Wesley in Georgia and throughout the British Isles; Thomas Coke in the United States, Great Britain, Nova Scotia, the West Indies, and Africa, and as missionary-designate for India; Francis Asbury *to* America and *throughout* the United States of his day.* The other "Asburian bishops" were forever pushing toward the frontier and beyond.

With the sending of Melville Cox to Liberia in 1832 (encouraged by Bishop Hedding and all the other bishops; commissioned by Bishop Andrew) American Methodism extended itself into foreign missions. Cox was followed by other pioneer missionaries to other countries. The very success of these ventures soon raised questions of episcopal

---

*It will be recalled that in 1787 an effort to elect Freeborn Garrettson as a "missionary bishop" for Nova Scotia, as suggested by Wesley, failed.

supervision in these regions. Originally limits of the general superintendency were restricted to the United States.* How could the needs of newly emerging churches be met and at the same time the accepted understanding of general superintendency maintained? Several approaches to this issue emerged as time went on.

In The Methodist Episcopal Church at first one bishop was assigned to the supervision of all foreign missions by correspondence. Later the Board of Bishops divided this responsibility among several of its members.[24] Then in 1853 Bishop Levi Scott visited Liberia for nearly three months, the first Methodist Episcopal bishop to exercise his authority outside the United States since Asbury's brief visit to Canada in 1811. This was followed by other such visitations to Europe and then through successive decades to places all over the world.

Bishop Scott's Liberian tour still did not meet the continuing need in American Methodism's oldest foreign mission field. The possibility of a missionary bishop for that country was discussed indecisively at the General Conference of 1852 and then renewed again in 1856, stimulated by Bishop Scott's report. This time a two-thirds vote approved a constitutional change to enable the consecration of a bishop to be elected by the Liberian Annual Conference, an exceptional mode of election. This was actually done by adding to the Third Restrictive Rule the phrase "but may appoint a Missionary Bishop or superintendent for any part of our foreign missions, limiting his episcopal jurisdiction to the same respectively."[25] The Liberian Conference did elect a black missionary, the Reverend Francis Burns. After the Annual

---

*In 1828 Canada's ties with American Methodism were severed by mutual consent of both parties. That same year The Methodist Episcopal Church of Canada was organized.

Conferences had sanctioned the General Conference action by their concurrence, for this was a constitutional matter, Bishop Burns was consecrated at the Genesee Conference (October 14, 1858) by Bishops Osmon C. Baker and Edmund S. Janes. Burns was our first missionary bishop, but he was not a general superintendent.

The second such bishop, John W. Roberts, was elected in 1866. There were naturally advantages to electing missionary bishops: their knowledge of the country or region and languages and their full-time supervision added greatly to the effectiveness of the mission.

Nevertheless this approach to the problem did not commend itself generally to the church, and for some years reliance was placed upon the occasional visit of one of the general superintendents from the United States to a given field. Then in 1884 William Taylor was elected missionary bishop for Africa.* Four years later James M. Thoburn was chosen for India. Both gave outstanding service. Other missionary bishops were to follow, among them for India: Edwin W. Parker (1900–died 1901), Frank W. Warne (1900–1920), John E. Robinson (1904–1920), William F. Oldham (1904–1912), John W. Robinson (1912–1920); for Africa: Joseph C. Hartzell (1896–1916), Eben S. Johnson (1916–1920); for Japan and Korea: Merriman C. Harris (1904–1912). Some of these, such as William F. Oldham (1916) and John W. Robinson (1920), were later elected general superintendents.

The last two missionary bishops elected were Edwin F. Lee (1928) for Malaysia and the Philippines, and John M. Springer (1936) for Africa. Although appropriate legisla-

---

*The 1892 General Conference of The Methodist Episcopal Church refused to approve an "assistant missionary bishop" for Africa.

tion for missionary bishops remained in the *Discipline* after the 1939 reunion of Methodism, because there were still continuing missionary bishops, the Judicial Council declared further election of missionary bishops by the General Conference to be unconstitutional.

As early as 1884 the General Conference affirmed its authority to fix the residences of any of its bishops in any part of the territory occupied by The Methodist Episcopal Church. It did not exercise this power until 1900 when it began sending general superintendents for residence in mission fields to China, Japan, Korea, Europe, South America, and India. This practice continued for some years. Thus missionary bishops and general superintendents sometimes served simultaneously in the same part of the world. Some observers felt strongly that it was not fair to have what were sometimes termed "second-class" bishops. Missionary bishops were, in fact, first-class persons. The legislation creating this office held that missionary bishops were not subordinate to but rather coordinate with general superintendents in their special fields.

In The Methodist Episcopal Church, South, a visitation program of mission lands began with Bishop Enoch M. Marvin's tour to China in 1876. Then years later, general superintendents were directed by the General Conference regularly to include foreign fields in their visitation. Just as the Northern branch of the church had done, so Southern Methodism also assigned general superintendents to residential work overseas. Bishop Walter R. Lambuth was a notable example, assigned first to residence in Brazil in 1910.

2. *Central Conference Bishops**

Another approach to episcopal supervision of work outside the United States was the Central Conference

---

*General Conference *Journal,* 1928, 716.

structure. Though initiated fifty years before Jurisdictional Conferences in the United States, the Central Conferences resembled them and may have been the model for the jurisdictional structure.

In 1884 the Methodist Episcopal General Conference constituted a Central Conference for India and Malaysia and authorized one for Japan. They were semiautonomous with power to supervise a number of activities prescribed by the General Conference. Other Central Conferences developed later in China, Africa, Europe, Latin America, and the Philippines, and of course, several of these continue to the present. Beginning in 1928 they were authorized to elect their own bishops who were not general superintendents.* The Methodist Episcopal Church, South, provided also for Central Conferences, but this legislation was not implemented.

Meanwhile in 1907 an independent Japan Methodist Church was established with Yoitsu Honda as its first bishop. Other affiliated autonomous Methodist churches, all with the office of bishop, were organized in Korea, Brazil, and Mexico (all in 1930).

After 1939 various Jursidictional Conferences were granted authority by the General Conference to elect general superintendents to serve in areas outside the United States.** For example, the Southeastern Jurisdictional Conference elected a bishop for the Geneva Area; the Central Jurisdictional Conference for Liberia; the Northeastern Jurisdiction for Central and Southern Africa. In these cases *Provisional* Central Conferences

---

*On this subject and especially on the international and ecumenical aspects of Methodist episcopacy, see Gerald F. Moede's fine study, *The Office of Bishop in Methodism* (Nashville: Abingdon Press, 1964).

**See *Discipline,* 1944, par. 439. See also Judicial Council Decisions 84, 182, and 210.

were provided with episcopal leadership, for they were not authorized themselves to elect bishops.

Furthermore, "The Council of Bishops may assign one of their number to visit each Central Conference."[26] This bishop may, if requested, exercise therein episcopal functions. In an emergency the Council of Bishops may assign a general superintendent or a bishop from another Central Conference to serve with a Central Conference, subject to the consent of a majority of the bishops therein.[27]

There have been instances of an anomalous nature in which a general superintendent and a missionary bishop and/or a Central Conference bishop have served simultaneously in the same Central Conference. This has usually worked all right insofar as personal relationships have been concerned. However, it has also revealed the discrepancy between bishops as to certain prerogatives. Considerable progress has been made in this matter largely because of careful monitoring of Central Conferences by a General Conference commission which has been in existence since 1940. There is no current instance of the mingling of general superintendents and Central Conference bishops in the same region. Moreover, all Central Conference bishops have membership in the Council of Bishops; all may attend all the Council's meetings; all may preside at General Conference; all participate in the international episcopal visit programs. The proper view is that Central Conference bishops and general superintendents are coordinate officers.

Enough has been said to indicate that episcopal Methodism has been quite flexible in adjusting to global realities. For what really needs to be done, a creative way can usually be found to do it.

3. *The Area Plan*

Any trend toward settling or localizing general superintendents has always been viewed with alarm.* This did, of course, raise constitutional issues, but the jeopardizing of long tradition and custom was also a potent factor in resistance. Therefore, the development of the area system needs to be examined briefly.

John Wesley was not enamored with the notion of diocesan episcopacy:

> Concerning diocesan episcopacy, there are questions I should be glad to have answered. First, Where is it prescribed in Scripture? Second, How does it appear that the apostles settled it in all the churches they planted? Third, How does it appear that they so settled it in a way so as to make it of perpetual obligation?[28]

We have observed that Thomas Coke's idea of dividing the episcopal work into two geographical areas to be served alternately by the two bishops did not find favor. Likewise, the 1807 New York Conference proposals, of which Ezekiel Cooper was probably the author, for what amounted to diocesan bishops, one for each conference, failed to secure the necessary support of all the Annual Conferences.[29] Whenever and in whatever form this proposal to localize episcopacy appeared it was beaten down.

Localization was by its very nature especially repugnant to Bishops McKendree and Soule and to the Southern and Western parts of the church generally. The Northern view expressed in 1844 and afterward tended to place this or any other matter related to the episcopacy in the hands of the General Conference, but even there that body was reluctant to move toward localizing the bishops.

---

*See *History of American Methodism*, 3:34. Also Thomas B. Neely, *The Bishops and The Supervisional System of The Methodist Episcopal Church* (Cincinnati: Jennings & Graham, 1912), passim.

In 1864 the General Conference of The Methodist Episcopal Church declared: "The bishops ought, and therefore are hereby *respectfully requested* to so distribute their residences as to be most accessible to and in the intervals of the conference, to be able to oversee every part of our extended work so far as possible"[30] (italics mine). The same session refused actually to assign bishops to districts. In 1872, however, when eight new bishops were elected, the General Conference expressed its judgment that "one of the newly-elected bishops should reside at or near each of the following places: San Francisco, Saint Louis, Boston, Atlanta, Chicago, Cincinnati, Council Bluffs or Omaha, St. Paul."[31] This did not involve the older bishops and was not mandatory. The new bishops themselves were to choose the residences according to seniority or order of election. Traditionally bishops, both North and South, had chosen their own residences and, as they gained in seniority, tended to move to what were regarded as the more attractive areas.

Further, in 1884 and upon recommendation of the Judiciary Committee,* the General Conference approved the General Conference's (constitutional) power of fixing "the residence of its Bishops in any part of the territory occupied by the Methodist Episcopal Church."[32] The General Conference refused in 1892 to "district the bishops." But in 1900 the action of 1884 was confirmed and extended in the following way: "the General Conference shall (through the Committee on Episcopacy) assign each Bishop to his residence for the ensuing four years"[33] (parenthesis mine). It was under this provision that *general*

---

*This powerful committee did for The Methodist Episcopal Church essentially what the bishops did in The Methodist Episcopal Church, South, until 1938 and the Judicial Council after 1939 for The Methodist Church regarding constitutionality of legislation.

superintendents were first assigned for residence in China and Europe. Strangely enough the Judiciary Committee in 1904 found that the actions taken in 1900 and 1892 were unconstitutional.[34] Even stranger was the fact that Thomas B. Neely proposed a motion that bishops be assigned to particular areas.[35] In contradiction of its own finding the 1904 General Conference elected Neely a general superintendent and assigned him to South America.

Thus every General Conference of The Methodist Episcopal Church in this century took action leading progressively toward the episcopal area system we are familiar with today. In 1908 the General Conference "suggested" to the bishops that they group Annual Conferences around the assigned residences for their special attention, even though they alternated in presiding at them.[36] The Episcopal Address of 1912 voiced strong opposition to *diocesan* episcopacy but quietly encouraged the practice of the bishops' presiding at the same conference for three out of four years. Bishop Francis J. McConnell was elected in 1912 and at the time was serving on the Episcopacy Committee of the General Conference considering the area system. He observed in his autobiography that the nationwide viewpoint which the general superintendency affords "was being paid for by too heavy a cost in lack of close supervision."[37] In other words, he favored an area system. The 1912 step was decisive in what came to be called "the episcopal area plan." It was further refined thereafter up till 1939.

In the Southern church a similar development took place but at a slower pace. By 1918 the bishops in that church also were essentially resident in episcopal areas. They were never called "areas" but for presiding the same conferences were assigned to one bishop for a whole quadrennium. Bishops were not required to *reside* within the bounds of their assignments.

All of this would have seemed very strange indeed in the eyes of Asbury who in 1798 wrote,

> It would be a disgrace to our episcopacy, to have bishops settled on their plantations here and there, evidencing to all the world, that instead of breathing the spirit of their office, they could, without remorse, *lay down their crown,* and bury the most important talents God has given to men! We would rather choose that our episcopacy should be blotted out from the face of the earth, than be spotted with such disgraceful conduct![38]

Bishops McKendree, Soule, Quayle,* and many others would have joined him in his lamentations. Thomas Coke might not have minded much, nor would Bishops George, Thoburn,[39] McConnell, and Blake. It is hard now to see how some of our brethren of blessed memory became so agitated about this. Episcopacy has survived the area plan and yet found ways to exercise general superintendency! They became not merely area bishops, for it was found that they need not be provincial.

4. *The Jurisdictional System*

When reunion of Methodism took place in 1939 it incorporated a new organizational feature, namely, the Jurisdictional Conference. There were six of them in the United States; five of them were geographical and one—the Central Jurisdiction—was racial.

There was something to be said for the sectional or regional unit. The whole denomination was large and in some respects unwieldy. There are, after all, sectional viewpoints and interests that are not all-important but they are important.

---

*Bishop Nolan B. Harmon cites an interesting letter in which Bishop William Quayle states his distaste for the area system. See *History of American Methodism* 3:33-34.

Along the road that led to reunion attention had to be given to such realities. Attitudes toward the jurisdiction have varied widely and have reflected regional attitudes. Some feared it would become a church within a church. Others were convinced that it offered opportunities to develop church programs more immediately responsive to local needs. The structure has worked to the degree a given jurisdiction has determined to work it.

So much for the factors of size and the reality of regional concerns. The creation of a racially segregated jurisdiction was sheer compromise. The nineteen black Annual Conferences and most black individuals voted overwhelmingly against it, as did a number of white leaders. Nevertheless they accepted it in as good grace as could be mustered, and they agreed to work for the fulfillment of an ideal of church unity. At the same time they began to work for its elimination. The most that could be said for it was that it gave opportunity to build up black interests, institutions, and awareness for developing black leadership. In this way a strong base could be laid for making and attaining larger demands for justice that were rightfully laid upon the church as a whole.

Until 1939 in episcopal Methodism bishops were elected by the General Conference. Since that time they have been elected by the six—later by the five—Jurisdictional Conferences. Although they were elected in this way, they were bishops of the whole church. Nevertheless it has often been insisted that this system has been detrimental to the concept of general superintendency.

In only three instances has a Jurisdictional Conference elected a bishop resident from a conference outside its borders. It is possible, though cumbersome, for a bishop to be transferred from one jurisdiction to another, but in practice this has never been done, except when the Central Jurisdiction was dissolved and its bishops assigned to the geographical jurisdictions. In this respect walls stand high around the jurisdictions. Possibly transfer should be tried deliberately in the event of a vacancy occasioned by death or other emergency, for fewer difficulties would arise in such an instance.

More than once it has been proposed that the Jurisdictional Conferences should meet prior to (or immediately before) the General Conference and even at the same location. Then *all* the bishops could be consecrated in one service by the General Conference. This proposal would have symbolic meaning but is attended also by practical difficulties and has never been accepted. Since 1968 *all* jurisdictions have met at the same time two months after the General Conference so possible transfers of bishops can take place. Also a bishop (usually retired) from another jurisdiction visits each Jurisdictional Conference, thus symbolizing unity and general superintendency.

As regards the Central Jurisdiction, after prolonged wrestling of conscience, vigorous debate, and meticulous planning the jurisdiction was dissolved. A crucial development was Amendment IX to the Constitution, passed by a two-thirds vote at the 1956 General Conference and, after approval by the Annual Conferences, included in the 1960 *Discipline*.[40]*

Racial segregation of this structural type came to an end by 1972. A church that segregated its members, ministers, and leaders racially was less than an ideal church. It could have no real *general* superintendency as long as bishops could serve only one or another race, for both races were segregated from each other. A more inclusive church is a more united one. All parties have gained in the process.

---

*A similar proposal was approved by the 1948 General Conference but failed to be ratified at the Annual Conference level.

The final reports on the jurisdictional system are not yet in. It is noteworthy that counterpart structures in other traditions—synods, provinces, and archdioceses—often do not perform up to expectations. However, the jurisdictional system has managed to mingle a degree of local and regional autonomy with a General Conference government. Writing from the perspective of nearly a half-century one can be grateful for the Herculean accomplishments of the architects of reunion. Some have surmised that more able bishops were elected by the old General Conference method. This would be hard actually to prove. In any event, general superintendency was not lost, and the body of bishops is more representative of the whole constituency today than it might otherwise have been.

5. *Terms and Tenure*

A term episcopacy would clearly limit the general superintendency with respect to time, just as diocesan episcopacy would limit with respect to space. We have seen how such a proposal has surfaced from time to time in episcopal Methodism and has always been defeated.[41] The Evangelical United Brethren at the time of the 1968 union with The Methodist Church had term episcopacy, but this had been the invariable practice of all its predecessor bodies. The rule for episcopal term was such that it allowed for reelection which was usually done until retirement.

While it is true that The Methodist Episcopal Church did grant authority for the Central Conferences to elect bishops for a term if they chose to do so, this was based on the fact of two types of bishops: (1) general superintendents elected by the General Conference; and (2) limited superintendents (i.e., limited as to territorial authority), bishops elected by Central Conferences.* This also

---

*See Judicial Council Decision 4, April 30, 1940.

allowed freedom for the Central Conference to adapt to local conditions and attitudes.[42] Not all of them have chosen term episcopacy.

In the United States, however, the consistent practice has been life tenure. Life tenure is provided for constitutionally in The United Methodist Church (1980 *Discipline,* par. 55). It would appear therefore to be doubly protected: by this provision and also by the Third Restrictive Rule itself, for the plan of general superintendency before 1808 was life tenure for bishops.

Life episcopacy at times has been defended rather crudely or arrogantly by such statements as, "Once a Bishop, always a Bishop."[43] There were, nevertheless, sound reasons for life episcopacy in addition to those already suggested:

—It does not differ in principle from academic freedom.

—It lends continuity and stability not only to episcopacy but to the denomination as a whole.

—It tends to depoliticize the office; that is, an *incumbent* does not have to concern himself or herself periodically about reelection.

—It offers the *possibility* that a bishop may act and speak boldly in fulfillment of the duties of office.

—It offers over the years the possibility that bishops may grow with the years in stature. Where are the giants of yesteryear? It takes time to grow them!

—It places our church in a strong posture vis-à-vis other episcopal churches in an ecumenical era.*

The limit of service for a bishop to reside in any one area

---

*See Report of the Co-ordinating Council to the 1964 General Conference, *The Study of the General Superintendency of The Methodist Church,* 71–73, and relevant portions of the 1972–76 *Report of the Quadrennial Commission for the Study of the Offices of Bishop and District Superintendent.*

was set at twelve years in 1956 and at eight years (with possible extension to twelve years) in 1976. This step has by its nature enabled itineration within a jurisdiction. We have seen that so far bishops are rather "locked in" to jurisdictions.

In the early days no age for retirement was set by the General Conference. Then a terminology of "effective" and "noneffective" bishops was instituted; later "effective" and "superannuated"; then the use of "retired."[44] A peculiarly Methodist way of stating this is, "Bishop . . . is released from the obligation to travel," this by the action of the General Conference. The retirement date has been lowered several times in recent years. He or she can be reactivated in cases of necessity. Bishops may resign for health or other reasons; early retirement may take place either voluntarily or involuntarily (1980 *Discipline,* pars. 508; 509).

Summary

We have examined a number of factors that have limited or are supposed to have limited the exercise of general superintendency in the Wesleyan tradition. Although, according to the Third Restrictive Rule the General Conference may not act constitutionally so as to "destroy the plan of our itinerant general superintendency," it may be that unintentionally or circumstantially this will be done. Although certain developments have undoubtedly changed the office in ways that are inevitable and even desirable, it has not been destroyed. Its flexibility and adaptability have been remarkable.

There are a multitude of ways open to the episcopacy to exercise general oversight and to supervise the temporal and spiritual welfare of the entire church. Therefore, a number of avenues for general superintendency are mentioned as examples without any elaboration:

—Presenting the Episcopal Address and presiding at General Conferences (1980 *Discipline,* pars. 15.11; 57).

—Active membership of bishops on the general boards and agencies. Nominations of others to the same. A bishop may also name a substitute bishop in the event of enforced absence from a session (par. 810.10).

—Involvement in ecumenical organizations at many levels (par. 512.3).

—In arranging the plan of visitation or episcopal supervision it would be possible at least once in a quadrennium to assign a bishop from another jurisdiction to preside at an Annual Conference in each area. This is urgent (par. 53)! Throughout our history such interchange has been the rule until recently.

—Possibility of a bishop's being reassigned (translated) for service from one jurisdiction to another (par. 54).

—Possibility of a bishop's being assigned for one year "to some specific churchwide responsibility deemed of sufficient importance to the welfare of the total Church" (par. 507.3).

—The transfer of ministers from one Annual Conference to another upon the request of the receiving bishop (pars. 59; 514.5). This practice has decreased of late.

—Involvement in initiating and promoting churchwide programs on emphases, including evangelism (par. 512.5). Not all promotion is demeaning or inimical to the episcopal office as some would insist.

—Speaking on current social and political issues in pastoral letters or otherwise. "The Church expects the Council of Bishops to speak to the Church and from the Church to the world" (pars. 524.2; 502).

—Working for a racially inclusive church in every possible way (par. 725.3 et al.).

These are only a few of the ways in which bishops today can and, for the most part, do exercise authentic general superintendency. For the bishops individually and corporately to fail to do such things would be for *them* to conspire in doing away with the office of general superintendent. I do not believe this is happening.

But particularly the bishops at the present time must effectively fulfill the general superintendency which collectively they *are* in and through the Council of Bishops.

The Council of Bishops

Important segments of the responsibilities of bishops can be fulfilled only in and as a *Council* of Bishops. This is not immediately obvious. It may even be taken for granted and therefore lost sight of or neglected in positive ways. That they are a *body* is seen in the way they are commonly referred to in a collective sense: "The Council of Bishops." Its mandate is broad, and bishops acting in concert antedates all other agencies of the church. It is the chief executive arm to carry out the mandates of the General Conference.

All United Methodist bishops are automatically members of the Council of Bishops. They are not elected *by* that body, but *to* and *for* membership in it.* The vows made by bishops at their consecration are not kept solely by their exemplary conduct as individuals nor by their outstanding performance in their assigned areas of residential and presidential responsibility. They must also participate wholeheartedly in the work of the Council of Bishops. This is not optional but obligatory (see Appendix A).

---

*An interesting sidelight on this is given by the late Roman Catholic theologian, Karl Rahner, who refers to the historical fact of the conciliar nature of episcopacy in the Church Universal (whether dispersed or in session at synods or councils): "Because someone is accepted into the episcopal college, he is a bishop." Cf. *Bishops: Their Status and Function* (London: Burns and Oates, 1964), 19.

The collegial nature of episcopacy was seen very early; in fact, it was designed in this way. As soon as there was more than one bishop it was expected that they would perform as a unit—no easy matter, as we have observed.

The 1824 General Conference adopted the following resolution:

> Resolved . . . 4. That it is highly expedient for the general superintendents, at every session of the General Conference, and as far as to them may appear practicable, in the intervals of the sessions, annually, to meet in council to form their plan of traveling through their charge, whether in a circuit after each other or by dividing the connection into several episcopal departments, with one bishop or more in each department, as to them may appear proper and most conducive to the general good, and the better to enable them fully to perform the great work and to exchange and unite their views upon all affairs connected with the general interests of the Church.[45]

This is the genesis of a "council of bishops." Note that it was regarded as "highly expedient"; it was voluntary, not mandatory.

In response to this resolution four of the five bishops did meet in Philadelphia on April 13 and April 18, 1826. Bishop Roberts was absent. The meeting was indecisive and even became deadlocked over the appointment of a fraternal delegate to the British Conference. From the very beginning, then, bishops in council were prepared to express their candid judgments.[46] At the 1832 session General Conference clarified the fact that the above resolution was not mandatory but advisory.[47] Nevertheless, the advice was accepted, and there were meetings together of the bishops till 1844 and beyond.

The Methodist Episcopal Church had a Board of Bishops and The Methodist Episcopal Church, South had a

College of Bishops. Neither of these was at that time mandated in any constitutional way, but they were official, for they are repeatedly mentioned in the *Discipline*. Unfortunately there were no repositories designated for the Minutes of these bodies, but reference is made to the meetings throughout relevant literature of the period (1824 to 1939). A diligent search finally uncovered Minutes of the Methodist Episcopal Board of Bishops for the years 1936–1940,[48] but not the earlier ones from either branch of Methodism.

Since 1939 both the Council of Bishops and the Colleges of Bishops of the jurisdictions and Central Conferences have had constitutional sanction. An even wider scope is provided by a quadrennial Conference of Bishops of the whole Methodist family, including those of autonomous Methodist churches.[49]

In addition, the General Conference has since 1939 provided increasingly extensive legislative guidance for the episcopacy.[50] This is in contrast to earlier practice which allowed large discretion to the bishops themselves as they pursued their broadly defined duties. For example, in the 1968 *Discipline* just over three hundred paragraphs—including ten in the Constitution—refer to bishops. In almost exactly one-third of these instances the reference is to the *Council of Bishops*.[51]

Great emphasis has been made in ecclesiastical history of the term *collegiality*. This has been especially reemphasized in the Roman Catholic church since Vatican II. Since the time of the apostles the corporate nature of the church has been a central emphasis.[52] Collegiality relates in a broad sense to the whole people of God; in a narrower sense it applies to the leadership body of the church acting in concert and as coequals. As we have noted, both Ignatius and Cyprian strongly emphasized this reality. So did Augustine, as in his famous maxim that he was "a bishop *for* you and a Christian *with* you."

The Council of Bishops, the Colleges of Bishops, and to a lesser degree the Conference of Bishops, are legitimate expressions of collegiality. We simply *are* collegial. Talents, interests, and concerns vary; wholehearted commitment to Christ and to one another is invariable. The Council's members do not all think alike nor act alike, but these bodies afford arenas for the debating and planning of modes for fulfilling the common tasks assigned to them as together they witness to the common faith they are also charged to defend.

But more than that, the Council of Bishops is a fellowship and a family. It is a circle of leadership that manages to be combined with friendship. This is not too far from the ideal exemplified by the primitive church. The practical and spiritual value of this cannot be overstated. It is the only body in United Methodism where the bishops can be said to have *membership*. This is true of retired bishops also, a forum where they have voice but not vote.* The Council is a principal support group for its members, and this includes on occasion the spouses of the bishops.**

It would be easy to be sentimental about this, but one colleague, Bishop William C. Martin, has said:

> I can only say that there is no human bond, beyond the range of one's family, that brings men (or women) into quite so close a communion of mind and heart as this. There are really no words known to me that are spacious enough fully to disclose the depth of this experience. . . . If some of us

---

*It is not infrequently said in jest that this should be reversed: they should have vote without voice!

**At present all spouses are wives. They are charged with no official duties but necessarily assume many adjunct ones. Eunice Mathews has made two studies of their roles (1972, 1976).

who sit in the Council meetings should appear, at times, to be a bit distracted, it may be that we see faces and forms and hear voices that the younger members do not see and hear.

The late Bishop Gerald Kennedy expressed the following thoughts:

As I think about it, the wonderful truth is that we all love one another. I do not want to put this on any sentimental basis, for it is something very deep. I know there are conflicting temperaments; and now and then two of the brethren may aspire for the same goal and only one of them attains it. We differ, but it came to me not long ago that there is not a single member of the Council I dislike. It would be my honest opinion that this testimony would be unanimous and that not a single bishop would ask for help from any other bishop without receiving it in full measure.

This is quite true, as any bishop can testify. Practical and pastoral help from a colleague is as close and readily available as the nearest telephone.

This may be the place to sound another note. Not all bishops have administrative assistants, but those who do have them are indebted to them for all they do. Every bishop is exceedingly grateful for office secretaries who greatly extend episcopal effectiveness. There is the support of families, too, for most bishops. To this must be added the close bonds of the cabinets—men and women chosen district superintendents by the bishop as extensions of the episcopacy. Beyond all this are the general affection and support offered by the great host of members and ministers they endeavor to serve. Among these must surely be counted those who serve in Annual Conference and Jurisdictional Committees on Episcopacy, not forgetting also the wider company of faithful laity.

We turn to the manner in which business is done by the

Council of Bishops. A wise voice from the not too distant past may well be heard from Bishop McConnell in his autobiography:

> It may be that here is as good as any to put down some of my impressions of the episcopacy as a working organization. To begin with, it does work. When I first came into it, there were hardly any rules at all as to the length of the sessions of bishops' meetings. We worked till we got through. Later on that was changed, so that the sessions accomplish more now than we did then. . . .
>
> An oft-repeated criticism of the present plan is that under it the bishop cannot know the needs of the whole church as his predecessors did. There is some truth here, but not much, for the bishops never did know the interests of the whole church as they know them today. The knowledge of the whole church, whose loss is allegedly important, is better met by sending men into areas other than their own at least once in four years, and seeing that at least once in about eight years each gets a glimpse of a foreign field.
>
> There are faults in the system, but it is better than it has ever been before. The difficulty in criticizing it is that if one does not know the system fairly well, one does not know how to criticize; and because of the ignorance of the criticism something that ought to be changed is ignored.[53]

As to internal organization and structure the details are left to the Council itself. A president serves for one year. A president-designate is chosen annually a year in advance by ballot without nomination. By custom and by rotation this officer is selected in turn from each of the jurisdictions in the United States. For a long time it seemed impossible or impractical—the distance from the most of the constituency—for the president to be one of the Central Conference bishops, but in 1984 for the first time one *was* elected. The president-elect serves as a member of the Executive

Committee from the time of his or her choice until he or she completes the year of active presidency. The secretary is elected quadrennially, also by ballot and without nomination.

The Council was reorganized extensively in 1971–72* and is constantly under greater or lesser refinement of organization and procedure. All of the bishops, active and retired, are members of one of four standing committees on Administrative Concerns, Pastoral Concerns, Relational Concerns, and Teaching Concerns. Each of these has a chairperson and a recorder elected by the standing committees for two years. These chairpersons also are members of an Executive Committee comprised of the officers and one representative from each jurisdiction and one from the Central Conferences. If racial balance is not achieved otherwise, an additional member is added to the Executive Committee to bring about a rightful ethnic representation.

The Executive Committee usually meets four times a year, once just before each spring and fall meeting of the Council and during both intervals. Its work is largely to prepare the agenda of the semiannual meetings of the Council as a whole. On very rare occasions the Executive Committee may act for the Council on some assigned matter or in the event of an interim emergency. Even less frequently the officers may speak, after consultation, in situations of extreme urgency that cannot await a regular meeting. The Council has approved carefully drawn bylaws to guide its deliberations.

An invariable part of every meeting is unhurried daily worship conducted by one or more of the bishops. This is planned in such a way that sooner or later every member

---

*See Appendix A.

has profited by being led in the life of the Spirit under the guidance of every other colleague.

Much of the Council's business is processed through the standing committees which have no final authority of their own. All recommendations they may propose must be considered by the Council as a whole before adoption. By custom there is no limit to the length of speeches nor the number of times a bishop may speak. Also by custom no proposal is ever "laid on the table." At one time it was the practice for bishops to speak in the order of their seniority in office, but that is no longer the case. It is now hardly known who is senior to whom!

The Colleges of Bishops also report on items that arise from their deliberations but affect the whole Council. During sessions all the Central Conference bishops form a "college" to consider their common concerns.

Episcopal members of general boards and agencies can bring to the Council matters that concern all bishops. On occasion special ad hoc committees are assigned particular responsibilities that do not readily fall into categories assigned to the standing committees. The Minutes are recorded and promptly shared with all bishops. Periodically the Minutes are bound and deposited in the church's archives.

Very frequently particular issues of vital concern to the entire church or society are presented to the plenary sessions either by bishops or by persons invited from outside the body. Not infrequently general secretaries of boards and agencies have met with the bishops. Periodically a message, pastoral letter, or resolution is issued by the Council. Specialists are sometimes involved in their preparation.

Although traditionally the bishops met in closed session, beginning in the early 1970s all the meetings have been open unless, for specific items, it becomes necessary to meet in executive sessions. On the whole the business is done with deliberation yet dispatch. On some matters there is lively debate; on others consensus is achieved readily. It is pleasant to think that, on occasion, agreement is reached according to the apostolic pattern: "It has seemed good to the Holy Spirit and to us" (Acts 15:28).

As to what the Council of Bishops does, it may be said that it has responsibility to be both reactive and innovative. It is the only body of the church charged with oversight of the complete range of denominational concerns and interests. As such it relates to the other councils and general agencies of the church. The Council's officers twice a year invite their counterparts from the General Conference on Ministries and General Council on Finance and Administration to unhurried meetings involving frank and fruitful interchange. Likewise, periodically there has been consultation with Judicial Council officers. The Council of Bishops is mindful of the importance of cultivating mutual and reciprocal trust and respect in the manifold and sometimes delicate relations with other councils and agencies of the connection.

Specifically since 1939, the Council of Bishops has had a part in the following endeavors:

—The Council has initiated or has been deeply involved in the great quadrennial programs and emphases such as the genesis of what has become UMCOR (United Methodist Committee on Overseas Relief); the Crusade for a New World Order (1939–44); promotion of the Crusade for Christ (1944–48); the Advance for Christ and His Church (1948–52); the Fund for Reconciliation (1968–72); the Bishops' Call for Peace and Self-Development of Peoples (1972–76); Ethnic Minority, Local Church Development (1976–84); to mention only a few.[54]

—The Council has emphasized evangelism and recruitment for ministry in churchwide programs.

—The Council has specific responsibility in the field of ecumenical relations, for instance, with the World Council of Churches, the National Council of Churches, the World Methodist Council, dialogue with the Roman Catholic church, and, not least, with the bishops of the black denominations of the Methodist family.

—The Council has far less nominating authority than once it had, but it fulfills this duty with the most detailed and meticulous care as its carefully prepared workbooks and procedures clearly show.

—The Council plans and carries out the bishops' program of international visitation, renewal leave, orientation of new bishops and spouses, and it participates in the training of new district superintendents and program council directors.

—The Council has prepared careful guidelines for the transfer of episcopal area leadership.[55]

—The Council has prepared and periodically brings up to date a "Manual for Bishops." It also prepares from time to time a compilation of the "digests" of the decisions of the Judicial Council, an invaluable tool for those who must rule in the Annual Conferences on questions of law.

—The Council very frequently affords a forum for interchange of information among the bishops for practical ways of performing the episcopal tasks in the areas and Annual Conferences, or upon parliamentary procedures and presiding.

—The Council has frequently worked on agreed-upon procedures for consultation in the appointment process— this before and since the extensive legislation passed on this subject by the 1976 General Conference.

—The Council has been a forum for discussions of and devising of programs for a more inclusive church.

—The Council has systematically considered concrete suggestions made to it from many quarters, most especially by the general commissions to study episcopacy and superintendency of 1960–64 and 1972–76, and before that the Survey Committee of 1952.

—The Council (or its representatives) has frequently spoken for the church in the halls of government.

—The Council has tried "to maintain the spiritual glow" and extend all that this means throughout the life of the church.

After itemizing such a catalogue there comes to mind the words of our Lord about after having done all, "We are unworthy servants; we have only done what was our duty." Bishops are thoroughly accountable in more ways than simply to the Jurisdictional and General Conferences, mostly to the One who is the "great shepherd of the sheep" and the "Bishop and Guardian of your souls."

Notes

1. *The Book of Discipline* of The United Methodist Church, 1980, par. 17.

2. Annotated *Discipline,* 1798, 39.

3. Cf. Asbury, *Journal* 2:470.

4. Horace M. Du Bose, *Life of Joshua Soule* (Nashville: Publishing House of The Methodist Episcopal Church, South, 1916), 60n; Richard Watson in *The Life of the Rev. John Wesley, A. M.* (1839 edition) supported this sort of episcopacy for America, 339ff.

5. *Discipline,* 1980, par. 42.

6. Thomas B. Neely, *The Bishops and the Supervisional System of The Methodist Episcopal Church* (New York: Eaton and Mains, 1912), 152. (I don't like his split infinitives!)

7. *Discipline,* 1798, par. 42.

8. Ibid.

9. Thomas Ware, *Sketches of the Life and Travels of Rev. Thomas Ware* (New York: Mason and Lane, 1839), 189.

10. Cf. Nicholas Snethen in *The Wesleyan Repository and Religious Intelligencer,* 1, no. 10 edition of October 16, 1821, 153, and signed by his frequent pseudonym "A Methodist."

11. Daniel Berger, *History of the Church of the United Brethren in Christ* (Dayton: United Brethren Publishing House, 1897), 214.

12. Cf. Asbury, *Journal* 2:59. See also Ware, *Sketches of Life,* 214.

13. Asbury, August 5, 1813, *Letters,* 477.

14. Ibid., 487; 491-92; 475.

15. Paine, *William M'Kendree* 1:349.

16. *Discipline,* 1785, answer to Question 26.

17. Annotated *Discipline,* 1798, p. 41.

18. Cf. Paine, *William M'Kendree,* 356ff.; Bishop Soule in Episcopal Address, General Conference *Journal,* 1840, 139. In 1807 Asbury wrote to Daniel Hitt: "In my opinion nothing can keep the body united; but a well regulated, and energetic general superintendency." *Letters,* 379. Bishop Soule made a similar point in the 1840 Episcopal Address.

19. Nolan B. Harmon, *Understanding The United Methodist Church,* rev. ed. (Nashville: Abingdon Press, 1977), 120.

20. *Discipline,* 1980, par. 59.

21. In 1976 Arthur G. Riewald, Ph.D., read a paper to the Council of Bishops stating: "As a consultant for the past twelve years I have worked closely with the leadership and the professional ministry of nine denominations. I have been a counsellor and therapist for several hundred ministers and ministers' (families). . . .

I can say as an outsider that from my perspective the appointive system has distinct advantages over any other system of deployment that I know of."

Later in the paper he says that our appointment process "leads to a much greater loyalty among your clergy than I find in any other denomination."

22. Asbury, *Letters,* 318-20; 334ff.

23. Paine, *William M'Kendree* 1:361ff.

24. Barclay, *History of Methodist Missions* 3:171.

25. General Conference *Journal,* (Methodist Episcopal Church), 1856, 146.

26. *Discipline,* 1980, par. 35.

27. Ibid., par. 54.

28. Wesley, *Works,* 16:35.

29. See Lee, *Short History,* 344ff. See also Buckley, *Constitutional and Parliamentary History,* 218. Buckley states clearly that a diocesan episcopacy would defeat itinerant general superintendency.

30. General Conference *Journal,* 1864, 359-60.

31. Ibid., 1872, 321.

32. Ibid., 1884, 160, 369.

33. Ibid., 1900, 424-25.

34. Ibid., 1904, 514.

35. Thomas B. Neely was a great constitutionalist and a staunch defender of the general superintendency. Later on in the 1904 General Conference he was himself elected a general superintendent and assigned to Argentina. Though he knew a great deal about episcopacy,

he did not prove very effective in the office. He was retired involuntarily in 1912 by action of the General Conference.

36. General Conference *Journal,* 1908, 456.

37. Francis J. McConnell, *By the Way* (New York: Abingdon-Cokesbury Press, 1952), 116-17.

38. *Discipline,* 1798, p. 44.

39. Bishop James M. Thoburn said, "The attempt to maintain the present systemless and outgrown policy must be abandoned. . . . It seems ridiculous to require sixteen men here in the United States to interchange their fields of labor annually." (Though he himself did well in the supervision he undertook in India, Burma, Malaya, the Philippines.) Cited by Drinkhouse, *Methodist Reform* 2:701–702. Bishop Edgar Blake once also declared: "I do not believe we ought to bind a Church of tomorrow to a plan of superintendency that was in vogue more than a century ago." Cited by J. H. Barton in "The Definition of the Episcopal Office in American Methodism" (Ph.D. diss., Drew University, 1960), 162.

40. *Discipline,* 1960, pp. 26-27.

41. Cf. Asbury, *Letters,* 491-92n.

42. General Conference *Journal,* 1932, 632-33.

43. General Conference of The Methodist Episcopal Church, *Daily Christian Advocate,* May 16, 1884, 107.

44. Thomas B. Neely, *Vital Points in The Methodist Episcopal Church* (Philadelphia: Methodist Episcopal Book Store, 1924), 61ff.

45. General Conference *Journals* 1:301-2.

46. Cf. Roy H. Short, *Chosen to be Consecrated* (Lake Junaluska, N.C.: Commission on Archives and History, 1976), 23ff. Bishop McKendree's informal notes on the first meeting are in the library of Vanderbilt University.

47. General Conference *Journals* 1:419-20.

48. See Library of Wesley Theological Seminary, Washington, D.C.

49. *Discipline,* 1980, pars. 52; 53; 525.

50. This is especially evident in the *Disciplines* of 1964 and 1976, in each case following extensive study of episcopacy or superintendency by quadrennial general commissions.

51. See Appendix A where this writer has provided extensive analysis of constitutional and legislative rules relating to the office and duties of episcopacy from the 1968 *Discipline.* This was updated in reports to the Council of Bishops in 1976 and again in 1980.

52. Cf. Kenneth E. Kirk, ed., *The Apostolic Ministry* (London: Hodder and Stoughton, 1946), 529, and passim. See also Edward Schillebeeckx, ed., *The Unifying Role of the Bishop* (New York: Herder and Herder, 1972); and Schillebeeckx, *Ministry.*

53. McConnell, *By the Way,* 129-30.

54. Bishop G. Bromley Oxnam in an address delivered in 1956 said: "Great movements emerge from creative thinking, and much of that thinking is being done collectively in the Council of Bishops. It is one of the chief services of the episcopacy to the church."

55. Unpublished paper prepared by and for the Council of Bishops, 1975.

VI

WHAT DO BISHOPS DO?

Of one thing I am convinced: most United Methodists are bishop-watchers. It is not that they would readily admit this even to themselves much less want to be caught in the act of bishop-watching! But it is nevertheless true. Perhaps it is as well that bishops are kept under scrutiny. It does not hinder them, I feel sure; it helps them.

Some years ago an African was ushered in for an audience with the pope. With naive and dissarming candor he is reported to have said to the pontiff: "What is Your Holiness *for?*" When one gets over the shock of it, it must must be acknowledged that that is a good question. Without being presumptuous, one may frame another question: What is a bishop *for?* Indeed, one time in Maine that very inquiry was addressed to me: "What are we to expect of a bishop?"*

According to the New Testament the expectation is very great. Paul writes to Titus in this way:

For a bishop, as God's steward, must be blameless; he must not be arrogant or quick-tempered or a drunkard or

------

*Hugo in *Les Miserables* gave one answer, "a bishop is only to bless."

violent or greedy for gain, but hospitable, a lover of goodness, master of himself, upright, holy, and self-controlled; he must hold firm to the sure word as taught, so that he may be able to give instruction in sound doctrine and also to confute those who contradict it (Titus 1:7-9).

Paul himself reports about his own fulfillment of episcopal obligations:

You yourselves know how I have lived among you all the time from the first day that I set foot in Asia, serving the Lord with all humility and with tears and with trials which befell me . . . I did not shrink from declaring to you anything that was profitable, and teaching you in public and from house to house, testifying both to Jews and to Greeks of repentance to God and of faith in our Lord Jesus Christ. . . . But I do not account my life of any value nor as precious to myself, if only I may accomplish my course and the ministry which I received from the Lord Jesus, to testify to the gospel of the grace of God (Acts 20:18-21, 24).

Most bishops cannot claim to have attained such standards of excellence, but perhaps by the grace of God they may say, "I am what I am."

Likewise, the church today expects much of its bishops. Among the traditional vows required of bishops at the time of their consecration are these:

Will you then faithfully exercise yourself in the Holy Scriptures, and call upon God through study and prayer for the true understanding of the same?
I will so do, by the help of God.

Are you ready with all faithful diligence to seek and to promote the truth of Christ and to defend the Church against all doctrine contrary to God's Word?
I am ready, the Lord being my helper.

Will you maintain and set forward, as much as lieth in you, quietness, love, and peace among all men; and faithfully exercise such discipline in the Church as shall be committed unto you?

I will so do, by the help of God.

Will you be faithful in ordaining and appointing others; and will you ever seek to deal justly and kindly with your brethren of the ministry over whom you are placed as chief pastor?

I will so do, by the help of God.

More recently in the newly proposed ordinal (1980) other questions have been raised:

As chief pastor, will you, in cooperation with the elders and deacons, encourage and support all baptized people in their gifts and ministries, pray for them without ceasing, proclaim and interpret to them the Gospel of Christ, and celebrate with them the Sacraments of our redemption?

I will, in the name of Christ, the shepherd and bishop of our souls.

Will you share with other bishops in the oversight of the whole Church; will you support the elders and take counsel with them; will you guide and strengthen the deacons and all others who minister in the church; will you be faithful in seeking, ordaining, and sending others to minister in Christ's name?

All this I will do, by the grace given me.

Will you be a faithful witness to Christ to those among whom you live and lead the Church to obey the gospel command to make disciples of all nations?

I will, by the help of God.

Will you lead the Church in its mission of witness and service to the world and in its concern for peace, justice and freedom among all people?
I will, God being my helper.

Will you be merciful to all, show compassion to the poor and strangers, and defend those who have no helper?
I will, for the sake of Christ Jesus.

The rereading of these vows is a sobering experience, and it is assuredly by the help of God alone that bishops can even attempt to fulfill them.

But what do bishops do? Perhaps it would be as well to try to say what they do *not* do, at least in The United Methodist Church:

—They do not speak (unless specifically invited to do so) nor vote at General and Jurisdictional Conferences. They may speak at Annual Conferences but have no vote there even to break a tie.

—They do not choose other ministers for the episcopal office.

—They do not determine constitutional amendments nor do they legislate.

—They do not have veto power over legislation.

—They do not make any rules governing Annual Conferences.

—They do not determine who shall be ordained.

—They do not confer orders but rather *confirm* and convey orders authorized by the ministerial members of the Annual Conference.

—They do not exclude ministers or lay persons from membership.

—They do not give final determination on matters of church law, but their rulings are subject to review by the Judicial Council and are either sustained or reversed.

In fact, in the Wesleyan tradition bishops are not regarded as being in the "apostolic succession" nor do they possess authority by "divine right." They are not *ordained* bishops but set apart and consecrated to serve in that office. As we have seen they are members of neither local churches nor Annual Conferences, nor are they delegates to Jurisdictional and General Conferences. This is part of what is meant by the saying, Methodism is not governed *by* bishops but *with* bishops.[1]

No wonder Bishop Hoss of The Methodist Episcopal Church, South, once said, "I have many duties but no prerogatives."[2] In an address given before the Council of Bishops Roy H. Short said, "The only real power that any United Methodist bishop has is that which flows out of the example of his/her life and character as well as demonstrated qualities of church leadership." Though it is popularly supposed to be quite different from this, bishops are not as all-powerful as is usually assumed. As the years have passed there has been no real increase in the powers they have. Rather, exactly the opposite is true: their authority has diminished.

What often are regarded as the powers of bishops are, in fact, the duties and responsibilities assigned to them. It has been suggested that when we speak of the *role* of bishops we are referring to the basic and general character of the office; the functions of bishops are their specific obligations and responsibilities.

Once again, episcopacy with us is not an order, honor, or privilege but a responsibility. It has already been said that bishops are given authority sufficient for the fulfillment of their responsibilities. It is conceivable that that authority could be so undermined as to make impossible such fulfillment. No bishop does or can dominate other bishops. Officers in the Council of Bishops are temporary. No United Methodist bishop is denomination head, for our church has no single head (save the Lord of the Church Universal)—a constant source of astonishment to leaders of other denominations. We also sometimes say, The United Methodist Church has no headquarters unless it be the General Conference in quadrennial session. All general superintendents have the same authority, the same responsibility, the same ecclesiastical status, the same salary; in effect, they share one office. The whole episcopal body is accountable to appropriate bodies, and each member is accountable for his or her life and conduct of office.

United Methodist bishops do have the duty to fix appointment of the ministers. We have already observed that this is unique with us (shared, of course, with other episcopally governed Methodist denominations). This is the crux of the whole matter. This is a very great power indeed, an authority that is clearly established and well known in United Methodism; therefore, those who are entrusted with the exercise of such authority are carefully scrutinized and held strictly accountable. Nearly all the struggles concerning bishops that have been recounted revolve around this very fact. We shall return to this matter shortly.

What do bishops do? Some suggestion comes from the Scriptures, as we have seen. Bishops of the Wesleyan tradition are obliged to be "scriptural *episkopoi,*" insofar as we understand this aright. Their work is not by any means identical with what bishops have done historically, but elements of the office bear clear resemblance to what bishops have always done—animating the people of God and guarding the doctrine and unity of the church.

More particularly, bishops among us have their role set forth in part by our own tradition and custom regarding the office. In some sense they are bound to display some characteristics derived from the fact that both John Wesley and Francis Asbury are role models. But even more specifically what United Methodist bishops do is defined in the *Discipline* by both constitutional and legislative definition and requirement. The latter is under almost constant revision, and bishops are required "to discharge such other duties as the *Discipline* may direct" (1980, par. 512.6). These may change from quadrennium to quadrennium. Their role is implied also with considerable specificity in the vows they make during the service of consecration. It is defined also in a measure by what history and circumstance demand of the office. The episcopate must therefore be open and adaptable.

Because one is a United Methodist bishop with the authority to "fix appointment of preachers"; because he or she is a general superintendent; and because of the prestige attaching to the office, many other duties automatically rest upon the incumbent. This includes membership in episcopal conciliar bodies, general board membership, ecumenical relationships, public roles, liturgical roles, leadership in fund-raising campaigns, and all manner of churchwide activities. Closer home it involves being pastor to pastors and people, counseling, disciplining, preaching, teaching, corresponding, and carrying out detailed administration of an episcopal area. The bishop constantly moves back and forth between local and general responsibility. Both are requisites of the office. Then there must be time, never enough seemingly, for being a human being and a family member, a student, and a prayerful, active servant of Jesus Christ. Many bishops have complained that community service, family life, prayer and devotions, recreation and leisure, and study and writing are quite often neglected more than they would prefer.[3]

The astonishing variety of activity is reflected in reports bishops make periodically to their Annual Conference, area, or Jurisdictional committees on episcopacy. So it is that what bishops do is defined in large measure by what individual bishops actually do. Their own interests, concerns, attitudes, attributes, aptitudes, and past experience help to shape the office. They help also to determine the nature of episcopacy by their behavior, much as Francis Asbury drew the map of Methodism with his horses' hoofprints.

This writer feels that too much emphasis has been placed on the suggestion that United Methodist bishops are merely promoters. It may well be that if that is where a given bishop places the emphasis of ministry, he or she will be mainly a promoter or at least seen to be a promoter. Much, much more is involved. We will look at a few episcopal duties. General superintendency has been dealt with at length in the previous chapter. With regard to other episcopal roles it is important that it be understood that these are not isolated from one another in watertight compartments but are extensively intermingled.[4] (See also Appendix B in which the bishops speak of the office as they understand it.)

Presiding Officer

From the very beginning of American Methodism bishops have been presiding officers. In the annotated *Discipline* of 1798 the very first duty stated is: "To preside in our conferences." Bishops do this in Annual Conferences and in many subsidiary meetings. Active bishops also preside by rotation at Jurisdictional or Central Conferences, and some of their number are asked to preside at General Conference sessions, for a bishop must always preside at every official session.

This duty requires a mastery of parliamentary procedure. Though the responsibility can be irksome, the more familiar the presiding officer is with such procedures, as well as the specific rules of a given body, the greater liberty will be attained by both the assembly and the bishop.*

Chairing a General Conference can be a demanding role. One bishop likened it to mounting the saddle of a bucking bronco! Usually, however, the body is courteous, and with the backup of a colleague when assistance may be required, it can be a pleasant and invigorating experience. Relaxed freedom on the part of the one presiding can be communicated to the whole body and make for an orderly assembly which discharges its work promptly. The one chairing a meeting needs to be fair, to know at all times what precisely is before the house, to remind the assembly constantly of this, and to be completely detached and objective as to the outcome of the voting.[5] Many bishops of our tradition have through the years discharged this responsibility in a superb manner.

A presiding officer does not merely *preside* but has certain legal responsibilities that attach to this role. At the Annual Conference level the bishop as president also has executive and administrative responsibility.

Stationing the Preachers

In earlier discussion it has been argued that a connectional church with an itinerant ministry requires an appointive system, its bishops equipped with authority to make the system work. A movement must be capable of moving. With United Methodists the bishop fixes the appointments or stations the preachers. The system also

---

*No bishop has a right to declare a motion properly made in General or Jurisdictional or even in Annual Conference to be "unconstitutional" and refuse to entertain it. He or she knows that if it is unconstitutional the Judicial Council will strike it down; as in Congress, since the days of John Adams, no Speaker listens to the charge of unconstitutionality, knowing that the Supreme Court will strike it if illegal.

involves a guarantee of a church or charge to every pastor and of a pastor to every church. It is not surprising that sometimes neither is pleased, but on the whole it has worked well. Most bishops would report that very few times have they had to use their full authority to make an appointment against the will of either pastor or parish. This is a tribute to all parties who are committed to a plan and covenant which have in view the larger interest of the whole connection.

On the other hand, Bishop F. Gerald Ensley used to speak of the process in the following terms: "Every church needs a pastor who is a good preacher. Every church needs a pastor who is a good pastor. The same church also needs a pastor who is a good educator. Likewise it needs one who relates well to youth; who is a good administrator; who is able in finance; and so on." Then he concluded: "To my observation ours is the only denomination that provides each church with a pastor who has all these abilities. We send them in succession." So, too, bishops as they succeed one another in a given area over a period of time provide it with leadership with a great variety of skills.

In many ways the deployment of ministers is a bishop's first responsibility. Years ago in the popular film *Going My Way,* a bishop in another communion transferred a pastor. When this function was under discussion, the familiar question—more likely a statement—was phrased, "What are bishops for?"* In our denomination, as we have already observed several times, ministers are deployed in the context of a covenant.

The bishop does have appointive authority. It is seldom used to the full. It is exercised not by one of superior order

---

*The same film affords another insight into what bishops are *for:* "To call the close decisions."

but by a representative elder who is vested by election and consecration with authority for this purpose. Nor may it be used arbitrarily, though in the frontier days it is hard to see how a system such as ours could have worked without a firm appointing officer. Bishop McKendree used to insist that a preacher was appointed by a *brother,* though he might not always have been perceived as such.

Yet "fixing the appointments" is not done by the bishops alone; the cabinet is very much a part of the process, as are others—the preachers themselves and the parish representatives. There lies behind it a prolonged and careful process.

Usually appointments are announced at an Annual Conference session, but they may be made at any time. The calendar of appointment making extends through much of the year prior to the conference meetings. This involves annual consultation with pastors (and usually their spouses); consultation with Pastor-Parish Relations Committees; evaluation processes; the following of a detailed procedure set forth in the *Discipline* (pars. 514.1-5; 527-31). This was mandated by the 1972 General Conference but reflected procedures that were already in place in some episcopal areas. The methods for doing all this have since been worked out in great detail in most areas, so that it is well understood and highly visible. A change of appointment presupposes an opening that is available. It also requires that an announcement of decision be made to the parties concerned before public announcement. The plan of itinerant ministry involves an annual review of all appointments; that is part of what *connection* means.

All this, in turn, is dependent on a broad first-hand knowledge of the pastors and the churches by bishops and, in greater depth because they work at closer range with the local church, by district superintendents. Most bishops work very hard at this, and many have systematically visited all the churches and parsonages in their areas to help equip them for this task.

The Council of Bishops is on record with the following statement:

> We strongly and unanimously affirm the consultative process in appointment making. This is a collective undertaking involving the local church through its Pastor-Parish Relations Committee; the pastor (and the pastoral family); the district superintendent(s); and the bishop. Each party may take appropriate initiative in the process.[6]

Though seemingly complicated these methods usually work smoothly and let it be repeated, with an amazing degree of compassion and understanding as anyone who has ever sat in a cabinet meeting can testify.*

Pastor of Pastors

A bishop is called "chief pastor" and also pastor of pastors as the ordinal makes clear. Many, perhaps most, bishops feel that they are not able to fulfill this role as adequately as they would like. Yet after years as pastors themselves in local churches it is almost instinctive with them to respond to their work in a pastoral fashion. Moreover, this is a biblical mandate. The Scripture lessons of the consecration service faithfully remind us "to feed the Church of God;" to "feed my sheep; feed my lambs."

How fully these admonitions are heeded is only partially observable. Bishops ordinarily do not have time to counsel individuals repeatedly and in depth, but they do try to deal redemptively with persons in deep trouble. Only bishops

---

*(One of the best brief descriptions of the appointive process is found in Nolan B. Harmon's *Understanding The United Methodist Church*, (Nashville: Abingdon Press, 1977), 120-24.

themselves and the recipients know of the hundreds of telephone calls made, notes of comfort and reassurance penned, words in season spoken, congratulations and commendations extended. Sometimes calling pastors by name or asking about the welfare of a spouse or child is all that is needed. In spite of limitations it is possible for a bishop to have a rich and rewarding pastoral ministry. Moreover, they may in part enable each minister to be more effective in the pastoral role. In the Council bishops are often pastors to one another.

Sometimes it is said that pastors will not seek counsel from bishops or district superintendents because they are "authority figures." There may be some truth in this but not much. Pastoral care is a reciprocal relationship, and bishops, too, experience very often what it means to be cared for by a fellow minister of Jesus Christ or by a lay person exercising a share in that ministry.[7]

To be chief pastor suggests the even further obligation of being pastor of all the people. The consecration vows relating to "concern for peace, justice, and freedom among all people" and to "show compassion to the poor and strangers, and defend those who have no helper" are directly pastoral. Righting social wrongs—and taking high risk in doing so—is a legitimate part of "shepherding," creative of atmosphere and conditions in which people may become more fully human and fulfill their greatest potential.

The Teaching Office

The episcopate has always involved the teaching office. The first apostles and other church leaders took seriously the command of the Lord to teach all nations (Matt. 28:18-20). Since the time of Irenaeus episcopacy has been seen in this way. Indeed, he understood that the consecration of a bishop conveyed a "special charism of truth."[8] The apostles were understood to have been similarly endowed at Pentecost.

This role has been continuous for bishops in the history of the church. For instance, in the age of Charlemagne the following was required: "In every bishop's See instruction shall be given in the psalms, musical notation, chant, the computation of years and seasons, and grammar." That the episcopacy was a teaching office was patent in these regulations addressed at a time when liberal education could not be taken for granted. But they were directed toward the concrete situation of that day. They did encourage the equipping of faithful Christian people to live in a real world, to study, to sing, to worship, to communicate. No less are similar charges laid upon us in terms appropriate to the times in which we live.

In the Roman Catholic tradition this idea was developed into a full-blown dogma of papal infallibility under certain conditions as defined by Vatican I and then further refined in Vatican II. It is generally viewed in that tradition as residing in the whole episcopal body whose *magisterium,* assisted by the Holy Spirit, is infallible (Matt. 18:15-20). But more sharply defined, this means the episcopal college with the pope as their head and not without the pope is the *magisterium.* Under certain carefully defined circumstances the pope is seen as infallible in and of himself. Naturally, this is not claimed for bishops in the Wesleyan tradition!

Nevertheless, it is a part of the episcopal office with us, as for the whole order of elders, to be charged with study and teaching of the Word of God and to defend the church against error.* This is explicit in the vows of ordination and

---

*The original Prayer Book vow was to "banish and drive away all strange and erroneous doctrines." Wesley kept that, but we finally changed it a bit. To "banish and drive away" all erroneous ideas today would be a vow to do the impossible!

consecration. The teaching of sound doctrine was a role that John Wesley took with great seriousness as his whole ministry makes clear, and he charged his preachers to do the same.[9]

The historical instincts of the 1816 General Conference were correct when it acted to charge the bishops with the teaching responsibility. Already there had been teaching and learning bishops. Asbury's study habits witness to this fact. We have seen also that the early bishops were publishers and editors of books. But the General Conference of 1816 adopted legislation making it "the duty of the bishop or bishops, or a committee which they may appoint in each annual conference, to point out a course of reading and study proper to be pursued by candidates for the ministry."[10] This supervised study was thenceforth to be a prerequisite for entry into ministry in full connection, but it took some years to refine and enforce this course of study. For a hundred years this approach served largely for training the ministry, only gradually giving way to seminary training.[11]

The bishops remained deeply involved in this task. Some of them, such as Bishop John Emory, made distinguished contributions to the process. By 1916, however, with the encouragement of some bishops, and considerable footdragging on the part of others, The Methodist Episcopal Church established a commission on the conference course of study.[12] Garrett's Professor Harris Franklin Rall and Boston's Dean (afterward bishop) Lauress J. Birney gave leadership in this office.

The bishops also were guardians of the purity of doctrine in the schools of theology. They did not always cover themselves with glory in theological judgment as, for example, in their failure to confirm the scholarly and saintly Dr. H. G. Mitchell as professor at Boston University School of Theology. Bishops were in 1912 relieved from investigational responsibility concerning theological teaching in the seminaries,[13] and after the quadrennium 1924–28 they no longer had to confirm theological faculty members.[14] At about the same time the bishops of The Methodist Episcopal Church, South, were in the midst of similar struggles regarding orthodoxy in the church and its institutions and with similar results.[15] It is worth noting in this connection that when the 1968 General Conference appointed a doctrinal commission, no bishop was on it. Later this was corrected by two bishops being added as consultants.

Bishops do continue to exercise the teaching office in their preaching and evangelism. Some have made regular teaching days every year in every district with every pastor a vital part of their episcopal ministry. Most have been good and instructive preachers. Some have been authentically and responsibly prophetic in their utterances. Through the years some of our bishops have been scholars and educators; among them were Henry B. Bascom, Levi Scott, Matthew Simpson, Francis J. McConnell, James C. Baker, Paul B. Kern, F. Gerald Ensley, and others.

Other ways have been found for fulfilling the teaching office. Pastors and people have a right to expect some intellectual leadership from their bishops. This, too, is a part of overseeing the temporal and spiritual welfare of the whole church. Of one contemporary bishop serving a largely rural area a farmer's wife reported: "Our bishop loves us; he reads to us from the Greek New Testament." It was indeed his custom to translate directly as he read the Scripture lessons.

On occasion also the *magisterium* has been fulfilled through statements to the church or through study programs under the auspices of the Council of Bishops. It has an obligation to judge many matters on the social and political scene by the criteria of Scripture, Tradition,

Experience, and Reason, and then address the people under their charge with careful teaching regarding them. Here again, theologians are at times called upon to lend their specialized assistance.

Administrator

Bishops are administrators. Sometimes this is by observers perceived to be their chief role.* Most bishops would themselves not rank it first among their duties, and they try not to become bogged down in it. They are, however, charged with carrying into effect the enactments of the General Conference (1980 *Discipline,* par. 52) as well as many programs of the Annual Conferences. Some are indeed skilled and effective in administration, a role they enjoy. The burden and variety of this task can be immense. It must be discharged as a necessary prelude to the other, and often more interesting, functions bishops must fulfill. Even administration is a gift of the Spirit, though apparently it does not rank high on Paul's lists. It is itself a dimension of ministry and by its very nature intends to reinforce other ministries.

At times the administrative function becomes very onerous. In 1952 Bishop Kern gave expression to this fact in the Episcopal Address:

> We are not entering a complaint. We want to do to the best of our several abilities the task the Church lays upon us. If we are to be arch administrators, super-promoters of the whole program of the Church, the General Conference

---

*One overly busy church executive said of himself that an appropriate epitaph would be: "Killed in committee!" Yet wise bishops will be selective about attending Annual Conference committees except where participation, *ex offico,* is expected. They are not, after all, Annual Conference members.

should gear its thinking into this interpretation of our responsibilities. It should bring under review the resources available in our episcopal offices for promotion. Today they are totally inadequate. We are without the facilities and the personnel to get done effectively the tremendous job the Church asks of us. We have a great task to perform in our world and we must not be parsimonious with the means required to accomplish it. We should not be beholden to the patterns of yesterday except in so far as they insure a vital episcopal leadership.[16]

Since that time considerable more help has become available. Conference staffs have been enlarged; some would now say they are too large. This means that the bishop is a team person and must work with a group, and the corporate style he or she follows becomes important. Most now follow a flexible method of reaching group decisions by consensus. This makes open-mindedness and flexibility indispensable.

The episcopal leader will find it necessary at various times to be personnel officer, missional planner and strategist, innovator, pioneer, promoter, fund-raiser, arbiter, enabler, custodian of records, writer of letters, all things to all people. All this is for the sake of the ministry and the mission of the church; for the sake of each local church and all local churches; for the unity and insofar as possible the harmony of the whole. The bishop needs in time to know the whole episcopal area in his or her charge better than any other person and thereby lend coherence to its program, imparting a basic direction or thrust and accent overall.

Liturgical Leader

Bishops are also liturgical leaders, traditionally guardians of the whole liturgical life of the church. In spite of this, it comes to them as a bit of a surprise—especially if they are elected from the pastorate—that they seldom baptize, solemnize marriages, or conduct funerals. Their time usage differs from the usual pastorate. Frequently they do preside at Holy Communion when they are present, the custom since the time of Ignatius, and are always expected to read the prayer of consecration when they are present for a Communion service.

United Methodist bishops are not required, as are their Anglican counterparts, to conduct services of confirmation, but not infrequently they do join local church pastors in receiving the young into full membership. Such episcopal participation can make these rituals both meaningful and memorable in the lives of those concerned. When this is done, it should not be seen as belittling those not confirmed by bishops.

The principal liturgical services in which bishops are necessarily involved are ordinations. (There has always been the possibility of new bishops being consecrated by the laying on of hands by three elders in the event that we should have no living bishops.) According to ancient custom, however, the bishop is the representative and operative elder in ordinations. In order that an "orderly" ministry may be maintained, bishops are the ordaining officers, laying on hands for deacons, elders, and consecration of bishops and leading in the prayer of ordination or consecration. As has already been stated, persons are elected to these offices by the appropriate conferences; deacons and elders by the ministerial members of the Annual Conferences and bishops by all lay and clergy delegates to the Jurisdictional or Central Conferences. Then the bishop *confirms* orders rather than *confers* their orders and inducts them into the same.

In our tradition the priestly function seldom is emphasized. We would subscribe to the Reformation understanding of "the priesthood of all believers"—that each Christian is a priest to every other brother or sister. Nevertheless, there are elements of the priestly in the liturgical dimension of our church's life.

Bishops can and often do lead these high services of the church with great dignity, and as good examples, they train and encourage the other ministers to do the same. In a time of universal liturgical renewal an opportunity is afforded greatly to enrich our services.[17] We would not want to press with Ignatius that "where the bishop is, there is the Church," but where the bishop goes, there the life of the church should be enlivened and enriched.

Ecumenical Liaison

The 1980 *Discipline* also charges bishops "to provide liaison in ecumenical activities and relationships" (par. 512.3). The Council of Bishops as a whole has the function of serving as "foreign ministry" for the church in cooperation with the standing General Commission on Christian Unity and Interreligious Concerns. Individual bishops are also engaged fully in this enterprise. They often are among those representing The United Methodist Church in general organizations such as the National Council of Churches, the World Council of Churches, the World Methodist Council, or in formal dialogue with other communions.

Nearly every bishop is involved deeply in state and local councils and conferences of churches. In 1978 the Council of Bishops issued a statement on *Christian Unity: Imperatives and New Commitments*. Likewise, they participated in a statement on relations with Judaism. In these activities the bishops are encouraged by the very temper of the times in which we live. They are reinforced by the support of the great majority of United Methodist people. They may take courage also from a long tradition stemming from John Wesley who enjoined Methodist and all Christians to a "Catholic Spirit." In an ecumenical period they are entitled to conduct themselves as elders and bishops of the Church Universal, while awaiting the time when this may be freely acknowledged.

Spiritual Formation

Of late the usage "spiritual formation," long characteristic of the Catholic tradition, has become current in United Methodist circles. The bishop has an important part in this development. If we are committed to spreading scriptural holiness, then the holy life must be a continuing emphasis among us.*

Bishops must themselves "maintain the spiritual glow." If their lives sag at this point, then the consequences show up in every dimension of their work. The life of prayer and devotion relates to every element of episcopal work and undergirds the whole. It enters into pastoral counseling as a caring ministry which is demanded in particular measure and of those chosen to be chief pastors; but also it relates to administration. A vibrant life of prayer, then, is essential to the office. Fortunately many of our bishops have shown themselves exemplary to such an end and still do. Doubtless those most disciplined in this respect would be least likely to think of themselves exemplary!

During the early 1980s spiritual formation has become a special emphasis of the Council of Bishops. Its members have been active in teaching the Bible and in sharing methods in the areas of meditation, contemplation, and

---

*This emphasis on the holy life has been a subject for formal dialogue between Roman Catholics and United Methodists in the United States.

prayer. One area for two years studied a different spiritual "classic" in each district and then compiled a "daily office" as a result. All this can be an antidote for much that seems to ail us in the present secularized age.

Being at one's best in the life of the Spirit is only a part—an indispensable part—of caring for one's self as a whole person, including care of the body and continuous training of the mind. Bishops must be strong. Asbury felt they should be persons who "can ride three thousand miles and meet ten or eleven conferences a year."[18] It is important that bishops and other ministers be at their best. They are under no necessity to be infallible but should be humble and never lose their temper! Recall the exclamation: "I have never met a person who was entirely sanctified, save one—and she did not know it!"

Bishops are, after all, persons—Christians in the making—or, to borrow a phrase uttered in jest, they are only human beings trying to be divine. They must play many roles. Most of them enjoy the supporting roles of families. Sometimes those in the episcopate neglect families and pay a price for doing so. Among other things, family members usually do not allow bishops to take themselves too seriously. They need a sense of humor. If they seem to lack something to laugh about, they always have themselves! Occasional relaxation and renewal are required to maintain balance in those to whom heavy and varied responsibilities are entrusted.

Bishop Herbert Welch, to whom United Methodists are indebted for many things, offers, as relates to the inner life, a recipe he called the "Welch Quadrilateral":

1. Moderation in work—when circumstances permit.
2. Prohibition of worry.
3. A little play along the way.
4. Trust in God.

The Matter of Image

The *Discipline* beginning in 1976 included a paragraph (par. 502) entitled "Guidelines for Superintending in this Age." It suggests several intangible but clearly recognizable matters relating to the office charged with overseeing the temporal and spiritual affairs of the entire church. They are "mode," "pace," and "skill." Bishops will vary with respect to all three factors that color and accent the way in which each person may actually perform in the office. These factors, in turn, help to set the tone of a conference, an episcopal area, perhaps the whole church.

For example, how would one conceive of a diagram of the church? Usually it would be drawn as a triangle with a broad base and some hierarchical figure at the top. Why not turn the diagram on its side, that is, lay it flat? Then the base would be seen at the front—at the task in the local church. It would then be seen that supervisory ministries are in a backup or support position.

There is such a thing as image. For the bishop shall it be "democratic overseer," "board chairman," "placement officer," or "systems manager"? Image may be formed and informed in part by the very doing of the various duties of the episcopate as set forth in what has been written above.

Victor Frankl has somewhere suggested that a person possesses a sense of meaning when one feels that there is a vital connection between the goals one values and the activities and relationships in which one is involved. A balance must be reached between what one intends and what one does. For example, a leader may adopt a *style,* an intentional mode of conducting himself or herself. Image is the way in which one's style is *perceived* by the observer. The two—style and image—ought to coincide, but this is not always true. Some would want further to talk about *model*—the replication of one's style or image—but that is not a great concern here.

Possible images for bishops are numerous: leader; father- or mother-in-God; better still, brother (or sister); above all, *servant.* This is being written on Holy Thursday; *servanthood* is the only authentic model for leadership among Christians. And only One has shown that model with complete authenticity. Bishops cannot be more than that and ought not to be less: servants; for they are *set apart to serve.*

Finally, we may learn what servant-bishops do as we borrow wisdom from Lao Tzu in ancient China:

> Leaders are best when people barely know they exist, not so good when people obey and acclaim them, worst when people despise them. Fail to honor people, they fail to honor you. But of good leaders who talk little, when their work is done, their aim fulfilled, people will all say: "We did this ourselves."

Notes

1. Cf. Neely, *Vital Points,* 54.
2. Cf. *Joint Commission on Unification of The Methodist Church and The Methodist Episcopal Church, South* (New York: Methodist Book Concern, 1918), 3:116.
3. See A Report to the General Conference of 1964, *The Study of The General Superintendency of The Methodist Church,* 43.
4. Reference may be made to a story about a bishop in the Church of England which has become a classic in Great Britain. It is entitled "The Curate's Egg" and appeared as a cartoon in the very first issue of *Punch* more than a century ago. A young minister is invited to breakfast with his elderly and somewhat pompous bishop. The curate is served a softboiled egg which proves to be of dubious vintage. The prelate, observing the young man's hesitancy over it, remarked: "What's wrong, Jones, is your egg bad?" To which the curate replied: "On the contrary, my Lord, parts of it are very good indeed!" (Some episcopal roles are very good indeed!)
5. All recent bishops have been helped by a letter from their highly

respected colleague, Bishop Wiliam C. Martin, on presiding. It has eased the way for many grateful bishops.

6. Part of a statement adopted unanimously by the Council of Bishops in Dallas, January 14, 1976. It is interesting that *The Decree on the Pastoral Office of Bishop* of Vatican II sounds similar notes, although in a very different context.

7. Cf. Ruth B. Caplan, *Helping the Helpers to Help* (New York: Seabury Press, 1972).

8. Cf. Irenaeus *Against Heretics* 4:26.2.

9. Early American Methodism was not unaware of the importance of study. The 1798 *Discipline* gives helpful suggestions regarding sermon preparation. Accompanying notes expand on this (See pp. 84-89.)

10. General Conference *Journal*, 1816, 1:151.

11. The first seminary was established in Newbury, Vermont, in 1840 (now Boston University School of Theology).

12. McConnell, *By the Way*, 250-51.

13. *Discipline*, 1912, par. 206.

14. *Discipline*, 1924, par. 456.5. (This was the last time this provision was made.)

15. Cf. Sledge, *Hands on the Ark*, 138-64.

16. *Daily Christian Advocate*, 1952, 69.

17. Cf. Gregory Dix, *The Shape of the Liturgy* (1945; reprint, Westminster: Dacre Press, 1946, 1947, 1949, 1952, 1954), 104. Dix gives the wonderful account of the offertory. Monetary gifts are brought by the faithful. Laity brings the bread and wine. Then the *orphans*, who have "nothing to bring," carry to the altar *water* to be mingled with the wine. This really makes liturgy the "work of the People of God."

18. Asbury, *Letters*, 541.

VII

THE ROAD AHEAD

We have examined the meaning and role of episcopacy in the Wesleyan heritage. This has involved an examination of the scriptural usage of the term *bishop;* a tracing of the office through history; a closer scrutiny of this role in our own experience over the last two centuries; a consideration of some of the critical appraisals of it and resulting changes because of this criticism. Here we have seen in operation once again the fourfold Wesleyan guidelines: Scripture; Tradition; Experience; and Reason. We have observed both norm and practice as they relate to the episcopate among United Methodists.

In turning toward the future it is necessary to be brief. There is said to be an ancient Chinese proverb to the effect that it is extremely difficult to prophesy, especially with respect to the future. At one and the same time we are fascinated with it and we fear it. These are the two forces that, according to Rudolf Otto, when they meet create awe. We do indeed experience awe as we contemplate the future. Someone has said that the future is too important to leave to the future. An Hispanic poet even goes so far as to refer to "remembering the future."

The ancient Hebrew prophets were not so much foreseers as forthseers. They did not try to probe the future in the sense of predicting it in detail. Rather they saw the future as a consequence of what is going on in the present. Simply stated, they were saying, "If you do not change, doom lies ahead. If you do change—repent, turn around —there is hope."

This seems to suggest that we can tell a good deal about the future by looking more acutely than usual at what is actually going on now. Here we tend to divide into two camps. Some would recite a long list of woes that no doubt characterize the present scene. They would imply that even worse is to come.

It would indeed be folly to ignore the terrible peril we now face with the possibility of nuclear holocaust and the end of civilization. To succumb utterly to such a prospect, however, would be to inhibit our doing what we could and should be doing to try to prevent it. On the other hand, there are less dismal prophets who would regard the present as one of "humankind's better moments"; therefore, for them the future is not devoid of promising possibilities.

All of this would appear to be particularly relevant to Christians who are committed to a theology of hope. This makes what we do now not only justifiably worthwhile but may result in very positive consequences for the future. It was Arnold Toynbee who said that "there is nothing inevitable about history." From the Christian perspective we may see ourselves cooperating with God and choosing from among options that may help to shape the future. This is as always a venture of faith, in which the *community* of faith must of necessity be involved.

It is time to state what all of this may have to do with United Methodism and, more specifically, with episcopacy in United Methodism. It is simply that we are a part of the community of faith that is making decisions now which will affect the future.

The contemporary Dutch Roman Catholic theologian, Edward Schillebeeckx, says, "The new type of bishop cannot be invented by theologians or bureaucrats, but must issue from new communities of faith."[1] In the context from which he is speaking he suggests that leadership may be combined with friendship; authority with family relationships; "father" tempered by "brother." Granted that he writes from a different tradition, nevertheless insight is afforded here for the rest of us, too. People are ready for bishops to change all right, but on the record they change in a correlative way as the faith community changes. We have seen this repeatedly in our history which has been anything but immobile.

I have often reflected upon the fact that in a constitutional episcopacy such as ours the function of bishops becomes what the people, under God's guidance and in response to the demands of history, determine it shall be. Rather than having an *historic episcopate,* ours may therefore be termed a *futuric episcopate.* * It is flexible, experimental, pragmatic, and functional. We can and do change in respect to the episcopal office.

If the idea of *historic episcopate* is of value on the current scene, so too is a *futuric episcopate.* In the past we have demonstrated repeatedly that polity is subordinate to mission. This very characteristic is a current demand upon the whole church. The unity and good order of the church may depend in considerable measure upon this fact. For our part, we have always understood that, while doctrine and sacrament are of the *esse* of the church, ministry and

---

*By this term we mean what episcopacy may, under God, become as it responds to the demand history places upon it.

government are of the *bene esse*. We are profoundly committed to sound church government, including episcopacy, but we see that the mission of salvation is primary.

Bearing these considerations in mind we turn to three areas of decision that lie along the road ahead:

1. Ecumenical Interchange;
2. Structure for Mission; and
3. Elements of Mission.

1. *Ecumenical Interchange*

It is reasonable to suppose that The United Methodist Church will continue to be involved in the conciliar movement and maintain membership in the World Council of Churches and the National Council of Churches in the United States and in counterpart organizations in other countries, as well as in numerous state and local councils. This involvement would be with appropriate critical attitudes with respect to their programs but also with deep commitment to their goals. Such commitment is a part of our heritage and is expressed clearly in our Constitution.[2] We cannot go it alone.

It is desirable also that we should keep in close relationship with other branches of the Methodist family, especially with autonomous churches formerly related integrally to The United Methodist Church or its predecessors. We also have not only a fraternal relationship with British Methodism but are linked with that fellowship by a solemn concordat which is a part of our Constitution.[3]

Moreover, we are linked by a special historical tie with The Christian Methodist Episcopal Church (1980 *Discipline*, par. 2007). By direction of the General Conference, the Council of Bishops is in quadrilateral dialogue and cooperation not only with that church but also with sister denominations, namely, The African Methodist Episcopal Church and The African Methodist Episcopal Zion Church. All four denominations have a similar episcopacy. It is at present not possible to say exactly where these relations will lead, but some observers believe that there might gradually emerge a federal union of these bodies which would at one and the same time allow for a high degree of oneness linked with as much autonomy as any party might wish to reserve.

The United Methodist Church also continues as a part of the Consultation on Church Union (COCU). So far the Consultation has been an instrument within which several organic unions have already taken place (Methodist-Evangelical United Brethren, 1968; United Presbyterian Church in U.S.A. and Presbyterian Church in U.S., 1982) or are under discussion (United Church of Christ and the Christian Church, Disciples of Christ; The African Methodist Episcopal Zion Church and Christian Methodist Episcopal Church).

Beyond this and by a complicated process COCU has for more than two decades been laying careful groundwork for possibly a more comprehensive union that might result finally in a "Church of Christ Uniting." It has labored for what is called "interim eucharistic fellowships" and "generating communities." Currently it is working along lines of covenanting for a complete mutual recognition of sacraments and ministries.* What final shape this might take is difficult to imagine. Perhaps here again a federal union model would be most promising. A huge monolithic union is not very attractive.**

---

*In November 1984 the plenary of COCU meeting in Baltimore voted unanimously to proceed along this line.

**But here again we may recall Lord Donald Soper's suggestion that Methodism's future may lie in its becoming a preaching order in the Church Universal.

Meanwhile the principal challenge to all the churches is a new possibility embodied in the document, *Baptism, Eucharist and Ministry (B.E.M.)*. It is the product of ecumenical exploration which may be said to date from 1927 with the first Faith and Order conference in Lausanne. The Faith and Order Movement is now a commission related to the World Council of Churches but has membership that reaches beyond that body. This document was after long and careful collaboration unanimously approved by the commission in Lima, Peru, in January 1982. This represents an almost unbelievable ecumenical milestone. It invites the possibility of an universal and reciprocal recognition of the sacraments of Baptism and Holy Communion as well as of Ministry among the churches. This does not mean that every denomination will actually walk on this open road but at least it *is* open. The United Methodist Church is at this writing preparing a first reaction to the document. It is worth observing that in 1784 American Methodists became a church precisely over concern for sacraments and ministry. We have traveled this road before.

Somewhere in the discussion the mingling of ministries must be considered. This would involve a possible mingling of an Anglican type of episcopacy with the Methodist type. We have referred to them as *historic* and *futuric,* respectively. These terms do not altogether cover the subject of course, nor need they be seen as antagonistic terms. There remains to be determined an understanding of what bishops are expected to do in any new church.

In 1966 at a COCU meeting in Dallas I brought up, for the first time, the appointive function of bishops as practiced in the Methodist tradition. It should be noted that the three black Methodist churches, the Evangelical United Brethren Church and The Methodist Church, all members of COCU, also had appointive systems, but up till that time this method of deploying ministry had never really been put on the agenda of the Consultation for serious discussion. My purpose in raising the matter was not with the intention of removing it *from* negotiation but to introduce it *for* negotiation. The issue is still not resolved, and although we should not be inflexible about it, at the same time it would be inappropriate to yield the point without discussion. That is to say that we are not obliged to adjust our polity in advance by what we may know may be required by possible union. These are matters for reciprocal agreement during the process of negotiation.

It is worth noting that Anglicans in their celebrated Chicago (later Lambuth) Quadrilateral of 1886 set forth their standards for restoration of unity: (1) the Holy Scriptures; (2) the Nicene Creed; (3) the two Sacraments, Baptism and the Lord's Supper; and (4) the Historic Episcopate. We should have no difficulty with the first three, but with the fourth there would need to be discussion.

There has been interchange on this topic before, for example, between our British Methodist brothers and sisters and the Church of England. This was in response to the open invitation of the Archbishop of Canterbury's famous Cambridge sermon in 1946 for free churches to consider episcopacy. The former did show its readiness to accept the historic episcopate, howbeit with the same latitude of interpretation that it already enjoyed *within* the Anglican fellowship. It seemed that reunion was just around the corner, but the Anglicans turned it down in 1969 and again in 1972.

Yet again a few years later British Methodists joined with other free churches to consider covenanting for church union in Great Britain. This, too, would have embraced the historic episcopate, but once more in July

1982 the Synod of the Church of England voted negatively on the matter. The effect of this on the free churches has been disappointing to say the least and may have a negative influence on union movements elsewhere in the world.

Thus far The United Methodist Church has not, as such, been confronted with a decision on this matter. Methodists of Pakistan, however, did make the decision and are now in a united church that acknowledges the historic episcopate.

The ecumenical mood today seems to lean toward acknowledging this notion of episcopacy as a symbol of the church's unity and continuity. In 1984, however, a study by ten United States Lutheran theologians concluded that this teaching is "not necessary for the validity of the church's ministry."[4] Two branches of American Lutherans have accepted episcopacy into their polities in recent years. This was a fulfillment of the long desire of many of their leaders, one of whom remarked some years ago, "I believe in bishops for my church—even if they don't make me one of them." Their view of bishops now coincides rather closely with our own.

It is worth noting also that an increasing interest in "connectionalism" has characterized Lutherans and others in the United States during recent years. Our denomination need not be ashamed of the gifts it brings to the ecumenical negotiating table—not its connectionalism, nor its episcopal experience, nor its doctrinal emphasis, nor its emphases on personal and social holiness, nor its sense of *ecclesiola in ecclesia*.

On the other hand, our tradition should be particularly congenial to ways in which the Holy Spirit has been at work in other traditions, including the historic episcopate. If the Roman pontiff can in our day be open to truth emphasized by Luther, the daughters and sons of Wesley might well display a similar spirit. We would claim a succession to gospel truth since the time of the apostles. We should be open to a powerful sign of continuity of ministry with the apostles.

2. *Structure for Mission*

The mere mention of *Structure for Mission* is likely to create anxiety in the United Methodist camp. During recent years a strange compulsion has appeared to afflict Christian churches and councils. Our own church has not escaped. It is a disorder that seemingly may manifest itself at any time and at any level: restructuring. We have tried this any number of times.

There is something to be said for this tinkering with machinery but not very much. Usually by the time we have agreed upon what structure we shall have for mission, the opportunity for mission has slipped away. The sad fact is that we do not so much engage in restructure *for* mission as in restructure *instead* of mission. If that is a severe indictment, perhaps it will help our Christian humility to live with it.

The last time we had an overall restructuring of our general agencies was during the quadrennium 1968–72. The General Conference of 1972 approved extensive reorganizational proposals, and we have been living with the results ever since. It left us with an extremely unbalanced set of general agencies. Far from being of commensurate size, one was a colossus and another comparatively minuscule. Apparently none of the four general boards has been very happy with the result, for all of them have undergone further intensive internal reorganization since 1972—some of them more than once. If restructuring were the answer to our ills, we should have been in sound health long ago!

I do not propose further reorganization but simply choose to address briefly a more basic issue. I refer to what

Professor Albert Outler and the late Dr. Jameson Jones, among others, have called a general superintendency *versus* a "curial or bureaucratic general superintendency." Another way of putting it is that we have a constitutional "general superintendency" and a "localized superintendency for certain broad areas of church-wide concern," which strives to be a general superintendency. This need not be stated in adversarial form, but here is an ambiguity that must be noted. Nor need we understand the terms *curial* and *bureaucratic* pejoratively but descriptively. This fact has been around for a long time, but there has not been much dialogue about it. Perhaps the best way to deal with it is just to discuss it candidly.

A little historical perspective on the development of agencies and boards may be of some help. It used to be said that Mahatma Gandhi *was* India. In a similar sense we could say that Bishop Asbury *was* early Methodism in this country. He embodied and activated every concern. He was educator, publisher, social conscience, and recruiting agent for the whole church. He and all the other preachers were missionaries. Lay leaders, whether local preachers or class leaders, were partners in mission.

The Methodist Book Concern was established in 1789, and John Dickins was named book steward or book agent. The array of early publications is impressive. In 1796 the General Conference stated: "The propagation of religious knowledge by means of the press is next in importance to the preaching of the gospel."[5] The preachers, in turn, distributed and sold books, and the proceeds undergirded ministerial support and charity. Later Ezekiel Cooper was book agent; later still Joshua Soule, Nathan Bangs, and other notables. Much later on it became the practice to name two publishers, one lay and one ministerial. So it was that such designations as "Phillips and Hunt" or "Curts and Jennings" appeared on title pages. A ministerial publisher naturally related to the appointive system and ensured some episcopal supervision.

Then in 1819 John Stewart, a man of mixed Negro and Indian ancestry, was appointed as the first "home missionary" to the Wyandot Indians at Upper Sandusky, Ohio. The following year the first Methodist Missionary Society was founded. As to its overseers it could be said that originally the bishops collectively *were* the missionary society. The organized society itself could only recommend action; the bishops and Annual Conferences were to act upon and implement their suggestions. Thomas Mason, a general book steward, was the first Corresponding Secretary. Some years later Nathan Bangs held that office, and the bishops appointed him to it.

Then organizations arose for Church Extension, for Education, for Pensions, and others for social causes such as Freedmen's Aid and Temperance. Bishops were deeply involved in establishing and governing all these agencies. As time went on their secretaries or chief executive officers were elected by General Conference just as bishops were. These organizations increased in size, range, effectiveness, and prestige and came to resemble their successor boards we know today.

After the 1939 reunion at first *all* bishops were voting members of both the Board of Missions and the Board of Education. Thus the two main functions of the church— outreach and nurture (mission and *magisterium*)—were immediate concerns of every general superintendent who was likewise informed about and involved in the formulation of policy.[6] Then in 1952 their involvement was reduced to approximately one-half in each agency, although for the first time six overseas' bishops were made members of the Board of Missions.[7] In 1964 the number was reduced to fifteen bishops on each, with five overseas' bishops on the Board of Missions,[8] and since then their number has been reduced further. As a member of the Coordinating Council in 1964, I opposed further reduction simply because nurture and outreach by their very nature were appropriate concerns of *all* bishops.

Nowadays bishops are designated as members of *one* general agency; their experience there is generally positive and constructive; and they report regularly to the Council of Bishops or its standing committees. Meanwhile, all the boards have a more representative and inclusive membership chosen from the entire church. These agencies themselves have increasingly become centers of power and influence throughout the church as they have endeavored to serve the general concerns of the whole denomination.

At the same time they share the shortcomings of any large organization: more and more time is required for internal conferences and in-house communication so that less energy and resources are available to fulfill their stated goals. So it is that, simply stated, the Board of Church and Society concerns itself with advocacy; the Board of Discipleship with nurture; the Board of Global Ministries with outreach; and the Board of Higher Education and Ministries with vocation. Furthermore, growth in size and influence of general agencies has been concomitant with growth in their counterpart agencies at the Annual Conference level. This has been true of both staff and budgets.

We have repeatedly observed that the bishops, as individuals and as a body, have for decades been subjected to criticism by the church that elected them. It might be supposed that general agencies, as they have increased in size and influence, would also be targets of criticism. This has indeed been the case, especially of late. At times this has been uninformed and unwarranted. Some of this criticism has been directed toward top-heavy centralization;[9] toward the alleged ineffectiveness of centralized bureaucracies as such;[10] or toward their alleged extravagance in the use of resources and power.[11]

Dr. Outler went so far as to state in the article just referred to that "the monarchical power of the Methodist bishops and *their* bureaucratic curias is no longer believed to be of divine right" (italics mine). His point of "*their* bureaucratic curias" is one that neither bishops nor general secretaries would concede. It must be said that much of this criticism of boards has come at a time of general malaise in all the churches; but whereas once in United Methodist circles the bishops were pointed to as the principal cause, now the general agencies have become the main targets of blame. The arrest, first, of growth of our church and, then, decline in membership have served to accentuate all this.

Another dynamic has also been at work. There have been blurring and overlapping of the discrete roles once assigned to the general agencies. During the 1960s and 1970s it became popular to say in substance that "everything is mission." Sooner or later this was believed by local churches who *themselves* engaged in mission. Therefore, they were understandably reluctant in seeking funds for what *they* conceived to be mission to have to apply to the Board of Global Ministries for grants of mission funds that they themselves had generated in the first place: much more direct involvement in mission was undertaken by Annual Conferences, by other general agencies, by new missionary agencies, the latter on the grounds that private agencies could do it better and cheaper. Likewise, it came to be said that "everything is social concerns," and the Board of Global Ministries was sometimes caricatured as an "International Board of Social Concerns." So, too, it was concluded that "everything is evangelism." Therefore the Board of Evangelism was, for all intents and purposes, dismantled, with predictable results, for as Henry P. Van Dusen used to say, "When everything is evangelism, nothing is evangelism." Naturally this has led to defense of the agencies including some "defense of turf." The bishops, as general superintendents, have joined in the defense. I, myself, in a response to Professor Outler's article cited above spoke to his insistence in decentralizing general agencies:.

> Decentralization ought not to be pushed to the point of jeopardizing the value of our connectionalism. The two forces—centralization and decentralization—should be kept in balance. The Church is local *and* the Church is world-wide. Though the whole Church is present in the local congregation, the local congregation is not the whole Church. Nevertheless, if the Church *is* mission, then the various structures enabling effective mission should be kept as close to the local church as possible. Likewise, agency programs should reflect real concerns and awaken real concerns at the local level. They should be evident expressions of compassion in forms relevant to the Twentieth Century and realizable by ordinary committed Christians and congregations.[12]

To sum up, bishops are elected by delegated bodies as general superintendents. They do not sit as members of General Conference nor do they debate legislation. The general secretaries, on the other hand, are elected or confirmed by agencies authorized by the General Conference. They *do* sit at the General Conference with voice but not vote. They may, moreover, in their own right be elected delegates to this body. Sometimes they are elected.

In either case they participate deeply in legislative formulation. In fact, the legislative committees of the several general agencies actually draft most of the legislation for their agencies, which after General Conference approval becomes their mandate.

General secretaries become in effect general superintendents for specialized concerns; indeed, they are *more* general than general superintendents. In some respects the general agencies function as an interim General Conference. Both bishops and general secretaries are accountable to General (or Jurisdictional) Conference. Bishops become executive officers of the General Conference, charged with carrying out *all* General Conference legislation and programs, just as general secretaries are charged with executing their particular areas of concern. This is what is meant by referring to "constitutional general superintendents" versus "curial or bureaucratic general superintendents."

In calling this section "Structure for Mission" we mean essentially the resolution of this issue. Bishops, as bridgebuilders, acknowledge their responsibility to help to do so. First of all, the issue must be understood. Flexibility, often demonstrated in the past, will help toward facilitating solution. All concerned are *servants* of Christ, and this in itself will go a long way toward resolution. All parties are team members experienced in and committed to working together. But all parties also are prone to self-interest and doubtless have low tolerance for change and relaxation of self-interest for the benefit of the larger interest.

Bishops *are* closer to the local scene: collectively they can immediately reach into every local church, community, and crossroads in the country (or countries). They do personally, and through the district and conference organizations, "know the territory" and are more acutely aware of grass-root concerns and attitudes than general secretaries can be. The general secretaries have deep knowledge of special Christian concerns. The two must try to work this matter through cooperatively, in a way that will encourage a high degree of mutual trust and will be always for the good of the whole church.

Early in the last century when the presiding elder

question was current, there was also a polarization in the life of the church, essentially between episcopal leadership and General Conference prerogatives. For a time this situation was mollified by a third party's appearing which was perceived as inimical to both. Therefore as we have observed, they did not really face and resolve the issue that divided them because there then emerged a third issue: a tripartite situation. The two poles, for expediency's sake, joined forces to oppose their common "enemy," namely, the assertion of laity's rights. The issue between them, which had not been resolved, erupted later with the devastating result of schism.

Today a certain polarization is present between two types of superintendency, and our church is also again confronted with a new assertiveness from the grass roots for a greater share in decision making. Expediency may be tempting once again. Would it not be wiser to work together and really hear what the Spirit may be saying to and through the churches? Then the specialists and the general overseers may work together, both be more receptive to the general will, and both unite to serve the good of the whole connection.

Having resolved any polarization in top echelons of leadership, we shall be prepared to move forward more effectively in mission that relates to the authentic issues of our time. Our church need not *react* to events but effectively intervene in events for the sake of mission. We need to marshal and husband our total resources to this end. This calls for effective use of research and modern technologies which the general agencies are equipped to supply.

3. *Elements of Mission*

Again and again it has been emphasized that, as overseers and guardians of the temporal and spiritual welfare of the entire church, bishops have a principal role in advancing the common life of our whole church. They have also a share in responsibility for the Church Universal. This would suggest that bishops should be characterized by a peculiar openness to the needs of people and be peculiarly focused on the basic realities of the faith. They are charged with sensing and articulating a coherent vision for the whole and a coherent vision for the future. Francis Asbury never seemed to lose this quality. For example, we find him toward the end of his life speaking in this way:

> Should my life be spared a few years, I shall push to preach the gospel in all the world of America, though I should find it three thousand miles in length and as many in breadth. I long to preach the gospel to all the British, Spanish, and the United States of America.[13]

What would be our counterpart today to such a continental vision of the future? For one thing ours would be global vision. For another, we might try to keep our aims as sharply focused as Asbury managed to do. We tend to be more diffuse with too many "vital concerns" and priorities before us at one time. When we try to address many priorities, we probably address *no* priority.

A. If we are to be true to our heritage and calling, surely our first priority is and should remain *evangelism*. Strange to say, the word *evangelism* does not appear in Scripture. *Evangelist does* occur. Evangelism is what evangelists do; it is "the work of an evangelist."

If I knew exactly how this is to be done, I should now reveal it. I do not know, but all bishops need somehow to sense that we must seek the ways in which evangelism can be done effectively in our day. Some fear the so-called numbers game and do not take church growth seriously, but total human need must be taken in all seriousness. The field of need is there in all its agonizing intensity. And it is "white unto harvest."

If we become freshly aware of the holiness of God and of the depth, the hurt, and the exceeding sinfulness of sin, then perhaps the healing balm can be applied. This demands our relentless energy and focus. Meanwhile we should be exceedingly grateful that we have inherited no narrow conception of what evangelism itself means.

We may in this connection very well recall the words of John Wesley:

> I am not afraid that the people called Methodists should ever cease to exist either in Europe or America. But I am afraid, lest they should only exist as a dead sect, having the form of religion without the power. And this undoubtedly will be the case, unless they hold fast both the doctrine, spirit, and discipline with which they first set out.[14]

B. When evangelism is first, then all the rest will follow. We are aware of human hunger(s) and of continuing racial inequity; of the rights of the aging and of women and children; of the continuing erosion of religious liberty; of the massive need for economic and social justice; of regard for the whole of humankind throughout the whole world. At the same time we are inescapably addressed by the possibility of nuclear destruction and faced by a multitude of other causes. Furthermore, we are assigned the task of being constructive critics of society and the state; of scrutinizing the rights and limits of government. We cannot mount every bandwagon, but we can be present to human need wherever it is found.

Jesus did not emphasize a merely individual dimension of life before God. Rather he preached about and offered the Kingdom of God, a corporate dimension. Indeed in the

Gospels he refers to the Kingdom—the active Kingship, or Reign of God over all—exactly one hundred times! Today the Church scarcely mentions the Kingdom at all! Bishops and the whole People of God need to recover this message: the Gospel of the Kingdom.

Jesus *combined* ministering to such real needs of people *and* proclaiming the good news of the Kingdom, for the two cannot be separated. Each demands the other. The Council of Bishops is charged with the necessity of pointing out the overarching issues of our time and of helping to mount the programs that would help meet them. In the midst of all these demands we are upheld by a quiet confidence that this is the Church of Jesus Christ and the gates of hell shall not prevail against it!

One of our most respected bishops was the late William C. Martin, who had this to say to his colleagues shortly before his death:

> And there is one thing about which each one of us can be perfectly certain; and that is that in all the long history of man's life on this planet, there has never been a time when the world was in greater or more urgent need for the message in the ministry for which the Church was created and commissioned to give.[15]

An old Russian priest once said, "The Church remains the church despite its bishops and because of its bishops." The criticism is accepted. Perhaps it would not be entirely self-serving to recall also the words of General Matthew Ridgway when he said that the critics should speak frankly "but don't do away with generals"—nor general superintendents!

Bishops are, after all, servants of the servants of God and of God's people. If they are to be "scriptural *episkopoi,"* they need the blessing of the Holy Spirit and need to pray:

Anoint and cheer our soiléd face
With the abundance of thy grace.

Notes

1. Schillebeeckx, *The Unifying Role of Bishop*, 27.
2. Cf. *Discipline*, 1980, Division One, Article V, par. 5.
3. Ibid., Division Two, Sect. II, Article I, par. 12.3.
4. Cf. Ecumenical Press Service, February 1–10, 1984, item 21.
5. General Conference *Journals*, 1796–1836, 17.
6. *Discipline*, 1948, pars. 1172; 1326.
7. *Discipline*, 1952, pars. 1172; 1326.
8. *Discipline*, 1964, pars. 1180; 1326.
9. Albert Outler, "Reform in the Methodist Manner," *Christian Advocate* (March 7, 1968), 7. This was given as a speech in Dallas on November 10, 1967.
10. Jameson Jones, "United Methodism: A Cautious Mood," *Christian Century* (September 20, 1978), 853.
11. See widely circulated but apparently unpublished article by layman, Edwin L. Jones, Charlotte, North Carolina, March 26, 1968.
12. Speech in response to Dr. Outler, Dallas, November 10, 1967. Published in part as "Appointments and Morale," *Christian Advocate* (April 18, 1968), 11-12.
13. Asbury, *Letters*, 456.
14. Wesley, "Thoughts Upon Methodism," in *Works* 13:258.
15. Message to the Council of Bishops meeting in Little Rock, Arkansas, May 3, 1983—the forty-fifth anniversary of his having been chosen a bishop.

APPENDIX *A*

ON BEING THE COUNCIL OF BISHOPS

—James K. Mathews

Presented to the Council of Bishops at San Antonio, April, 1971; later updated for 1976 and 1980 legislation. Most of the recommendations made herein were later implemented.

Introduction

If there is a thesis for this paper, it is that large and important segments of our responsibilities as bishops can be fulfilled only in and as a *Council* of Bishops. This may seem obvious, but if it is merely taken for granted, it is likely to be neglected and in fact often has been. Neither as exemplary individual bishops nor by outstanding performance in our particular area assignments do we entirely keep our vows made at consecration. To participate wholeheartedly in the Council's work is no less a demand laid upon us. This is not optional but obligatory. It is not open to us to "sit lightly" to it. It is a principal way in which we can together exercise our general superintendency, for this cannot be done just in our being so many separate general superintendents. If all this is true, then only by our unremitting united efforts can we be the kind of Council the Church authorizes and intends us to be.

This paper is not meant to be a formal or exhaustive essay on the Council of Bishops. Rather, it is a kind of outline of the nature and function of the Council. It has been based on: the 1968 *Discipline* in both its constitutional and legislative portions; the documents from the study of the episcopacy undertaken by the Coordinating Council, 1960–1970; various essays and articles by members of this Council; several books dealing with our episcopacy and that of our traditions.

Clearly, United Methodism expects much from its bishops. It provides for a strong episcopacy. This is set forth in the Constitution of our church and is powerfully reinforced and safeguarded by a Restrictive Rule. The Constitution also reconciles and harmonizes the various episcopal traditions now present in United Methodism (par. 50).

In some respects, the classic and traditional roles of bishops throughout Christendom attach to our bishops. We are chief pastors; teachers; defenders of the faith; exercising discipline and general supervision of the church and especially of the ministers. We ordain; fulfill liturgical roles; have a prophetic office; have particular responsibility for the unity of the church. In addition, we, too, maintain symbolic roles, nor do we hesitate to adapt them. Yet we lay no claim to apostolic succession unless that concept be defined properly as exercising apostolic functions. We are an office, not an order. We are not prelates on the one hand, nor diocesan officers on the other. We exist for the whole connection and are a kind of cement uniting the whole denomination.

In United Methodism, our point of reference is not solely to the past. As a constitutional episcopacy, our function is what the people under God determine it shall be. Rather than an *historic* episcopate, ours may therefore be termed *futuric*. It is flexible, experimental, functional. Collectively, the Council of Bishops is amenable to the General Conference (par. 15.5) and individually the bishops are accountable to the Jurisdictional or Central Conferences (par. 623). "Checks and balances" similar to those in the United States federal structure are evident in our church. Our bishops have no direct legislative authority and no final judicial authority. Their basic role is executive and this is itself subject to appropriate review from time to time.

Ours is indeed a goodly heritage and the office we now hold has been honored by the caliber of men and the quality of service of most of our predecessors. This foundation we have not only gratefully to receive but to adapt and build upon. Our essential duties of travelling, presiding, fixing appointments, ordaining and directing the spiritual business of the societies have been continued from the very beginning of our traditions in this country. Episcopacy is essential to our ethos as a denomination. But two aspects of this function are evident in our tradition in unique measure; namely, general superintendency and collegiality.

It is specifically the episcopacy in the form of "our itinerant general superintendency" which is protected by a Restrictive Rule. Though our obligation to our assigned areas is of fundamental importance, it does not relieve any of us from a responsibility for the whole Church. This is scarcely understood by bishops and officers of other churches, not to speak of many among our own constituents. It is a role reserved in unique degree for the bishops according to our practice. Many feel that this dimension of our responsibility has diminished, that our general overseership has been replaced by our function as promoters. To the degree that this may be true, we have only ourselves to blame. We can either bog down in trivia or give leadership in larger things: what issues must our church face together with other churches, in what direction shall we proceed. To matters of such magnitude general superintendents must devote their energies. But we must do it together.

The general superintendency is not exercised merely, or even mainly, by the individual bishops but chiefly by the Council as a whole. The collegiality other communions seek is amply provided for us through the Council of Bishops as well as through such other collective contexts as the Colleges and the Conference of Bishops. This has been so at least since 1824. The fact that we have no denominational "head" is heard with never-ending astonishment by the leaders of some of our sister churches. We are a fellowship, but a fellowship with collective responsibilities. We need not all think alike nor act alike and this is good. We possess many talents and are a balance, at least at times, of a variety of interests and concerns. As individualists we are not necessarily drawn together by natural affinities but because we have been elected to commonly shared responsibilities. The very fact of our conciliarity is a corrective of the temptation for us to work in area-tight compartments and is therefore a force working for fuller unity within our church. Our collegial nature affords opportunity for united consultation, problem-solving, review, common planning and projection of programs. The manner in which we discharge these functions is particularly important now as we look to 1972 and beyond. The way we interpret the issues of our times and understand the effects of our behavior and proposals upon others will determine, in turn, their participation and partnership in what we may propose. For we do not function in a vacuum.

Quite evidently the episcopacy, like every other institution and authority in our culture, is under erosive criticism from many quarters: the laity, other ministers, leaders within the bureaucratic structure, the general public. It is complained that we are not aggressive enough in affairs of the church as a whole; not sufficiently effective in promotional effort; not adequately aware of nor articulate about the problems of our society. Fortunately some of the criticism of yesteryear of insensitivity, authoritarianism, arrogance, is less seldom heard today. Each one of us can fill in the details of the presentday critiques. Some of this must be expected and borne valiantly and even gratefully. We may get some comfort from General Matthew Ridgway who somewhere says that the critics should speak frankly "but don't do away with generals." Yet it must be observed that even our severest critics tend to speak with respect and nearly every study expresses the hope that we will be bishops! Undoubtedly our own failures and hesitation have eroded our office far more than its critics have done. Our inescapable obligation for advancing the well-being of the common life of the entire church is very great indeed.

Meanwhile the meaning of episcopacy is under considerable discussion in the currents within and among the churches in our day. One need only mention COCU, COSMOS, dialogue with the Roman Catholics, the work of the Commission on Structure as examples of this. The earthshaking events of our global society, the tragedies and tumults that rock mankind, the agonies of war, the drastic changes wrought by revolution of every kind can scarcely leave the venerable office of bishop untouched. In fact, such forces should help to remold episcopacy. The rapid development of autonomy within our own world-wide fellowship would seem to call for an even more effective Council of Bishops.

Examining Our Mandate

We now turn to an examination of our mandate as a Council of Bishops. Here we will not be dealing with the responsibilities of bishops either as individuals nor in the other concerted settings of the Jurisdictional and Central Conference colleges nor in the world-wide Conference of United Methodist Bishops, which meets quadrennially.

Our mandate is set forth in both the constitutional and legislative portions of the *Discipline.* In all, bishops are referred to one or more times in just over three hundred paragraphs of the *Discipline.* Among these almost exactly *one-third* refer to the *Council of Bishops,* ten times in the Constitution itself.

I. *The Constitution*

Paragraph 52 reads: "There shall be a Council of Bishops composed of all the bishops of The United Methodist Church. The council shall meet at least once a year and plan for the general oversight and promotion of the temporal and spiritual interests of the entire Church and for the carrying into effect the rules, regulations, and responsibilities prescribed and enjoyed by the General Conference and in accord with the provisions set forth in this Plan of Union."

Here quite clearly the sweeping *collective* responsibility of bishops is set forth with regard to oversight, promotional, and executive functions.

Specifically, the Constitution authorizes the Council of Bishops to do the following:

1. To call a special session of a General Conference (13).

2. To select the presiding officer of the opening session of a General Conference (15.11).

3. To determine the dates for the Jurisdictional Conferences (25).

4. To assign episcopal visitors to the Central Conferences (35; 630.4).

5. To assign bishops for temporary presidential or other service or to fill episcopal vacancies in the Jurisdictional or Central Conferences (54). (See also pars. 384; 395; 396; 399.)

6. To appeal by majority vote to Judicial Council to determine the constitutionality of an act of the General Conference (61). (See also 1701.1, 2; 1709.)

7. To canvass results of votes by Annual Conferences on constitutional amendments and announce that those passed are effective (64).

8. By implication other responsibilities, such as to prepare and present the Episcopal Address to General Conference (50).

II. *Legislation*

The legislation regarding the Council of Bishops based on the constitutional provision in paragraph 52 is broad and extensive. The administrative role of the bishops antedated the establishment of any of the general boards and agencies. The role of the Council between the sessions of the General Conference is such that the necessity for a General Council or Council of Administration might be questioned on this ground alone, not to mention other weighty considerations.

A. *General authorizations*

1. To set aside a bishop for a specific church-wide responsibility, for a period of a year (385). (Note: In my view we should soon use this authority or lose it.)

2. To grant a sabbatical to a bishop (386).

3. To promote evangelism (387).

4. Annual orientation for new district superintendents (388).

5. Quadrennial Conference of United Methodist Bishops (389).

6. Assign work to bishop temporarily impaired in health (394).

7. Approve division of seats at General Conference between former E.U.B. and Methodists (602.5).

8. Approval and inauguration of autonomous status for overseas churches (647.3, 4).

9. Relations with Missionary Conferences (656.1).

10. Suggest supplemental questions for Annual Conference agendas (663.4).

11. Special days; special financial appeals; and other fiscal matters (833.6; 833.7; 858.5; 869; 877; 878).

12. Relating to UMCOR (1304; 1311.1.*e*).

13. Relating to Commission on Chaplains (1389. 1.*a*).

14. Commission on Archives and History (1648. 2.*b.f.*).

15. Requests for declaratory decisions, Judicial Council (1707.2; 1715.2).

B. *Visitation or representation* (see 35; 630.4)

1. Mission fields outside Central and Provisional Central Conferences (639).

2. Affiliated Autonomous Churches (644; 647.5).

3. General Conferences of Affiliated Autonomous Churches (642.4).

C. *Convening of meetings*

1. *At General Conference:* Interjurisdictional Committee on Episcopacy—by president of Council (612.1).

2. General Agencies: Program Council (827.2); Social Concerns (988.1); Education (1010.6); Evangelism (1135.1); Missions (1353.1); Quadrennial Commissions (1419.3); (1420.3; 1421.6).

D. *Administration*

1. Council of Bishops *an* agency of administration (801).

2. Relation to Program Council (822.1; 831.12; 836.7).

3. Relation to the Advance (876.6).

4. Remuneration for reactivated retired bishops (890).

5. Report from president of Board of Evangelism (1131).

6. Report and recommendations from Commission on Ecumenical Affairs (1390.2).

7. Annual report of Council of Secretaries to Council of Bishops (1413.2).

8. Authorizing seating of alternate representative, with vote, for bishop absent from agency meeting (812).

9. Presumably the following assignment is in error and should refer to "bishops" rather than "Council of Bishops" (643): "When an Annual or Provisional Annual Conference becomes a part of an affiliated autonomous Methodist church, the Council of Bishops may at its discretion transfer its members who so desire to the conferences from which they went to the mission field." E. *Nominations,* etc. (Does not include roles of Colleges of Bishops)

1. *General:* Allocation of seats on general agencies for former Methodists and former E.U.B. (815.1.*e*).

2. *Nominate:* Secretary of General Conference (606); Council on World Service and Finance (850); Board of Pensions (1375.1.*a*); Commission on Worship (1384.1); Commission on Chaplains and Related Ministries (1389.2); Ecumenical Affairs (1390.1); Methodist Information (1392); World Methodist Council (1414.1); National Christian Council (1415.2); World Council of Churches (1416.2); Religion in American Life (1418); Quadrennial Commissions (1419.2); (1420.2; 1421.4); COSMOS (1422.2); Judicial Council (1701); Trustees (1509); The Methodist Corporation (1518.1).

3. *Elect:* Bishops on Program Council (827.1); Bishop for Committee on Official Forms and Records (855); Bishops on General Board of Publication (930); Bishops on Board of Social Concerns (983); Bishops on Board of Education (1011.1); Bishops on General Committee on Family Life (1077.2); Bishops on Board of Evangelism (1130.1); Bishops on Board of Health and Welfare Ministries (1164); Bishops and laymen at large on Board of Laity (1188); Bishops and some laymen on Board of Missions (1281); Bishops on Board of Pensions (1375.1.*a*).

4. *Name:* Bishops on Interboard Committee on Enlistment (1084.2); Joint Commission on Cooperation and Counsel of the Board of Missions (1356.2).

5. *Appoint:* Ten members of University Senate (1056.1); Bishops on Commission on Archives and History (1401.2); Bishops on Commission on Religion and Race (1423).

6. *Choose:* A Bishop for Committee on Deaconess Service (1324.2).

7. *Vacancies:* Secretary of General Conference (606); Bishops on general agencies unless specified otherwise (813); nominate for vacancy among members at large of Commission on World Service and Finance (850); Bishops on Board of Education (1011.4); same: Board of Laity (1192); Commission on Worship (1384.1); Commission on Chaplains (1389.2); Commission on Ecumenical Affairs (1390.8); N.C.C. (1415.2); W.C.C. (1416.2); Board of Trustees (1509).

Toward a More Effective Council of Bishops

If our thesis is correct that in considerable measure our responsibilities as bishops are fulfilled as and in the Council of Bishops, it follows that we ought constantly to strive to make it as effective as possible. Here all of us will have our thoughts as to how this is to be accomplished. From what I have been able to cull from our records, together with my own reflections, I offer the following:

1. Clearly we ought in every respect to fulfill the abovementioned Disciplinary enactments. This is not just a matter of carrying out an agreed methodology. That only begins the task of oversight of "the temporal and spiritual interests of the entire church." Surely we must find the means of moving more fully into this vaster mandate, and this should now engage our specific and concerted attention.

2. Even such a matter as nominating procedures can be of great significance. Thanks to the careful labors of our secretary we have improved in this respect. Nevertheless it is proposed by many United Methodists that this function should be assumed by a special committee of the General Conference. The bishops should be and are best situated to do this job. I suggest that our Executive Committee bring to our next meeting detailed procedures to be used for 1972. These might be reported to the church for information and we can prepare ourselves to complete this task still better than we have in the past and we can see to fair and equitable representation as well as the infusion of "new blood" into the general agencies. To this end we should come equipped at the appropriate session with specific "profiles" of those whose names are to be considered.

3. We should examine once more the detailed suggestions made to the Council in the Report of the Study of the Episcopacy to the 1964 General Conference, together with any similar study which may have been made by the former E.U.B. Church. Some of these have been acted on but others remain such as:

   a. A handbook for bishops. Could not one of the bishops available under paragraph 395 be assigned to this task?

b. Initiation of a study commission on some crucial contemporary issue. Why not try this?

c. Plan specifically for interchange between the jurisdictions of the annual conference presiding function once during a quadrennium.

d. Initiate systematic and regular liaison with the Council of Secretaries. Perhaps at least *one* day in joint session could be held during a quadrennium. Receive regularly the reports of that body in accordance with paragraph 1413.2.

e. More study of inter-conference transfer of ministers and other appointment matters.

4. In the handbook mentioned in 3.2*a* above, perhaps we could include some by-laws of the Council. These are somewhat mysterious; frequently referred to, they seem to depend on memory and "oral tradition." They might well be reduced to writing.

5. Arrange specifically for annual regional seminars for newly appointed district superintendents, rather than relying on quadrennial meetings which in the past have been excessively promotional in nature (cf. par. 388).

6. The Church has a right to expect us to "speak out" periodically. Therefore let us continue efforts to improve procedures for making "statements" in the name of the Council as well as the caliber of the statements themselves. Bishop William C. Martin has suggested that the Executive Committee and the Message Committee meet jointly in the fall, to choose a suggested theme and that in the interim the statement be worked on and given primary attention in the spring. Why not seek expert help of theologians on a draft when necessary and then make it our own?

7. Continue our overseas visitation but reexamine our procedures periodically.

8. Continue and extend our endeavors in common study as in the visits of professors or the seminar at the

United Nations. Bishop Holloway in 1967 suggested the following issues for our detailed attention: *(a)* racial equality; *(b)* economic justice; *(c)* international affairs; *(d)* the ecumenical movement; *(e)* the new theology. These will need updating from time to time. The research facilities of the general agencies should be understood as being at our disposal for such study and resultant action.

9. Abandon low-risk postures and work at establishing elements of a new style. Possibly we should let it be known that at an announced time during each session our doors are open for those who have a concern to lay before their chief pastors.

10. De-emphasize our having to be involved, constantly *as a Council* in multitude of routine decisions and emphasize the clarification of purpose and the direction to be taken by the Church.

11. In the past we have not hesitated to propose the launching of new efforts. One of our predecessors stated, "Great movements emerge from creative thinking. . . . It is one of the chief services of the episcopacy to the church." Examples from the past are: establishment of the Commission on Chaplains, the Advance, the Crusade for World Order. We should not hesitate, through the Episcopal Address or other channels, to propose specific legislation to the General Conference. Four examples:

a. Legislation to implement the concordat approved by constitutional amendment in 1970 for relations with British Methodism.

b. Consider taking specific initiative *at this session* to meet the request for an Hispanic bishop. This could afford far-reaching evangelistic advance.

c. Correct paragraph 643 mentioned above.

d. Propose a "policy reference" committee for General Conference, so evidently needed at Dallas and St. Louis.

12. Give constant attention to our ecumenical involvement. Two "far out" illustrations: *(a)* Since we meet both fall and spring the same week as the Roman Catholic bishops, why not explore meeting once in the same city and plan one occasion together? *(b)* Why not propose and participate in national gathering on some occasion of all the bishops of all the "episcopal" churches in the U.S.A. or other country? Or at least with our brethren in the black Methodist churches?

13. In situations in which the presence of a representative of the Council of Bishops is urgent or crucial, implement paragraph 812 under which *voting* alternate representative can be present.

14. Consider implementing paragraph 386 for sabbaticals in the near future. Has it so far been used only once?

15. Consider implementing paragraph 385 in the near future; that is, to release one of our number for an important church-wide responsibility. Why not at least release our secretary for this purpose from November till General Conference to serve as full-time secretary—assuming his readiness so to function on our behalf?

16. Endeavor having the agenda for each session of the Council of Bishops sent out several weeks in advance.

17. At each session of the Council have a period set aside for working subcommittees. This we have done to some extent, but let us now assign *every* bishop present to some working committee, either a standing committee or a committee simply designated by number—I, II, III, etc. These could be made to represent every region and concern. These groups would then consider in detail assigned items of business, subsequently making their report and recommendations to the whole Council. This should save time and involve more of our members in depth in the work.

18. In keeping with the above, the Executive Com-

mittee would preferably *not meet during* the regular sessions of the Council but only *ad interim.*

19. The working groups could, among other things, receive reports from bishops who serve on the various general and ecumenical agencies. This would help us in our task of general oversight. These groups might also on their own initiative propose recommendations to the Council as a whole and might themselves on occasion meet *ad interim.*

20. The Council of Bishops ought to be circumspect about referring to other bodies items which they may be best equipped to deal with themselves as general superintendents. An example might be the matter of church union in India which was before us in November 1970.

Conclusion

Such possibilities, among many others, may fruitfully be explored. We could become far more effective spiritual and temporal leaders of our Church and the Church Universal. None of us who heard Bishop Oxnam's final speech in the Council pleading for us to *be* the Council of Bishops could hope for anything else.

We need not be oppressed by any over-riding concern for ourselves and our status but rather continuously yield ourselves to the really significant matters: of seeking and doing God's will and of looking to the total welfare of all men. Our proper posture could scarcely be better than Luther described it for the Christian as free man—"perfectly free lord of all, subject to none . . . perfectly dutiful servant of all, subject to all." To this end may the Holy Spirit empower us and "anoint and cheer our soiléd face, with the abundance of thy grace."

APPENDIX *B*

During 1982–83 a short survey by questionnaire was circulated among United Methodist bishops concerning episcopacy. Although no great claim is made for scientific accuracy in the devising of the instrument and its interpretation, the results show something of how current United Methodist bishops—both active and retired—rate the various aspects of their duties.

I. In the order of importance, as they looked objectively at episcopacy, they listed the following roles:

1. Chief Pastor
2. Appointing Officer
3. General Superintendent
4. Preacher-evangelist
5. Ordaining Officer
6. Teacher
7. Presiding Officer
8. Spiritual Director tied with Ecumenical Leader
9. Promoter
10. Enabler-energizer

There were, of course, other options—thirty-two in all.

II. In response to the question as to which of the possible roles were most satisfying to them, they responded:

1. Chief Pastor
2. Preacher-evangelist

3. Teacher
4. General Superintendent
5. Appointing Officer
6. Presiding Officer
7. Ordaining Officer; Pastoral Counselor; Enabler-energizer; Missional Advocate (all tied)
8. Responsible Prophet
9. Spiritual Director
10. Ecumenical Leader

III. On the other hand, they rated as most distasteful or frustrating the following roles:

1. Troubleshooter
2. Board Member
3. Appointing Officer
4. Public Figure
5. Board Chairman
6. Spokesperson
7. Negotiator-reconciler
8. Promoter-interpreter
9. Father (or Mother)-in-God
10. Social Planner; Responsible Prophet; Manager-administrator; Symbolic Leader (all tied)

Some bishops listed frustrations not appearing on the list: too large an area; too many conferences; too little study time; having to appoint persons who should not be in the ministry; mediocrity in ministry; excessive correspondence; letters of complaint; attendance at so many meetings; clergy couples; moral problems; divorce.

IV. Attention was then turned to *role expectations* from bishops in the view of clergy and laity. Nearly all bishops strongly agreed that ministers had an adequate understanding of what should be expected of episcopal leadership. On the other hand, it was judged that among laity there was about an even division between those who did understand and those who did not understand the episcopal role. Then the bishops listed their own judgment as to the order of most important and least important of episcopal roles as perceived by ministers and laity:

Ministers:

Roles Most Understood:	Roles Least Understood:
1. Appointing Officer	1. Limited power of bishop
2. Presiding Officer	2. Responsible Prophet
3. Chief Pastor	3. Teacher
4. Ordaining Officer	4. General Superintendent
5. Preacher-evangelist	5. Liturgical Officer

Laity:

Roles Most Understood:	Roles Least Understood:
1. Appointing Officer	1. Work load; demands on time
2. Presiding Officer	
3. Chief Pastor/ Preacher-evangelist	2. Responsible Prophet
	3. General Superintendent
4. Ordaining Officer	4. Teacher
5. General Superintendent	5. Scholar-writer

V. *Episcopal Authority*

A. The bishops themselves reported that they were able to live with their episcopal authority relatively well. The majority agreed strongly with this. Only three felt otherwise and three were neutral.

B. They also perceived that most *ministers* of their areas were able to live with episcopal authority relatively well. One disagreed strongly and five were neutral.

C. As to *laity* on the same question, again the majority agreed, and some strongly. One disagreed and three were neutral.

VI. The next question concerned support groups related

to bishops. The bishops listed in the order of importance the following support groups:

A.   1. Family
      2. Cabinet
      3. Council of Bishops
      4. College of Bishops
      5. Conference Staff
      6. Individual Bishops
      7. Friends
      8. Committee on Episcopacy
      9. Counterparts in other Denominations
     10. Lay Leaders; Clergy

B. On the other hand, the bishops compiled a long list of factors of support/satisfaction they had enjoyed in their work before their election as bishops, and which they now miss. Strongly stressed were:

—Caring congregation and sense of community on college campus; closeness with faculty in seminaries
—Camaraderie of fellow pastors
—Close, long-term, and in-depth relationship with laity

In lesser degree were listed:

—Miss pastoral involvement
—Scholarly study which seemed more readily possible before becoming bishop

Three bishops felt they missed nothing of their preepiscopacy experience.

VII. In response to a question of value of the Annual Conference/Area Committee(s) on Episcopacy, bishops overall felt this was satisfactory. Two were negative with respect to the value of these committees, one strongly so, and seven were neutral.

VIII. The bishops reported overwhelmingly that they regarded the structures of accountability for United Methodist bishops to be adequate. Almost all reported affirmatively; only six negatively.

IX. The bishops were then asked to react to frequently reported areas of conflict or frustration. Not all responded to this question, but to those who did the following seven areas of conflict or frustration were high on their lists:

1. Time for study and reflection
2. Time for adequate spiritual discipline
3. Clergy divorce
4. Clergy moral problems
5. Time management
6. Inadequate time with families
7. Morale of ministers

To a lesser degree were

—"Working" the consultative process
—Loneliness and isolation
—Issues of a political nature
—Adequate secretarial help

X. Each bishop was asked to list three goals for personal continuing education. The great majority (95%) stressed spiritual growth—formation—renewal and a more disciplined spiritual life as their first goal. This was followed by

—More adequate biblical studies
—Management skills
—Mission of church in world and in society
—Time for research; reading
—Disciplined study of theology
—Wesleyan theology
—Study of contemporary issues facing church and society
—Keeping up with current theological thought and changing patterns of ministry
—Ethical and social questions and resolutions
—Possibilities of spiritual healing
—To provide fresh vision for Annual Conferences
—To study computer science
—Church growth and evangelism.

—Appreciation for those who represent different priorities

One commented: "We need help in experiencing connectionalism."

XI. A. The bishops were asked to indicate whether or not they had found the Renewal Leave (par. 510.1 in *Discipline,* first provided for in 1976) helpful. All but two of those who had so far had opportunity to have such leave reported affirmatively on it.

B. All reported affirmatively on the usefulness of overseas visitation (provided for once a quadrennium since 1948).

C. The following areas were listed as those in which bishops, particularly recently elected ones, would welcome help or open discussion, possibly through the Council of Bishops:

—More corporate study of issues facing church and society

—Changing role of women, especially as it affects clergy marriage

—Consultative process, especially as it deals with spouse professions

—Sharing experiences dealing with crisis and difficult decisions

—Discussion of area administration—too many "administrative assistants" and "conference executives"

—Planning for long-range future

—Administration and management

—More scholarly presentations on theological, ethical,

and substantive matters from Council of Bishops members

—Time scheduling.

XII. The last item read: "You are inivited to write a

paragraph on 'What is a Successful Bishop?' " Most did not like the way the question was put. They were understandably reluctant to respond in terms of *success*. Some preferred the adjective *faithful* rather than *successful*. A few of the responses follow:

. . . "one who can and does interpret and exemplify the Church's own best nature—a covenant community of Christ's people. He/she takes his/her ministry with great seriousness, himself/herself with not too much."

. . . "one who renews continuously ordination vows— and reflects seriously on consecration vows."

. . . "one who recognizes that he/she is only one link in the chain of continuity of the church. His/her oversight of temporal affairs is important but the oversight of spiritual affairs is critical."

. . . "one who provides spiritual and dynamic leadership in those places where their gifts, training and experience best qualify them, but not neglecting either their general superintendency or their area's assignments."

. . . one who "is consecrated as an episcopal leader who maintains intimate contact with God and also with humanity; one who is more concerned with the agony and suffering of the world around about than in maintaining a position of prestige."

. . . "one who was leading (by teaching and example) both laity and pastors into a deeper convenantal relationship with God, Christ and the Holy Spirit."

. . . "one who is effective when he/she empowers and enables other persons to be effective in ministry."

. . . "we do the best we can, lay it at the foot of the cross—let Him have it, hopefully, to make some divine or gracious use of it."

. . . one who "accepts his/her election both as a mandate from the Church and with a joyous expression in giving of self freely for the cause for which elected."

. . . one who "accepts responsibilities of the episcopal office with a firm conviction that there is available from divine and human resources sufficient strength for each task."

. . . one who "never loses the human touch in the labyrinth of episcopal duties."

. . . one who "can be identified by four standards: first is the leadership capability of the District Superintendents appointed; these 'lieutenants' determine the morale of both pastors and congregations more than any other factor. Second is the accessibility of the bishop to both pastors and laity; the more the bishop is known personally the more influence that bishop will have both in programming and in the interpretation of Christian faith. Third is the commitment of the bishop to the program of the church; both in mission promotion and in spiritual growth, the Bishop's declared support merits cooperation by pastors and people. And fourth, the ecumenical involvements of the bishop and the resulting relationship with the wider religious community reflect the response to the bishop's stature by a community external to the immediate associations."

. . . "one who is a senior pastor and holds in his/her concerns the needs of pastors and families. The role must include decision making, administrative responsibilities, and leadership. These and other assignments must be carried in the context of a pastor. Preaching is important as an image of the role for other ministers. He/she must lead by proclamation, and example."

. . . "one who is genuinely dedicated to the Gospel, the Universal Church, and the United Methodist Church. . . . He/she takes seriously the responsibilities of appointment-making, including the Consultative process, works closely with Cabinets and Staffs, speaks clearly on vital issues, and offers himself/herself as a servant of God and His people."

. . . "one who takes as his first duty the supervision of his own area and the Conferences entrusted to him/her. That means both the temporal and spiritual leadership of the area. . . . The bishop should . . . work with his cabinet but should not be dominated by them. His is the responsibility."

Finally a word from the late Bishop Gabriel Sundaram: "A successful or faithful bishop is not selfish and does not use his authority to secure material benefits for himself or his family. He is modest, and does not parade his position or use excessive episcopal regalia. He is fearless and does not make decisions to mollify people. He does not encourage flattery. He is just. He is not revengeful. He is willing to take advice from people and is a good listener. He has the intelligence and vision to plan for the development of the various departments of the church. He does not take upon himself too many burdens and shares responsibility with others. He picks out intelligent and devoted young men and helps them to get the best ministerial training. He is interested in world evangelism and a world church. He is a deeply devoted man and has time for Bible study and prayer. He works and prays hard for evangelism. He is the Chief Pastor of his Area."

SELECTED BIBLIOGRAPHY

This bibliography includes all works cited in the text and a selection from the vast array of materials examined as a background for this study.

Source Books

Asbury, Francis. *The Journal and Letters of Francis Asbury.* Ed. Elmer T. Clark et al. 3 vols. London: Epworth Press; Nashville: Abingdon Press, 1958.

Bangs, Nathan. *A History of the Methodist Episcopal Church.* 4 vols. New York: Mason & Lane, 1839.

Boehm, Henry. *Reminiscences.* New York: Nelson & Phillips, 1875.

Coke, Thomas. *A Sermon.* New York: Mason & Lane, 1840.

———. *Extracts of the Journals of the Rev. Dr. Coke's Five Visits to America.* London: G. Paramore, 1793.

Cooper, Ezekiel. Papers. Garrett-Evangelical Theological Seminary, Evanston, Illinois.

Garrettson, Freeborn. *The Experiences and Travels of Mr. Freeborn Garrettson.* Philadelphia: John Dickins, 1791.

King, Peter. *An Inquiry into the Constitution, Discipline, Unity and Worship of the Primitive Church* (first 300 years). New York: Lane & Sandford, 1841.

Lee, Jesse. *A Short History of the Methodists.* Baltimore: Magill & Clime, 1810.

Pilmoor, Joseph. Journal. The Historical Center Library, Old St. George, Philadelphia.

Stillingfleet, Edward (Bishop). *Irenicum.* Philadelphia: M. Sorin, 1842.

Ware, Thomas. *Sketches of the Life and Travels of Rev. Thomas Ware.* New York: Mason & Lane, 1839.

Wesley, Charles. *Journal.* 2 vols. 1849. Reprint. Grand Rapids, Mich.: Baker Book House, 1980.

Wesley, John. *Explanatory Notes Upon the New Testament.* London: Bowyer, 1755.

——. *Explanatory Notes Upon the Old Testament.* 3 vols. Bristol: Pine, 1765.

——. *The Sunday Service of the Methodists in North America.* Intro. by James M. White. Commemorative reprint. Nashville: United Methodist Publishing House, 1984.

——. *The Journal of the Rev. John Wesley, A.M.* Ed. Nehemiah Curnock. Standard ed. 8 vols. London: Epworth Press, 1938.

——. *The Works of the Rev. John Wesley, A.M.* Ed. Thomas Jackson. 14 vols. London: John Mason, 1856.

——. *Wesley's Standard Sermons.* Ed. Edward H. Sugden. 2 vols. London: Epworth Press, 1921.

——. *The Letters of the Rev. John Wesley, A.M.* Ed. John Telford. Standard ed. 8 vols. London: Epworth Press, 1931.

——, ed. *Arminian Magazine.* London: Fry, Paramore, etc., 1778–1797. Continued as the *Methodist Magazine,* 1798–1821, and as the *Wesleyan Methodist Magazine,* 1822–1913.

——, ed. *A Christian Library,* 30 vols. London: Blanshard, 1750ff.

Doctrines and Discipline of The Methodist Episcopal Church in America, with explanatory notes by Thomas Coke and Francis Asbury, 1798.

Daily Christian Advocate. Proceedings of the General Conference of The Methodist Church, 1940–1968.

Documents of Vatican II. Ed. Walter M. Abbott, SJ. New York: America Press, 1963.

General Conference *Journals,* 1792–1980.

Minutes of the Council of Bishops, 1939–1984.

Minutes of the Methodist Conferences from 1744–1798. London: Mason, 1862.

Report of Debates in the General Conference of The Methodist Episcopal Church, Held in the City of New York, 1844. New York: Lane & Tippett, 1844.

Biographies of John Wesley

Ayling, Stanley. *John Wesley*. Nashville: Abingdon Press, 1979.

Cell, George C. *The Rediscovery of John Wesley*. New York: Henry Holt & Co., 1935

Green, V. H. H. *John Wesley*. London: Nelson, 1964.

Haddal, Ingvar. *John Wesley*. Nashville: Abingdon Press, 1961.

Lean, Garth. *John Wesley, Anglican*. London: Blandford Press, 1964.

McConnell, Francis J. *John Wesley*. New York: Abingdon Press, 1939.

Schmidt, Martin. *John Wesley*. 2 vols. Nashville: Abingdon Press, 1962.

Southey, Robert. *The Life of Wesley; and the Rise and Progress of Methodism*. Ed. Maurice H. Fitzgerald. 2 vols. London: Oxford University Press, 1925.

Thompson, Edgar W. *Wesley: Apostolic Man*. London: Epworth Press, 1957.

Tyerman, Luke. *The Life and Times of the Rev. John Wesley, M. A.* 3 vols. London: Hodder and Stoughton, 1870–71.

Watson, Richard. *The Life of the Rev. John Wesley, A.M.* New York: Waugh and Mason, 1836.

Other Books on John Wesley

Baker, Frank. *John Wesley and the Church of England*. Nashville: Abingdon Press, 1970.

Cannon, William. *The Theology of John Wesley*. Nashville: Abingdon-Cokesbury Press, 1946.

Heitzenrater, Richard P. *The Elusive Mr. Wesley*. 2 vols. Nashville: Abingdon Press, 1984.

Lawson, A. B. *John Wesley and the Christian Ministry*. London: S.P.C.K., 1963.

Piette, Maximin. *John Wesley in the Evolution of Protestantism*. Trans. J. B. Howard. New York: Sheed and Ward, 1937.

Stephen, David S. *Wesley and Episcopacy*. Pittsburgh: Methodist Protestant Publishing House, 1892.

Williams, Colin W. *John Wesley's Theology Today*. Nashville: Abingdon Press, 1960.

Miscellaneous Biographies and Autobiographies

Allen, Richard. *The Life Experiences and Gospel Labors of the Rt. Rev. Richard Allen, Written by Himself.* Intro. by George A. Singleton. Bicentennial ed. Nashville: Abingdon Press, 1960.

Candler, Warren A. *Life of Thomas Coke.* Nashville: Publishing House of the Methodist Episcopal Church, South, 1923.

Clark, D. W. *Life and Times of Rev. Elijah Hedding.* New York: Carlton & Phillips, 1855.

Crooks, George R. *The Life of Bishop Matthew Simpson.* New York: Harper & Bros., 1890.

Drew, Samuel. *The Life of the Rev. Thomas Coke.* New York: J. Soule and T. Mason, 1818.

Du Bose, Horace M. *Life of Joshua Soule.* Nashville: Publishing House of the Methodist Episcopal Church, South, 1916.

Feeman, Harlan L. *Francis Asbury's Silver Trumpet (Nicholas Snethen).* Nashville: Parthenon Press, 1950.

Flood, Theodore L., and John W. Hamilton, eds. *Lives of Methodist Bishops.* New York: Phillips and Hunt, 1882.

Gill, Frederick C. *Charles Wesley, the First Methodist.* Nashville: Abingdon Press, 1964.

Graveley, William B. *Gilbert Haven.* Nashville: Abingdon Press, 1973.

Grose, Geroge R. *James W. Bashford.* New York: The Methodist Book Concern, 1922.

Harris, C. D. *Alpheus W. Wilson.* Louisville: Board of Christian Extension, Methodist Episcopal Church, South, 1917.

Hoss, E. E. *William McKendree.* Nashville: Publishing House of the Methodist Episcopal Church, South, 1916.

MacClenny, W. E. *The Life of Rev. James O'Kelly.* Raleigh, N.C.: Edwards and Broughton, 1910.

McConnell, Francis J. *By the Way.* New York: Abingdon-Cokesbury Press, 1952.

Maser, Frederick E. *Robert Strawbridge.* Baltimore: Strawbridge Shrine Association, Baltimore, 1983.

Paine, Robert. *Life and Times of William M'Kendree.* 2 vols. Nashville: Publishing House of the Methodist Episcopal Church, South, 1874.

Phoebus, William, ed. *Memoirs of the Rev. Richard Whatcoat.* New York: Joseph Allen, 1828.

Rudolph, L. C. *Francis Asbury.* Nashville: Abingdon Press, 1966.

Spellman, Norman W. *Growing a Soul: The Story of A. Frank Smith.* Dallas: Southern Methodist University Press, 1979.

Taylor, William. *Story of My Life.* New York: Hunt and Eaton, 1895.

General Books

Albright, Raymond W. *A History of the Evangelical Church.* Harrisburg, Pa: Evangelical Press, 1942.

Anciaux, Paul. *The Episcopate in the Church.* Staten Island, N.Y.: Alba House, 1965.

Anderson, William K., ed. *Methodism.* Nashville: Methodist Publishing House, 1947.

Asheim, Ivar, and Victor R. Gold. *Episcopacy in the Lutheran Church.* Philadelphia: Fortress Press, 1970.

Augustine. *City of God.* Edinburgh: J. Grant, 1909.

Bacon, G. C. *The Polity of the Methodist Episcopal Church and Proposed Modification.* Baltimore: Baltimore Methodist Conference, 1895.

Baker, Frank, ed. *Representative Verse of Charles Wesley.* Nashville: Abingdon Press, 1962.

Baker, Gordon Pratt, ed. *Those Incredible Methodists.* Baltimore: Baltimore Annual Conference, 1972.

Baker, Osmon C. *A Guide-book in the Administration of The Discipline.* New York: Phillips and Hunt, 1884.

Barclay, Wade C. *History of Methodist Missions.* 4 vols. New York: Board of Missions, The Methodist Church, 1949, 1950, 1957.

Barton, Jesse H. *"The Definition of the Episcopal Office in American Methodism."* Ph.D. diss., Drew University, 1960.

Bassett, Ancel H. *Concise History of the Methodist Protestant Church.* Pittsburgh: James Robison, 1877.

Behney, J. Bruce, and Paul H. Eller. *The History of the Evangelical United Brethren Church.* Nashville: Abingdon Press, 1979.

Benson, Joseph. *An Apology for the People Called Methodists.* London: Story and Whitfield, 1801.

Benson, Robert L. *The Bishop-elect: A Study in Medieval Ecclesiastical Office.* Princeton, N.J.: Princeton University Press, 1968.

Berger, Daniel. *History of the Church of the United Brethren in Christ.* Dayton: United Brethren Publishing House, 1897.

Bertrams, Wilhelm. *The Papacy, the Episcopacy and Collegiality.* Westminster, Md.: Newman Press, 1964.

Bibbins, R. M. *How Methodism Came.* Baltimore: Baltimore Annual Conference, 1945.

Bowen, Elias. *History of the Origin of the Free Methodist Church.* Rochester, N.Y.: B. T. Roberts, 1871.

Bowen, John. *Robert Strawbridge and the Rise and Progress of Methodism.* Westminster: privately printed, 1856. Reprint. Baltimore. Strawbridge Shrine Association, n.d.

Bowmer, John C. *The Sacrament of the Lord's Supper in Early Methodism.* London: Dacre Press, 1951.

Brandreth, Henry, R. T. *Episcopi Vagantes and the Anglican Church.* London: S.P.C.K., 1961.

Brannan, Emora T. *"The Presiding Elder Question."* Ph.D. diss., Duke University, 1974.

Brown, Raymond E. *The Community of the Beloved Disciple.* New York: Paulist Press, 1979.

―――. *Priest and Bishop, Biblical Reflections.* New York: Paulist Press, 1970.

Brown, Raymond E., and John P. Meier. *Antioch and Rome: New Testament Cradles of Catholic Christianity.* New York: Paulist Press, 1983.

Bucke, Emory Stevens et al. eds. *The History of American Methodism.* 3 vols. Nashville: Abingdon Press, 1964.

Buckley, James Monroe. *Constitutional and Parliamentary History of the Methodist Episcopal Church.* New York: Eaton & Mains, 1912.

Cameron, Richard M. *Methodism and Society.* Vol. 1, *In Historical Perspective.* Nashville: Abingdon Press, 1961.

Caplan, Ruth B. *Helping the Helpers to Help.* New York: Seabury Press, 1972.

Carey, Kenneth M., ed. *The Historic Episcopate.* Westminster: Dacre Press, 1954.

Carrington, Philip. *The Early Christian Church.* 2 vols. Cambridge: University Press, 1957.

Congar, Yves. *Lay People in the Church.* Westminster: Newman, 1957.

Cooke, George Alfred. *The Episcopacy and the General Conference of the Methodist Episcopal Church.* Baltimore: W. V. Guthrie, 1912.

Cooke, R. J. *The Historic Episcopate.* New York: Eaton and Mains, 1896.

————. *History of the Ritual of the Methodist Episcopal Church.* New York: Eaton and Mains, 1900.

Core, Arthur C. *Philip William Otterbein.* Dayton: Board of Publication, Evangelical United Brethren Church, 1968.

Cross, Frank M., Jr. *The Ancient Library of Qumran and Modern Biblical Studies.* Garden City, N. Y.: Doubleday, 1958.

Cullmann, Oscar. *Peter.* Philadelphia: Westminster Press, 1953.

————. *Early Church.* Philadelphia: Westminster Press, 1956.

Davies, Rupert E. *Methodism.* London: Pelican Books, 1963.

Davies, Rupert E., and Gordon E. Rupp, eds. *A History of the Methodist Church in Great Britain.* Vol. 1. London: Epworth Press, 1965.

Dix, Gregory. *The Shape of the Liturgy.* 1945. Reprint. Westminster: Dacre Press, 1946, 1947, 1949, 1952, 1954.

————. "The Ministry in the Early Church." In *The Apostolic Ministry.* London: Hodder and Stoughton, 1946.

Douglas, C. E. *Constitutional Episcopacy.* London: Faith Press, 1932.

Du Bose, Horace M. *A History of Methodism, 1884–1916.* Nashville: Lamar and Smith, 1916.

Durrwell, F. X. *The Apostolate and the Church.* Denville, N.J.: Dimension Books, 1973.

Easton, Burton Scott. *The Apostolic Tradition of Hippolytus.* London: Archon Books, 1962.

Ehrhardt, Arnold. *The Apostolic Ministry.* London: Oliver and Boyd, 1958.

Elliott, J. H. *The Elect and the Holy.* Supplements to *Novum Testamentum.* Leiden: Brill, 1966.

Emory, Robert. *Early Disciplines of the Methodist Episcopal Church.* New York: Nelson & Phillips, 1876.

Empie, Paul C., and T. Austin Murphy. *Eucharist and Ministry: Lutherans and Catholics in Dialogue.* Vol. 4. Minneapolis: Augsburg Publishing House, 1979.

Fitzgerald, W. B. *The Roots of Methodism.* London: Charles H. Kelly, 1903.

Gagarin, S. J. *The Russian Clergy.* Reprint. New York: AMS Press, 1872.

Gerdes, Egon W. *Informed Ministry.* Zurich: Publishing House of the United Methodist Church, 1976.

Goodloe, Robert W. "The Office of Bishop in the Methodist Church" Ph.D. diss., University of Chicago, 1929.

———. *The Principles and Development of Methodist Church Government.* Nashville: Cokesbury Press, 1932.

Gregory, J. Robinson. *A History of Methodism.* 2 vols. London: Charles H. Kelly, 1911.

Guirey, William. *The History of Episcopacy.* London: Charles H. Kelly, 1911.

Hand, J. W. *One Hundred Years of Zion Methodism.* Charlotte: African Methodist Episcopal Zion Publishing House, 1895.

Harmon, Nolan B. *The Rites and Ritual of Episcopal Methodism.* Nashville: Publishing House of the Methodist Episcopal Church, South, 1926.

———. *Understanding The United Methodist Church.* Rev. ed. Nashville: Abingdon Press, 1977.

Harnack, Adolph von. *The Constitution and Law of the Church in the First Two Centuries.* New York: G. P. Putnam and Sons, 1910.

Harris, William L. *The Constitutional Powers of the General Conference.* Cincinnati: Methodist Book Concern, 1860.

————. *Rulings of Bishops.* Cincinnati: Cranston and Stowe, 1886.

————. *The Relation of the Episcopacy to the General Conference.* New York: Eaton and Mains, 1888.

Hatch, Edwin. *The Organization of the Early Church.* London: Rivingtons, 1881.

Headlam, Arthur C. *The Doctrine of the Church and Christian Reunion.* New York: Longmans, Green and Co., 1920.

Heal, Felicity. *Of Prelates and Princes.* Cambridge: Cambridge University Press, 1980.

Herbert, A. G. *Apostle and Bishop.* London: Faber and Faber, 1963.

Hooker Richard. *Of the Laws of Ecclesiastical Polity.* London: printed for W. Clark, 1821.

————. *Works.* Ed. John Keble. Revised by R. W. Church and F. Paget. 3 vols. Oxford: University Press, 1881.

Hughes, Philip. *The Church in Crisis: A History of the General Councils, 325–1870.* Garden City, N.Y.: Hanover House, 1960.

Hurst, John F., ed. *The History of Methodism.* 7 vols. New York: Eaton and Mains, 1892.

Irenaeus, Saint. *Five Books of St. Irenaeus Against Heresies.* London: W. Smth, 1872.

Kelley, Francis C. *Sacerdos et Pontifex.* Patterson, N.J.: St. Anthony Guild Press, 1942.

Kerley, T. A. *Conference Rights* (Methodist Episcopal Church, South). Nashville: Publishing House of the M.E.C., South, 1898.

Kirk, Kenneth E., ed. *The Apostolic Ministry.* London: Hodder and Stoughton, 1946.

Kleist, James A. *Ancient Christian Writers.* Westminster, Newman Press, 1961.

Konidaris, D. G. I. *Of the Supposed Difference of the Forms of Constitution in Primitive Christianity (34–156).* 3 vols. Athens: Akademie of Athens, 1956.

Koontz, Paul R., and Walter E. Roush. *The Bishops, Church of the United Brethren in Christ.* 2 vols. Dayton: Otterbein Press, 1950.

Küng, Hans. *The Church.* New York: Sheed & Ward, 1967.

Lawson, John. *Methodism and Catholicism.* London: S.P.C.K., 1954.

Leete, Frederick D. *Methodist Bishops.* Nashville: Parthenon Press, 1948.

Lightfoot, J. B. *The Apostolic Fathers.* (2 parts. 3 vols. London: Macmillan, 1890.

————. *Saint Paul's Epistle to the Philippians.* London: Macmillan, 1890.

Lindsay, Thomas M. *The Church and the Ministry in the Early Centuries.* London: Hodder and Stoughton, 1902.

M'Caine, Alexander. *Letters on the Organization and Early History, of the Methodist Episcopal Church.* Boston: Norris, 1850.

McKenzie, John L. *Authority in the Church.* New York: Sheed & Ward, 1966.

McLeister, Ira F. *History of the Wesleyan Methodist Church of America.* Syracuse: Wesleyan Methodist Publishing Assn., 1934.

McTyeire, Holland N. *A Manual of the Discipline of the Methodist Episcopal Church, South.* Nashville: A. H. Redford, 1874.

————. *A History of Methodism.* Nashville: Publishing House of the Methodist Episcopal Church, South, 1894.

MacVey, William Pitt. *The Genius of Methodism.* Cincinnati: Jennings & Pye, 1903.

Magee, J. C. *Apostolic Organism.* New York: Hunt & Easton, 1890.

Manson, Thomas W. *The Church's Ministry.* Philadelphia: Westminster Press, 1948.

Marshall, John. *General Conference Powers.* New York: Methodist Book Concern, 1930.

Mason, A. J. *The Church of England and Episcopacy.* Cambridge: Cambridge University Press, 1914.

Mathews, Donald G. *Slavery and Methodism.* Princeton, N.J.: Princeton University Press, 1965.

Merrill, S. M. *A Digest of Methodist Law.* Cincinnati: Methodist Book Concern, 1912.

Meyendorff, John. *Orthodoxy and Catholicity.* New York: Sheed & Ward, 1966.

————., ed. *The Primacy of Peter in the Orthodox Church.* London: Faith Press, 1963.

Milhouse, Paul W. *Nineteen Bishops of the Evangelical United Brethren Church.* Nashville: Parthenon Press, 1974.

————. *Theological and Historical Roots of United Methodists.* Oklahoma City: Cowan Printing and Lithographic Co., 1980.

Mills, Frederick V. *Bishops by Ballot.* New York: Oxford University Press, 1978.

Mitchell, Joseph. *Episcopal Elections in the Southeastern Jurisdiction of The United Methodist Church.* Troy, Ala.: Troy State University, 1972.

————. *There is an Election!* Troy, Ala.: Leader Press, 1981.

Moede, Gerald F. *The Office of Bishop in Methodism.* Nashville: Abingdon Press, 1964.

Moffatt, James. *The First Five Centuries of the Church.* Nashville: Abingdon-Cokesbury Press, 1938.

Monk, Robert C. *John Wesley, His Puritan Heritage.* Nashville: Abingdon Press, 1966.

Moore, John M. *The Long Road to Methodist Union.* Nashville: Abingdon-Cokesbury Press, 1943.

————. "The Story of Unification." In *Methodism,* ed. William K. Anderson. Nashville: The Methodist Publishing House, 1947.

Morris, Joan. *The Lady was a Bishop.* New York: Macmillan, 1973.

Muelder, Walter G. *Methodism and Society.* Vol. 2, *In the Twentieth Century.* Nashville: Abingdon Press, 1961.

Neely, Thomas B. *The Bishops and the Supervisional System of the Methodist Episcopal Church.* Cincinnati: Jennings & Graham, 1912.

————. *The Evolution of Episcopacy and Organic Methodism.* New York: Phillips & Hunt, 1888.

———. *A History of the Origin and Development of the Governing Conference in Methodism*. New York: Phillips & Hunt, 1892.

———. *Vital Points in The Methodist Episcopal Church*. Philadelphia: Methodist Episcopal Book Store, 1924.

Neill, Stephen C. *Anglicanism*. Harmondsworth, Middlesex: Penguin Books, 1958.

Niebuhr, H. Richard. *The Social Sources of Denominationalism*. New York: Henry Holt & Co., 1929.

Niebuhr, H. Richard, and Daniel D. Williams. eds. *The Ministry In Historical Perspectives*. New York: Harper & Bros., 1956.

Norwood, Frederick A. *The Story of American Methodism*. Nashville: Abingdon Press, 1974.

Norwood, John N. *The Schism in the Methodist Episcopal Church, 1844: A Study of Slavery and Ecclesiastical Politics*. Alfred, N.Y.: Alfred University Press, 1923.

Outler, Albert C. *The Works of John Wesley*. Vol. 1. Nashville: Abingdon Press, 1984.

———., ed. *John Wesley*. New York: Oxford University Press, 1964.

Porter, Joseph. *The Revised Compendium of Methodism*. New York: Phillips & Hunt, 1875.

Power, David N. *Ministries of Christ and His Church: The Theology of the Priesthood*. London: G. Chapman, 1969.

Rahner, Karl. *The Episcopate and the Primacy:* New York: Herder & Herder, 1963.

———. *Bishops: Their Status and Function*. London: Burns & Oates, 1964.

Ramsay, W. M. *The Church and the Roman Empire*. New York: G. P. Putnam's Sons, 1893.

Rattenbury, N. Morley. *Episcopacy*. London: Epworth Press, 1964.

Rattenbury, J. Ernest. *Wesley's Legacy to the World*. London: Epworth Press, 1938.

———. *The Eucharistic Hymns of John and Charles Wesley*. London: Epworth Press, 1948.

Richardson, Cyril C. ed. *Early Christian Fathers*. Philadelphia: Westminster Press, 1953.

Robinson, J. Armitage, "The Primitive Ministry." In *Essays on The Early History of The Church and The Ministry,* ed. H. B. Swete (1921).

Romanides, John S. *The Ecclesiology of St. Ignatius of Antioch.* Atlanta: International Printing Co., 1956.

Sanford, Arthur B., and Henry W. Rogers. *Reports of the Committee on Judiciary of the General Conference of the Methodist Episcopal Church.* New York: Methodist Book Concern, 1924.

Schillebeeckx, Edward. *Ministry.* New York: Crossroads, 1981.

―――., ed. *The Unifying Role of the Bishop.* New York: Herder and Herder, 1972.

Short, Roy H. *Chosen to be Consecrated.* Lake Junaluska, N.C.: Commission on Archives and History, United Methdist Church, 1976.

―――. *History of the Council of Bishops of The United Methodist Church, 1939–1979.* Nashville: Abingdon Press, 1980.

Sledge, Robert Watson. *Hands on the Ark.* Lake Junaluska, N.C.: Commission on Archives and History, United Methodist Church, 1975.

Snethen, Nicholas. *Essays on Lay Representation.* Baltimore: John J. Harrod, 1835.

Spaulding, John Franklin. *The Church and Its Apostolic Ministry.* Milwaukee: The Young Churchman, 1887.

Spayth, Henry G., and William Hanby. *History of the Church of the United Brethren in Christ.* Circleville, Ohio: Conference Office of the United Brethren in Christ, 1851.

Spellman, Norman W., *"The General Superintendency in American Methodism, 1784–1870."* Ph.D. diss., Yale University, 1961.

Stevens, Abel. *History of the Methodist Episcopal Church.* 4 vols. New York: Nelson & Phillips, n.d.

―――. *An Essay on Church Polity.* New York: Carlton & Phillips, 1853.

Stone, D. *Episcopacy and Valid Orders in the Primitive Church.* London: n.p., 1926.

Straughn, James H. "The Episcopacy." In *Methodism,* ed. William Anderson. Nashville: Methodist Publishing House, 1947.

———. *Inside Methodist Union.* Nashville: Methodist Publishing House, 1958.

Strawson, William. *Salvation—By Faith or By Bishops.* London: Epworth Press, 1964.

Streeter, B. H. *The Primitive Church.* New York: Macmillan, 1929.

Sundkler, Bengt. *Nathan Soderblom.* Lund: Gleerups, 1968.

Sweet, William W. "Religion on the American Frontier." In *The Methodists,* vol. 4. Chicago: University of Chicago Press, 1946.

———. *Methodism in American History.* Nashville: Abingdon Press, 1964.

Swidler, Leonard and Arlene Swidler, trans. and eds. *Bishops and People.* Philadelphia: Westminster Press, 1970.

Sykes, Norman. *Church and State in England in the XVIIIth Century.* Cambridge: Cambridge University Press, 1934.

———. *Old Priest and New Presbyter.* Cambridge: Cambridge University Press, 1956.

Tees, Francis H. *The Beginnings of Methodism in England and in America.* Nashville: Parthenon Press, 1940.

Telfer, W. *The Office of Bishop.* London: Darton, Longman and Todd, 1962.

Thompson, Robert Ellis. *The Historic Episcopate.* Philadelphia: Westminster Press, 1910.

Tigert, John J. *The Making of Methodism.* Nashville: Publishing House of the Methodist Episcopal Church, South, 1894.

———. *A Constitutional History of American Episcopal Methodism.* 6th ed. Nashville: Publishing House of the Methodist Episcopal Church, South, 1916.

Tuell, Jack M. *The Organization of the United Methodist Church.* Rev. ed. Nashville: Abingdon Press, 1982.

Turner, H. M. *Methodist Polity.* Northbrook, Ill.: Metro Books, 1972.

Von Campenhausen, Hans. *Ecclesiastical Authority and Spirit-*

ual Power in the Church of the First Three Centuries. Stanford: Stanford University Press, 1969.

Wade, W. N. "A History of Public Worship in the Methodist Episcopal Church." Ph.D. diss., Ann Arbor, Mich.: University of Minneapolis International, 1981.

Warren, William F. *Constitutional Law Questions.* New York: Hunt and Eaton, 1894.

Washburn, Paul A. *An Unfinished Church.* Nashville: Abingdon Press, 1984.

Williams, George H. *The Mind of John Paul II.* New York: Seabury Press, 1981.

Williams, James R. *History of the Methodist Protestant Church.* Baltimore: Book Committee of the Methodist Protestant Church, 1843.

Wood, E. M. *Bishops and Legislation.* Pittsburgh: Joseph Horner Book Co., 1903.

Worley, Harry Wescott. *The Central Conference of the Methodist Episcopal Church.* Foochow, China: Christian Herald Mission Press, 1940.

Wright, John A. *People and Preachers in the Methodist Episcopal Church.* Philadelphia: J. B. Lippincott, 1886.

Controversy

Bangs, Nathan. *Methodist Episcopacy.* New York: Tract Society of the Methodist Episcopal Church, n.d.

———. *Vindication of Methodist Episcopacy.* New York: Bangs and Mason, 1820.

———. *The Reviewer Answered.* New York: Emory and Waugh, 1830.

———. *An Original Church of Christ (or a Scriptural Vindication of the Orders and Powers of the Ministry of The Methodist Episcopal Church).* New York: Mason & Lane, 1837.

Bolles, James A. *The Episcopal Church Defended.* Batavia, N.Y.: Frederick Follett, n.d. (ca. 1842).

Bronson, Asahel. *A Plain Exhibition of Methodist Episcopacy.* Burlington: Chauncey Goodrich, 1844.

Colhouer, Thomas H. *Non-episcopal Methodism.* Pittsburgh: Methodist Book Concern, 1862.

————. *Republican Methodism Contrasted with Episcopal Methodism, and the Polity of the Methodist Church.* Philadelphia: J. W. Daughaday and Co., 1868.

Drinkhouse, Edward J. *History of Methodist Reform . . . with Special and Comprehensive Reference to . . . the History of Methodist Protestant Church.* 2 vols. Baltimore: Board of Publication of the Methodist Protestant Church, 1899.

Emory, John. *A Defense of "Our Fathers" and of the Original Organization of the Methodist Episcopal Church.* New York: Bangs and Emory, 1827.

————. *The Episcopacy Controversy Reviewed.* Ed. John Emory (his son). New York: Lane and Tippett, 1945.

Graves, James Robinson. *The Great Iron Wheel.* Nashville: Graves, Marks and Rutland, 1856.

Hamill, E. J., and Samuel Henderson. *A Discussion on Methodist Episcopacy.* Charleston: So. Baptist Publication Society, 1856.

Hawley, Bostwick. *The Methodist Episcopacy Valid.* New York: Hunt and Easton, 1892.

Henkle, Moses M. *Primitive Episcopacy.* Nashville: Stevenson and Owen, 1857.

Kilgore, Charles F. *The James O'Kelly Schism in the Methodist Episcopal Church.* Mexico City: Casa Unida de Publicaciones, 1963.

M'Caine, Alexander. *The History and Mystery of Methodist Episcopacy.* Baltimore: R. J. Matchett, 1827.

————. *A Defence of the Truth.* Baltimore: R. J. Matchett, 1829.

O'Kelly, James. *The Author's Apology for Protesting Against the Methodist Episcopal Government.* Richmond: John Dixon, 1798.

Disciplines

Disciplines of the Methodist Episcopal Church, Methodist Episcopal Church, South, and the Methodist Protestant Church (passim).

Doctrines and Discipline of the African Methodist Episcopal Zion Church. Charlotte: A.M.E.Z. Publishing House, 1978.

Doctrines and Discipline of the Christian Methodist Episcopal Church. Memphis: C.M.E.C. Publishing House, 1974.

Book of Discipline of the African Methodist Episcopal Church. 41st rev. ed. Nashville: A.M.E. Sunday School Union, 1976.

Discipline, 1973 of the Evangelical United Brethren Church. Dayton: Board of Publication of Evangelical United Brethren Church, 1963.

General Encyclopedias

The Encyclopedia Britannica, 14th ed., 1942.

The Encyclopedia Britannica, 15th ed., 1982.

The Catholic Encyclopedia. New York, 1907–1922.

The New Columbia Encyclopedia. Columbia University Press, 1975.

A Concordance to the Septuagint. Ed. Hatch and Redpath. Oxford, 1897–1907.

An Encyclopedia of Religion. Ed. Vergilius Farm. New York: Philosophical Library, 1945.

The Interpreter's Dictionary of the Bible. 4 vols. Nashville: Abingdon Press, 1962. Supplemental vol. 1976.

Encyclopedia of Religion and Ethics. Ed. J. Hastings. 13 vols. Edinburgh, 1908.

Sacramentum Mundi. New York: Herder and Herder, 1968.

The New Schaff-Herzog Encyclopedia of Religious Knowledge. 12 vols. New York: Funk and Wagnalls, 1908.

Theologische Realenzyklopadie. Band 4. Berlin: De Gruyter, 1980.

The Encyclopedia of World Methodism. Gen. ed. Nolan B. Harmon. 2 vols. Nashville: United Methodist Publishing House, 1974.

Articles, Pamphlets, Manuals

Burgess, James A. "Lutherans and the Office of the Bishop." *Ecumenical Trends* (April 1981).

Davies, Rupert E. "Episcopacy: Its History and Value." *The London Quarterly and Holborn Review*, no. 181 (1956).

George, A. Raymond. *The Sunday Service 1784*. Annual Lecture 2, The Friends of Wesley Chapel, Teesdale Mercury Ltd., Barnard Castle, 1938.

Holloway, Fred G. "What is the Future Role of the Bishop?" *World Outlook* (March 1968).

Huston, Robert W. "What's a Bishop?" *Michigan Christian Advocate* (March 1, 1979).

Jones, Jameson. "United Methodism: A Cautious Mood." *Christian Century* (September 20, 1978).

Kennedy, James W. *Anglican Partners*. Cincinnati: Forward Movement Press, 1978.

Outler, Albert C. "The Pastoral Office." *Perkins Journal* (Winter 1977).

———. "The Mingling of Ministries." Privately printed (November 26, 1973).

Roberts, Harold. *Anglican-Methodist Conversations*. London: Epworth Press, 1963.

Roumann, John. "A Further Report on the Title and Office of Bishop in the Lutheran Church of America." Philadelphia: Division for Professional Leadership (September 1980).

Tsoumas, George. *The Greek Orthodox Review*, Christmas issue, no. 2 (1956).

A Manual for Bishops of The United Methodist Church, issued 1978 under direction of Secretary, Council of Bishops, United Methodist Church.

Episkopé and Episcopate in Ecumenical Perspective. Faith and Order Paper 102. Geneva: World Council of Churches, 1980.

"Episcopal Transition." *The Center Letter* 10, no. 5, 6, 7. Naperville: Center for Parish Development, n.d.

Guidelines for the Transfer of Episcopal Leadership. Council of Bishops, United Methodist Church, 1975.

In Quest of a Church of Christ Uniting. Ministry. Princeton, N.J.: COCU, 1980.

Joint Commission on Unification of The Methodist Episcopal

Church and *The Methodist Episcopal Church, South.* New York: Methodist Book Concern, 1918.

Reports to 1964 General Conference on General Superintendent Study; Report of Quadrennial Committees: 1972–1976 on Study of Bishops and District Superintendents.

The Final Report. Anglican-Roman Catholic International Commission, Windsor, September 1981. London: S.P.C.K., 1982.

Christian Advocate Articles

Cox, Alva I. "We Must Redistribute the Load . . ." December 6, 1962.

Garrison, R. Benjamin. "Bishops Are Also Human." May 26, 1960.

Mathews, James K. "Appointments and Morale." April 18, 1968.

Outler, Albert C. "Reform in the Methodist Manner." March 7, 1968.

Rice, Charles E. "Will Methodists and Episcopalians Get Together?" January 5, 1961.

Seidenspinner, Clarence. "Should Methodism Go Diocesan?" May 26, 1960.

Spencer, Harry C. "Should the Bishops Speak for Us?" June 27, 1968.

Welch, Herbert. "Wise Words to a New Bishop." June 7, 1960.

Williams, Walter G. "We Need Bishops for the Whole Church." May 26, 1960.

Occasional Papers (United Methodist Board of Higher Education and Ministry):

Castuera, Ignacio. "Coming to *Terms* with the Episcopacy" 1, no. 8 (February 25, 1970).

Dunlap, E. Dale. "The United Methodist System of Itinerant Ministry: Its Nature and Future," no. 30 (January 15, 1980).

Moede, Gerald F. "Limited Term Episcopacy?" 1, no. 8 (February 25, 1976).

———. "Episkopé in Common," no. 40 (March 15, 1982).

———. "The Reconciliation of Ministries," no. 56 (February 7, 1984).

INDEX